STEEPLEJACK

BY JAMES HUNEKER

MEZZOTINTS IN MODERN MUSIC $1.50

CHOPIN: THE MAN AND HIS MUSIC $2.00

MELOMANIACS $1.50

OVERTONES $1.50

ICONOCLASTS: A BOOK OF DRAMATISTS $1.50

VISIONARIES $1.50

EGOISTS: A BOOK OF SUPERMEN $1.50

PROMENADES OF AN IMPRESSIONIST $1.50

FRANZ LISZT, ILLUSTRATED $2.00

THE PATHOS OF DISTANCE $2.00

NEW COSMOPOLIS $2.00

IVORY APES AND PEACOCKS $1.50

OLD FOGY $1.25

UNICORNS $2.00

BEDOUINS $2.00

STEEPLEJACK. TWO VOLUMES $4.00

CHARLES SCRIBNER'S SONS

BY JAMES HUNEKER

MEZZOTINTS IN MODERN MUSIC (1899)

CHOPIN: THE MAN AND HIS MUSIC (1900)

MELOMANIACS (1902)

OVERTONES (1904)

ICONOCLASTS: A BOOK OF DRAMATISTS (1905)

VISIONARIES (1905)

EGOISTS: A BOOK OF SUPERMEN (1909)

PROMENADES OF AN IMPRESSIONIST (1910)

FRANZ LISZT. ILLUSTRATED (1911)

THE PATHOS OF DISTANCE (1912)

NEW COSMOPOLIS (1915)

IVORY APES AND PEACOCKS (1915)

UNICORNS (1917)

BEDOUINS (1920)

STEEPLEJACK. TWO VOLUMES (1920)

CHARLES SCRIBNER'S SONS

JAMES GIBBONS HUNEKER
(1890)

STEEPLEJACK

BY

JAMES GIBBONS HUNEKER

"I find no sweeter fat than sticks to my own bones."
—Walt Whitman.

VOLUME II

NEW YORK
CHARLES SCRIBNER'S SONS
1921

CONTENTS

PART III

NEW YORK
(1877–1917)

CONTENTS

ILLUSTRATIONS

ILLUSTRATIONS

PART III

NEW YORK

(1877–1917)

I

I CAPTURE THE CITY

I was forced to drain my dree. My sudden little enthusiasms were beginning to pall. Stung by the gad-fly of necessity, I had to follow my market: all newspaper men must. I was to learn that versatility is not heaven sent, but is largely a matter of elbow-grease. Some one has written that genius is mainly an affair of energy, which puts the blacksmith, Theodore Roosevelt, and the baseball player in the same category. If it were only so, then the man of genius would rub elbows with mediocrity. I have always had the courage of my friendships. Not to envy some particular person for his accomplishments is to proclaim yourself hopelessly self-satisfied; nevertheless, I've never met anyone with whom I would change places, except a dead man. You may have the desire of the moth for the star and remain a happy insect. It demands something more than technical heroism to write your autobiography. The life of Samuel Johnson, that ranks its author among the greatest of the world's biographers, canny James Boswell, a portrait-painter without parallel, has also presented us with a self-portrait that matches his masterly delineation of the great Cham. Who reads Rasselas nowadays, or consults the once celebrated dictionary? I confess to liking the Tour to the Hebrides by this most perfect of John Bulls. But Boswell's Johnson! After all, autobiography is superior fiction. Nietzsche has warned us

3

against accepting the confessions of great men—meaning
Wagner.   Writing one's history is a transposition of the
embalmer's art to the printed page.   Like the Egyp-
tians we seek to preserve our personality.   The Egyptian
way has lasted longer.   We think of the mighty Milton
when he modestly confessed: "For although a poet, soar-
ing in the high reason of his fancies, with his garland
and singing robes about him, might, without apology,
speak more of himself than I mean to do; yet for me
sitting here below in the cool element of prose, a mortal
among many readers of no empyreal conceit, to venture
and divulge unusual things of myself, I shall petition
to the gentler sort, it may not be envy to me."   And
leaning heavily on the illustrious John, as must all soul-
spillers, I shall proceed with these avowals of a personal
pronoun.

Did you ever hear the story of the man who proposed
remarriage to his divorced wife?   She was one of the
old guard who sighs but never surrenders.   A skinny girl
with guilty eyes, her soul had become a slumbering
forest.   But she was faithful to her alimony.   Therefore, when her husband became imprudent, she calmly
answered: "You always were so impetuous!"   He was
one of those men to whom "God has given a forehead"
as Russian peasants say of the bald.   Her pent-up cascades of tenderness not freely flowing he went away in
a huff and remarried his other divorced wife.   But the
first lady's bank-account knew no husband.   She remained single and an alimonist in perpetuity.   It was
certainly the end of an imperfect day.   The moral is
not afar to seek.   I had been unfaithful to my birthplace.   I had hankered after the flesh-pots of Paris.
These failing, I had returned to my lawful first love,

and discovered that she was indifferent to me. I determined on another alliance. A third attack of that brief
epilepsy called love had begun. I was in the doldrums
of despair. I might have reproached Philadelphia as
De Quincey did "stony-hearted step-mother Oxford
Street." Anywhere, anywhere out of the town. I had
not even the consolation of those new cults, unscientific,
unchristian, and absurd, that elevate religion to the dignity of a sport. I dreamed of becoming a writer, but I
realised that splendour of style without spiritual elevation
is like a gewgaw in a pawnbroker's window. And the
sacrifices one must make are enormous. A leading-
motive in Faust, "Renounce thou shalt; shalt renounce!"
sounded for the first time in the symphony of my ego.
Suddenly one night I sat up in bed and thought: To-
morrow! New York! In the morning I packed my
bag and slipped away on an afternoon train without a
godspeed save from one faithful soul. I was to take
another bath of multitude. The month was February,
the year 1886.

It was nearing dusk when from the ferry-boat I saw
my new home, but unlike Rastignac in Balzac's fiction,
I did not shake my fist at the imposing city nor mutter:
"A nous deux maintenant!" I never even thought of that
duel with Paris in which no man was ever victor. I only
wondered where I should sleep. I soon decided. I
landed at Twenty-third Street ferry, caught a crosstown
car, alighted at Broadway and walked down to Fourteenth Street; there to get a lodging for the night in the
old Morton House. The room cost one dollar, the window was on the square, and from it I could see the Everett House, the Union Square Hotel, and the statue of
Lincoln. That section of the town was to become my

happy hunting-ground for over twenty-five years, and
New York my home for three decades, with the exception of excursions to Europe. A new Avatar! My
brother, Paul, had warned that if I became a resident of
Gotham then I should have no place to go to: an epigram
that has since been appropriated without due credit.
"J'y suis, j'y reste," said I in the immortal phrase of
Maréchal MacMahon. Besides, after Paris, the modu-
lation to New York was simple—and no city, not even
Philadelphia, is so unlike Paris as New York. I didn't
feel in the least provincial. Paris had lent me aplomb,
had rubbed off my salad greenness.

Thirty years ago the sky-line from Jersey City was
not so inspiring as it is to-day, but from the heights of
the Hudson the view was then, as now, magnificent.
Above Wall Street, on Broadway, and east of it, was
a congested business district. A few spires, Trinity
Church, the Tribune Building, the Times Building, were
conspicuous objects from the bay. Now you search for
Trinity between cliffs of marble, while in New Jersey you
catch the golden gleam of the World's dome. The Woolworth Building, among many, has distanced it in the
race skyward. What a difference, too, there was lower
down. The Battery, a clot of green, was surrounded
by a few imposing buildings, to-day mere impediments
for their loftier neighbours. Walt Whitman's Mast-
hemmed Manhatta had an actual meaning then; now
Manhattan is funnel-encircled, and in a few years it
may be the nesting spot of bird-men. You could see
churches then. Here and there a spire like a sharpened
lead-pencil protruded from the background. To-day, one
makes pilgrimages to them through stony canyons. The
city was torn up, as it had been fifty years earlier when

Dickens visited it, as it is in 1919. New York thrives best amidst excavations.

That first night is still vivid. A February thaw had set in. The evening was mild. I sauntered from my hotel, if not captain of my soul, anyhow of my slender purse. Leaving so unexpectedly I had not prepared for the inevitable. I had a few friends, but I preferred not troubling them. It was to be bareback riding for the future. But I had to eat my supper. I had dined at the unfashionable hour of 1 P. M. I went straight to a café; I had been there the previous summer. It stood on Fourteenth Street, east of Fourth Avenue, and faced Steinway Hall, a prime magnet for me. The café was kept by an old couple, the Lienaus, and was the headquarters of the musical aristocracy. The men sat below stairs in the café, and watched Mother Lienau count the cash or scold George, the fat bartender. She called him "Schorch," and he was simply a treasure, an adipose angel of amiability. To hear him address the irritable old woman as "Mamma" was touching, especially as he always winked at us when she asked for a drink. Upstairs was the drawing-room of the establishment, and there Papa Lienau reigned. He was as tall and massive as his wife was short and pudgy. His rule was clement. Not to raise a row over anything, that was the one law. And no one ever did. A room in the rear held a piano and from it I have heard music made by Joseffy, Friedheim, Mills, Neupert, Sternberg—who can do more amusing stunts on the keyboard than any pianist—Ansorge, and the herculean Rosenthal. But no one was present when I entered the café that evening and ordered a humble meal. Later in the evening I met nearly every man that later was to have a finger in my personal pie. I took a walk and got as far as Lüchow's, a few doors below. There I was introduced to Otto Floersheim, the editor of *The Musical Courier*. Hugh Craig introduced me. Hugh was a cultivated Englishman I had met at the "Keg" on Broad Street. I had sold my first story for five dollars to the editor of the West Philadelphia *Telephone*, and I promptly spent the money with that jolly chap, whose name I have forgotten. While doing this in strolled Hugh Craig and a friendship began that ceased with his death, twenty years afterwards. Craig was that ideal person, a scholar and a gentleman. A university man he was also a man of the world, of gentle breeding, and he was never in a hurry. No newspaper in which he worked needed an encyclopædia. He seemed to know everything, and could write without preparation on any topic. A linguist, he could speak no language fluently but his own, though he could translate from a dozen. He always had a cigarette in his mouth, and there was a slight burr on his speech, which may have argued a Scotch strain. He was a good friend, and like Sam Johnson, he was ever ready for a "frisk." He was of a dusty, indefinite age, about twenty years my senior. Otto Floersheim made no impression on me, except that he was fat, rather pompous, good-humoured, and perspiring.

We went back to Lienau's, there to meet the senior editor of *The Musical Courier*, chunky, shrewd, and with the most piercing and brilliant eyes I ever saw in a human's head. They were jewelled, gleaming, and as hard as agate. I had met Marc Blumenberg the summer of 1885 at the Academy of Music, New York, where a meeting of the Music Teachers' National Association was in session. Theodore Presser, of the *Etude* introduced me. I had liked the plump little Hebrew, and I continued to like him till the day of his death. He it was who gave me my first leg up over the fence in New York, and I shall never forget his kindness. We chatted. I can see him, napkin tucked under his chin, preparing to eat; he was a solid trencherman. He took me in with his cool, measuring glance, and when I told him that I wrote about music, he bade me drop into the office of *The Musical Courier*, then at 25 East Fourteenth Street. It was a year or so before I accepted that invitation. What Craig and I did that night has slipped me. The next morning I was up and doing, for I had slept well, thanks to my bad conscience. I went in search of a more suitable residence, and a cheaper. Jacques Reich, the engraver, had an atelier at Fifth Avenue and Fourteenth Street, and to him I explained my wants. He had lived in Philadelphia and I think did my father's head in crayon. He proved obliging. Soon I found a comfortable room, top floor, at the corner of Thirteenth Street and Seventh Avenue. In the row of houses with porches standing well away from the sidewalk, on Seventh Avenue, is No. 40. The row may be still seen looking as it did thirty-two years ago. Across the street was the Fanwood. S. B. Mills, a famous pianist, lived in the block, composed for the most, of boarding-houses. Mrs. Genevieve Ferris was my landlady, and the most motherly of women. She was handsome, and had a masterful way, which came natural as she was a custom-house inspector, and on the steamship docks every day. The boarders were only five or six young men. We paid eight dollars a week, and complained if we didn't get beefsteak at breakfast. O, the blessed time! No wheatless, meatless, heatless, sinless, thirstless days then. I

shook down at once in a tub of butter. But how to put
in my time was the problem.

At noon, after my belongings had been transferred
and I could look a policeman in the eye, feeling a home-
less vagabond no longer, I crossed Fourteenth Street to
University Place, then to the right and found myself at
the hospitable café of Billy Moulds'. It should not be
forgotten that in New York, as in Paris, the café is the
poor man's club. It is also a rendezvous for newspaper
men, musicians, artists, Bohemians generally. It is the
best stamping-ground for men of talent. Ideas circulate.
Brain tilts with brain. Eccentricity must show cause
or be jostled. If there is too much drinking, there is the
compensation of contiguity with interesting personalities.
In those abodes of prim dulness, so-called religious clubs
for young men without a thirst, I never saw any signs of
life except the daily newspapers. I am not concerned
with the salvation of my brother's soul, having my hands
full of my own, but if hedging a growing youth about
with moral wire-fences will keep him "straight," then his
intellectual growth is not worth a copper. At the first
puff of reality, of the world as it actually is, he will
collapse. Until mankind changes—which it hasn't since
the tertiary geological epoch—or something better is devised than the café, that institution will continue to form
and develop the adolescent male. Clubs are too expensive for the majority of us. The present interlude of
hypocrisy and bigotry from which our nation is now
suffering will surely be followed by a violent reaction,
and like such reactions, the pendulum will swing too far
in the opposite direction. Mankind can stand just so
much and no more. Recall the Restoration after the
reign of dreary Puritanism in England; and what were

the Puritans of those days compared with our oppressive breed! Heaven bless their bones! those roundheads consumed tankards of ale and plenty of beef. Their worst offence was their chronic howling of hymns, and their forbidding a man to covet his neighbour's wife on Sundays; also forbidding a man to embrace his proper spouse on the Sabbath; an edict that may have found favour with overworked husbands. But those Puritans with their "scarecrow" sins were also pious politicians. Beware a pious politician. He is more dangerous than one in petticoats (sometimes he is in petticoats). As to their droning, heaven, like hell, is paved with pious vocal intentions; otherwise how can the choir angelic, not to mention the Great White Throne, endure the ear-splitting bawling wafted upward from here below? Their deity must be very patient, or else as tone-deaf as his unmusical worshippers. Their sincerity is no excuse for sounds like a dog's cough, or the cackling of a hoarse parrot. God can't be worshipped beautifully enough. Little cause to wonder if a man with sensitive ears prefers the café to the church.

The first man I met at the Moulds Café was Francis Saltus, poet, wit, raconteur, and as brilliant as his brother, Edgar Saltus. With the solitary exception of Oscar Wilde, I never heard a human discourse so eloquently as Frank, nor have I ever known such a perfect Bohemian. William Dean Howells has told us of the group that gathered at Pfaff's several decades before; Fitz-James O'Brien who wrote the most horror-breeding short story since Poe, "What Was It?" or some such title, a story that is as vivid as de Maupassant's Horla, and one that furnished Ambrose Bierce with the motive for his best tale; Walt Whitman, who probably drank buttermilk, as he neither smoked nor touched alcoholic beverages, and a lot of chaps, Arnold among the rest, whose names are writ in water. The Moulds contingent was not so celebrated, but the actors, singers, painters, poets, newspaper men, and politicians were so numerous that a library might be filled with the recital of their accomplishments. Frank Saltus had lived the major part of his life in Paris. He was a member of the Théophile Gautier circle, and a protégé of "le bon Théo," whose polished technique and impassible attitude towards life and art he had assimilated. When I hear the frantic clamourings made by uncritical critics over some newly-arrived free-verse bard whose "poetry" is a jumble of Whitman and falling bricks, I wonder if they ever have read Francis Saltus. He was a poet, a pagan, therefore immoral. Now the "immorality" is taken as a matter of course by the young poetasters, but the poetry is left out. We have in this year of grace many "poets," but no Poet. (I must resort to obvious capitalisation.) Frank Saltus carved sonnets from the solid block. He wrote epigrams at fifty cents apiece for *Town Topics*, he composed feuilletons that would have made the fortune of a Paris boulevardier. His habits were irregular, though he got up earlier than Willie Wilde, Oscar's brother, who had married Mrs. Frank Leslie for a bedroom—so he said. And Frank Saltus was fond of absinthe, another imported habit and a deadly one. But I never saw him drunk, and I never saw him without a cigarette in his mouth. He usually arrived about noon and wrote and talked till the last trump, which was at two A. M.; sometimes later. The classic type of Bohemianism that has quite vanished. He was a ruin, and a gentleman, who had evidently been very handsome. The photographs taken in Paris revealed him as a Greek god; but when I knew him his good looks were historical. Edgar Saltus was handsome in a different style, dark, Italian, petit-maître, a prose-master and a philosopher.

There was a sufficing cause for the punctuality of Frank, and the rest of us at Moulds'. Free-lunch! Up at the Hoffman House you could eat a regular course dinner on one drink, but you had to tip the waiter a quarter; at Moulds' there were no tips, nor was there an assortment of dishes. The glory of the establishment was its bean soup, hot, savoury, plentiful. Oh! that bean soup. How many famished stomachs it soothed and nourished in the days that are no more! Pardon me if I shed a lyric tear over its memory. Billy Moulds retired years ago to darkest Brooklyn, and when I meet him I speak of the fabulous soup. His invariable answer is: "It saved some of you fellows' lives, didn't it? But do you remember Otto and his razzle-dazzle?" I did. He meant Otto Floersheim, who had devised a mixture of brandy, ginger ale, and absinthe, that was warranted to knock a horse down. It never fazed Floersheim, who introduced the concoction to Albert Niemann, the Wagnerian tenor, a drinker that would have pleased Pantagruel. To see this pair of monsters guzzle the poison made shudder a sensitive and beer-absorbing soul. Niemann could booze all night till next midday, and then sing Siegmund that evening in a marvellous manner. But not marvellous, vocally speaking. His acting, the assumption of the character, was the chief interest. His voice had gone before he visited us. In fact it was beginning to go at the first Baireuth Festival in 1876.

That bean soup was a mainstay for us when the weather

was unfavourable to our pocketbooks. And there were plenty of rainy days. The critical business is a precarious one. Writing of any sort still is unless you manufacture a "best-seller," and that is what we all try for. The cashier at Moulds' was a brother of the boss and had been a keeper at the Trenton State prison. Need I add that Tom Moulds was judge of human nature! Smiling, sympathetic, he would take my proffered check—not a bank cheque—and "hang it up" on my always growing account. "I see it's not Delmonico's to-day, bean soup, eh? Well, it's healthier and more filling—and it's on the house, like a tin-roof." He jested, but he had a warm heart and an open purse. I could fill pages with the names of illustrious actors who patronised Moulds'. Visiting English actors went there instinctively, it was homelike, quiet, few quarrels (before midnight), and good-fellowship was never absent. The old-timers I met were Frank Mordaunt, Frank Evans, J. B. Studley, Walter Turner, and an Englishman named Liston. I've seen Booth, Barrett, McCullough, and, once only, Lester Wallack, there. The musical crowd were unfailing visitors. I met, every evening, Augustus Brentano, the senior brother of the well-known book-sellers, whose big store was on Union Square next to Tiffany's. Joseffy and Franz Rummel—who married Leila Morse, the daughter of S. F. B. Morse—Sauret, Ovide Musin, Ysaye, Gerardy, Max Heinrich. Who didn't go to Moulds'? Many the commission to write I got in its shadowy back room. The music trade-journalists congregated there. In those days trade-journalism had not been standardised; the same with the weekly sheets devoted to theatricals. Each editor was a sharp-shooter—and often a free-booter—on his own account. Their pens knew no brother.

Dickens would have been delighted with the pages of personal vituperation that were published and without bloodshed ensuing. The vilest abuse was bandied. "If the bug-juice editor who was found by the police-patrol wagon early last Sunday morning as he sat on the curbstone with his watch dangling in the gutter, near the M——ds Cafe" (a subtle difference indeed) "does not abandon his worship of Bacchus"—this would be followed by a column devoted to the general habits of the aforesaid "bug-juice editor," who never turned a hair, but would report the following week as follows: "Our readers should not listen to the piteous appeals of a poor, decrepit barnstormer, bad actor, fugitive bankrupt, who is after the money of gullible piano manufacturers to keep his rotten little sheet from perishing. As the original pirate in the trade we have a portrait of him in top-boots, big hat, waving the piratical black flag which we would only be too happy to show our readers in case they drop in (and pay their new subscriptions) which accurately places him on the map." The pot calling the kettle black.

II

MUSICAL JOURNALISM

Theatrical journalism was even more personal, fisti-
cuffs being the last resort. To-day musical journalism
is greatly improved. It must always encourage mediocrity, else perish. And the same may be said of the
daily press. The music-critics when I came to New
York were Henry T. Finck, of *The Evening Post;* H. E.
Krehbiel, of *The Tribune;* William J. Henderson, of *The
Times;* this was 1887; later Mr. Henderson followed me
as music editor of *The Sun,* a position he still holds.
John T. Jackson, of *The World;* Bowman, of *The Sun;*
his wife, Mrs. Bowman, succeeded him; Albert Steinberg, of *The Herald,* then a real force in the musical
world, and other men on the afternoon newspapers, such
as Willy von Sachs, Edgar J. Levey, both dead. Jackson is dead, so is Steinberg, but the rest are alive, vigorous, and still "kicking." It is the function of a critic
to "kick," otherwise he is considered moribund. Add
Richard Aldrich to the list—for when I became dramatic
editor of *The Sun* in 1902, there was quite a displacement
in our frog-pond; Henderson left *The Times* for *The Sun;*
Aldrich, the assistant music-critic of *The Tribune,* went
to *The Times,* Edward Ziegler, my colleague, took over
my job on *Town Topics*—where for years I had more
fun than in a circus—and also assumed the musical
editorship of *The American* and afterwards *The Herald.*
And Leonard Liebling followed me on *The Musical*

Courier. To-day Ziegler is a young chap who dyes his hair iron-grey in order to appear older. At the Metropolitan Opera House he is closely allied to Director Gatti-Casazza. All these men—Ziegler excepted—I worked with from the beginning and they are still my friends. Something to boast about if you realise that the "artistic temperament" pervades the soul of the music-critic; that a more "touchier" set of humans would be difficult to find—except actors; a critic is thinner-skinned than his victims and hates to be criticised. We had our little tiffs but no serious embroilments. Albert Steinberg was the disruptive force. With a wit that was positively malignant he would place his surgical steel on your sorest place, and your vanity bled. He had a musical ear, much experience, sound taste, and his guesses were often as telling as riper knowledge. But he was lazy, a race-course gambler, though not a drinking man. When he was cremated at Fresh Pond a telegram from the De Reszke brothers, then on tour, was the only intimation that the dead man had once occupied a commanding position in the metropolis. Musicians, like actors, have a short memory. Steinberg was a powerful aid to Lillian Nordica at a time when she needed friends. Maurice Grau told me this. I knew it already; nor was Madame Nordica ungrateful. She possessed a big heart. Yet, there was Steinberg dead with no one to tender his remains a last salute except Theodore Stein—who, like Madame Frida Ashforth, took care of him through a long illness—and a few faithful friends, for the most part strangers to me. However, Steinway and Sons sent a representative. As for his absent colleagues, it must be said that Steinberg had estranged them by his savage tongue. But it was all desperately sad, this ending of a brilliant, cultivated, if wayward critic. Music-criticism as a profession—c'est du cimetière! Or the crematory. An ill-omen for me, this funeral.

I had attended one of the Music Teachers' National Association meetings at Indianapolis in the summer of 1887. These M. T. N. A. affairs were interesting to provincial professionals and, no doubt, useful; for New Yorkers, they smacked much of the local festival that blooms in the spring. But I was too young to be hypercritical and enjoyed myself with the rest. Frank Van Stucken, of Belgian stock, born in Texas, conducted the orchestra, and I again met Marc Blumenberg. We became more intimate. When I returned to New York, I visited his office and saw much of him and his partner, and presently I was writing for *The Musical Courier*, only for the fun of the thing. I didn't get salary till 1888. As my father often remarked, my specialty was working for other people at reduced rates. But I had nothing to complain of in regard to Blumenberg's generosity, nor Floersheim's either. Otto was improvident, an enraged gambler, plundered by the bookmakers, with a childlike credulity in "tips"; he was also the sort of friend who would take off his coat to help you. I judge these two men as I found them. I was a stranger to them, and they took me in. No doubt I was useful. Blumenberg was a pragmatic Jew, yet no more pragmatic than the average Gentile business man. Both had a certain reputation, like most trade-journalists; yet during my fifteen years' connection with *The Musical Courier* I was never asked to do anything that smelled queer, nor write anything but what I saw fit. Once only Blumenberg attempted to coerce me and, oddly enough, it concerned *The Sun* and not his own journal. I have saved the letter in which he told Driggs, the manager, that if I didn't cease praising Gadski in *The Sun* he would get Krehbiel, of *The Tribune*, to write my department, entitled "The Raconteur." This was such a joyous crack that the little editor had to laugh himself when I shrieked at the suggestion. Krehbiel smiled, too, for "The Raconteur" was a rag-bag, an olla-podrida page which I wrote from 1887 to 1902. Not only would Krehbiel have indignantly rejected the offer, but try as he might have he couldn't manufacture such a mess as my columns of gossip, crazy fantasy, and whirling comment. And that was the only time I had a disagreement with Marc Blumenberg. The joke of the matter lay in the fact that the season or two previous I had criticised Madame Gadski in *The Sun*, which newspaper I joined in 1900, and Blumenberg protested. The reason? Ask me not in gentle numbers, life is such a dream!

Well, for fifteen years I ran amuck in *The Courier*. Occasionally Hugh Craig, his literary taste outraged at my lack of method, would complain—he edited the "copy" of the staff—and an indignant subscriber would protest that "The Raconteur" should not be tolerated in a family where there were girls—Oh! what a lot of girl readers I had then. I know, because I received so many letters from them—but neither Blumenberg nor Floersheim bothered himself about me. I was "Crazy Jim, the Idealist"—let him have his fling. The truth was that musical journalists lived only because of the rivalries of piano manufacturers. The subscription list didn't much matter; indeed, the greater the number of subscribers the higher the bills for paper and printing.

One piano house could support a trade-journal. And logically the editorial policy of attacking the music-critics of the daily press was inexpugnable. There could be no rapprochement. They were the enemy! Crush them! "Get thee gone, girl, but the girl wouldn't get thee gone"—as Hughey Dougherty, or Lew Simmons, used to sing at the minstrel shows. The critics continued to write what they believed to be the truth, and they were attacked. Who was to blame for this system? The mediocrities who wished pleasant things written of them in the trade-journals, or their editors? As an ethical question, I fancy there isn't much doubt as to the answer, but as a business proposition there is something to be said for the musical journals—or the box-office. Business is such a ripe-rotten affair no matter where you go that these editorial gentlemen had their self-justification. I never judge, fearing judgment, so I can only say that to-day conditions are different. Music-trade editors ride in their motor-cars, are heavy bond-holders and don't bother about the music-critics, who are the same ill-paid pariahs they were thirty years ago. Who loves a critic? Once a music-critic, always a pauper; that is, if you don't marry a rich girl, or are not born to the purple, as was Reginald De Koven.

The world takes no interest in the quarrels of rival editors. We were up to our necks in scandals and libel suits. *The Musical Courier* was sued by Fred Schwab, former music-critic of *The Times* and *Town Topics*, for uttering a libel. Poor foolish Floersheim had picked the chestnuts out of the fire for other people, smarting under Schwab's attack on them in *Town Topics*, and he picked them so clumsily that *The Courier* had to retract its sentiments, or heavily suffer. The venerable owner of *The Times*, Mr. Jones, was subpœnaed, but turned so deaf in the witness-chair that he never told the jury why Schwab had been discharged, or allowed to resign from *The Times*. The musical town sniggered. *The Musical Courier* did not. Then I advised Blumenberg to engage Schwab to write criticism on the opera, and he did so. Fred Schwab, a practical man with a sly sense of humour, consented, and behold! the quarrel was forgotten. Krehbiel, Henderson, Finck, Irenæus Prime-Stevenson, and Edgar J. Levey were at one time contributors to *The Courier*, and their names were printed at the top of the editorial page. This was as early as 1887 or 1888. The collaboration didn't last long.

Blumenberg and Floersheim waxed rich, but I didn't. If there were "ill-gotten gains" they were scrupulously concealed from me. I got a plain living for my work, and I worked hard, the dreariest kind of labour, going to every tenth-rate concert, tramping out every night, wind or weather never deterring me, to Chickering Hall, to Steinway Hall, to the Academy, to the Metropolitan Opera House. Carnegie Hall was not built, nor was Aeolian Hall; we went to Mendelssohn Hall, or Madison Square Garden Concert Hall. In the nineties, when Floersheim definitely retired to Europe, I had a freer hand, and I edited the musical section in an easy-going fashion. I was mildly reproved once a week for mentioning the names of the other critics, and as I was with them day and night, I didn't heed the advice. "You are advertising these people throughout the country," Marc would say, but he didn't interfere till years had passed and the enmity became uglier. The quarrel seemed childish to me then, a tempest in a tin can.

Blumenberg got the notion that I could with training be made useful in the trade department of *The Courier*, and for many months he took me with him from Harlem to Brooklyn, interviewing piano manufacturers and dealers. I wrote grotesques and burlesques. I "created" fictitious firms. There was a certain Mr. Diggs, of Pilltown, whose adventures were chronicled weekly and, I dare say, amused or else saddened some readers. But I didn't have any flair for business. I was frivolous when I should have been solemn, and Blumenberg would look at me reproachfully or giggle—he was a grown-up boy. A man of musical talent, he possessed a well-lined intellect. He was a student of history and a patriot. One morning too bright and too early, for we had been up all night, we went over to the Ernest Gabler piano manufactory and there I was introduced to the head of the house, after being duly warned to be careful. I was very careful. In my lightest manner I said, after I shook hands: "Mr. Gabler, you make me think of an aunt of mine we always called an earnest gabbler." The man's face clouded, then turning to Marc he grimly said: "Bloomy, this young fellow would make a better piano-tuner than a trade-journalist, don't you think so?" We left in a few minutes and around the corner Blumenberg exploded. I was nervous, but when I saw him holding his sides and roaring with glee I felt relieved. The silly pun had tickled his risible rib, and even if he had lost the advertisement, he would have laughed. He was that kind of a man. He was also another; he gave much in charity; he lent money to the music-teachers he was supposed to bleed. I know this. I didn't go to piano-tuning. I was already a tuner of criticism. The ending of Marc Antony Blumenberg was not without that touch of irony inherent in matters mundane. Although he was up to his ears in criminal libels and lawsuits, he died at Paris in the odour of sanctity. The American colony, headed by the American Minister and musical Paris, honoured the bier of the dead man; the newspapers had naught but praise for his unselfish devotion to art. Even his most ferocious enemies in America would have been silenced by such an imposing demonstration. His faults no doubt, were many, but he boasted virtues that some of his opponents could not. Above all, he was not a hypocrite. If he called the kettle black he cheerfully admitted the sootiness of the pot. I never came in contact with a more agile intellect, nor with a cheerier nature than his. He was a politician born who had the misfortune to operate in a restricted field. Some of his schemes and dreams which seemed extravagant and Utopian at the time—for example, a piano manufacturers' trust—are to-day a commonplace. He had as many friends as enemies, and he raised merry hell his life long.

I remember speaking of a few cultivated families in Philadelphia which were my solace during the dark interval between my return from Paris and my hegira to New York. One of these families was the Houghs, on South Sixteenth Street. Mrs. Hough, before her marriage to Isaac Hough, was Mrs. Amelia Thibault, and the mother of three sons, my closest friends. They were all musical, and with their cousin, John T. Boyd, we were a phalanx of enthusiasms. The Thibault boys, Frank, Fritz, and Carow, were of French descent on the paternal side; Fritz died from fatigue and exposure in the Spanish War. Mrs. Hough was a fountain of affection. She was a benign influence in her circle. Dr. Thomas H. Fen-

ton and his wife, born Lizzie Remak, was another
musical family. Mrs. Fenton is an excellent pianist.
Dr. Fenton, a singer and member of the Orpheus.
The Mawsons, on Arch Street, were well known.
Mrs. Mawson, an Englishwoman of the old cultured
school, had an evening at home where you would meet
artistic people worth knowing. Her children have made
a name for themselves. Harry Mawson, playwright;
Edward Mawson, actor, who was a man with a lovable
personality; the young women were musical and intellectual. Lucie Mawson, a concert pianist, resides in London, where she plays in public and is well-liked. Through
the good graces of this family I was introduced to the
Garrigues, of New York. In the middle eighties they
lived on Seventeenth Street, near Union Square. To say
"109 East" sufficed for the musical elect. It was a centre of sweetness and light. The father, Rudolph Garrigue, a dynamic Dane, was president of an insurance
company. His daughters played, sang, and wrote. As
their mother said to me: "I never see them except at
meal-time, but I hear them day and night." This with
a gesture of mock despair; she belonged to a generation
less strenuous, a generation that did not take the kingdom
of heaven by assault. Several of them have attained
distinction as musical instructors. The eldest daughter
married Professor Thomas Garrigue Masaryk, of Prague,
just now in the public eye as first president of the
Czecho-Slovaks.

In this household I was gently encouraged in my various mild lunacies. The pianist, Eleanor Garrigue Ferguson, married to Henry Ferguson, a landscape-painter,
had advised me to come to New York; like most New
Yorkers she considered Philadelphia a pent-up Utica.

In 1885 I had witnessed the début of Fannie Bloomfield Zeisler, at the old Academy of Music—she played Rubinstein's D minor piano concerto with such fire and brilliancy that the conductor and orchestra pantingly followed her impetuous lead—and I met so many artistic people at the Garrigues' that I then and there renounced the city of my birth. I breathed an atmosphere ozone-charged. The idols of my youth were to be seen perambulating Irving Place, Union Square, Fourteenth Street. At Lienau's you might see William Steinway in the flesh, an immense political influence, as well as a musical. Theodore Thomas lived on East Seventeenth Street, opposite the Garrigues. William Mason would alight from the little blue horse-car, which ran across Seventeenth Street, at Union Square. He lived in Orange, N. J., and always stopped at Brubacher's, where he met S. B. Mills, before beginning his lessons at Steinway Hall. A polished pianist, delightful raconteur, Mr. Mason could discourse by the hour about Franz Liszt, with whom he had studied. And then there were to be seen at Lienau's, Anton Seidl, Mr. and Mrs. Charles F. Tretbar, Nahum Stetson, Joseffy, Sternberg, Rummel, Scharwenka, Lilli Lehman, Van der Stucken, Krehbiel, Mr. and Mrs. Victor Herbert, Rosenthal, Mr. and Mrs. Ferdinand von Inten, Charles H. Steinway, the present head of the house, and, of course, Max Heinrich. A few doors down the block was Augustus Lüchow's restaurant which outlived Lienau's, and a host of other hostelries.

III

IN THE MAELSTROM

After I left the quaint Seventh Avenue house—I had swarmed up a column from the second-story piazza to the third, and though it was a warm night my absence of superfluous attire and the general row that ensued (it was because of a bet)—made me seek lodgings elsewhere. A small family hotel at the northeast corner of Irving Place and Seventeenth Street, kept by an elderly couple, was noted for its cooking and cheerfulness. Werle's, too, was an artistic rendezvous, and its table-d'hôte dinner saw many celebrities. There were always entertaining companions. It was one of those houses where at any time before midnight the sound of pianos, violins, violoncellos, even the elegiac flute might be heard, and usually played by skilled professionals. There was also much vocal squawking. Across the street was, still is, the pretty Washington Irving house, and at another corner lived Victor Herbert. From the vine-covered entrance of Werle's I often heard string music made by Victor Herbert, Max Bendix—then concert-master of the Thomas Orchestra, and a Philadelphian—and others. I occupied on the ground floor a room about as big as the one I had lived in at Paris. It held a bed, an upright piano, a trunk, some books, and music. It had one advantage, it was easy of access, and one disadvantage— I never knew when I would be alone. Friends knocked on the window with their sticks at all hours of the night.

They also sang concerted noises. Finally, I stayed out
on purpose till dawn to escape their intrusions. The
dining-room was in the basement, a New York institution. I was soon introduced to my neighbour, the Red
Countess, Madame Von Shevitch. Her husband, a
pleasant Russian nobleman, was editor of a radical newspaper. She was a large, rather stout woman with red
hair of the rich hue called Titian. Her face was too
fleshy for beauty, but there were forms and accents that
told of its past; the fine, harmonious brow, the intense expression of the eyes, still splendid of hue and delicately set
like precious jewels, the pallor of her skin, sulphur-white;
her aristocratic bearing and the contours of her well-
moulded head attracted me at once. She spoke fluently
a half-dozen languages. I didn't know who she was, as
the name Von Shevitch was just one more Slav in
this abbreviated map of Europe. But when Mother
Werle whispered to me: "The Red Countess, otherwise
the Golden-crested Serpent, otherwise the Princess Racowitza, otherwise Helena von Doenniges"— "Stop," I
cried. "You mean Clotilde Rüdiger, the heroine of
George Meredith's novel, The Tragic Comedians." The
moment was almost historic. It sent me back to Meredith and this exasperating clever fiction, written in his
most crackling, incendiary style. This woman opposite
me at table who ate suet dumplings as she discoursed
art, philosophy, fiction, and politics, was the direct cause
of the death of Ferdinand Lassalle, of whom Bismarck
had said: "When he goes into the field I'll shut up
shop." He said this in the fifties. Lassalle was a fol-
lower of Karl Marx acharné, though he soon set up
a rival socialism, a democratic socialism with a new
brand, of which he was the agitator. This handsome,

audacious Jew, brilliant as to attainments, an orator who
could wind a mob around his voice, had made love to
Helena Von Doenniges, the daughter of a rich, aristocratic Munich family, one of those blown-in-the-glass families that exist to make plain people foam at the mouth.
Not only did she win the homage of this leader of men,
but Richard Wagner had admired her too much for the
peace of Cosima von Bülow, afterwards his wife, Cosima
Wagner.   But the haughty Von Doenniges family showed
Lassalle the door.   They also set a cousin on him, the
Rumanian Prince, Yanko Racowitza.   A duel followed,
and Ferdinand Lassalle, the one great force of the Social
Democrats, one apparently born to lead the German
people from the jungle of absolutism—Heinrich Heine
proclaimed this—was killed.   Worse followed.   She married the poor Prince, and when he died of galloping con-
sumption five months later (a form of her revenge), she
married a handsome actor, Friedmann, but soon divorced
him.   Two prima donnas in one family!   Then she married Serge Von Shevitch, who had fled from Russia after
some revolutionary enterprise.   Although an aristocrat
he was a liberal, too liberal, like Prince Krapotkin, for the
autocracy on the Neva.   She had lived what is called
"a full life."   Her published recollections of Lassalle fell
into the hands of George Meredith.   The Tragic Comedians followed.   She was bitter over that book, a libel,
she told me, of her relations with the grand Democrat.
She had known intimately Bulwer, Dickens, Liszt—
always philandering after girls—Napoleon and Eugénie,
Bismarck, and a forest of other celebrities.   She came to
America in 1877, and remained till 1890, when she returned to Munich, and after sundry vicissitudes she com-
mitted suicide in 1911, a few days later than her hus-

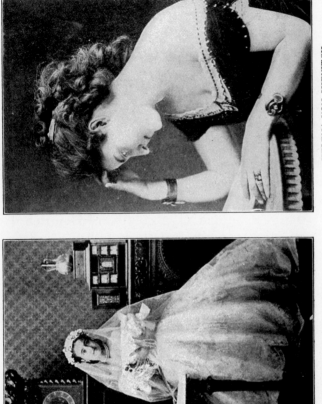

HELENA VON SHEVITCH
Heroine of "The Tragic-Comedians"

ADELINA PATTI AT SIXTEEN
Début as "Lucia," 1859

band's self-murder. Truly a Tragic Comedian. I suppose I was influenced by her version of the case and wrote of her as a woman abused, but Mr. Meredith stuck to his guns and amicably informed me that some day I might be brought to his way of thinking. Frank Swinnerton in his authoritative work on George Meredith treats of the matter and wonders whether I am a Jew! Possibly because I had quoted the word "Chutzpe ponem," applied to Lassalle by some of his co-religionists—meaning impertinent—Mr. Swinnerton jumped to the conclusion that a driver of fat oxen must himself be fat. Lassalle had been known as "The Social Luther," and his fighting motto was: "State Support for Co-operative Production." He was not in sympathy with "passive resistance" as a weapon against the government. A fallacy, he said. "Passive resistance is the resistance which does not resist."

And this "citizen of the world," as he called himself, fell before "The shaky pistol of the unhappy Danube Osier," Prince Racowitza, though himself a dead shot and a professed anti-duellist. To show you that Meredith had sounded the insincerity of Helena, when I asked her why she hadn't eloped with Lassalle, she calmly replied that she had enjoyed a brief elopement. He was at Righi-Kaltbad for his health, and she slipped away from her parents at Geneva and went to her lover. At the age of nearly sixty-eight she wrote another volume of memoirs. Unblushingly she admitted this passionate intermezzo. Perhaps it accounts for the tragic ending. Something happened—incompatability of temperament may be discovered in five minutes—and the lovers never met again. I asked her whether her family had disliked Ferdinand Lassalle merely because of his Jewish blood, and she smiled. "My grandmother was a Jewess and secretly aided our affair. No, he was a social firebrand feared by Bismarck, hated by Richard Wagner, and then that Countess Hatzfeldt affair"—he had been very friendly with this woman, "and many other things, also his impetuous manner of wooing." I have her picture, after the celebrated portrait by Von Lenbach, which she sent me in the keeping of Frida Ashforth. Her beauty in youth must have been exquisite, for exquisite in this pale transcription are her features and eyes. I saw in life the glory of her hair. Why did the Von Shevitch pair kill themselves. Poverty for one reason, self-disgust and boredom for another. They had lived in their flush times like nabobs. The decadence began in New York. Werle's house was not precisely palatial, though for lean purses a paradise. A few days before their death Madame Ashforth—who is, I need hardly add, a famous vocal teacher in New York—saw the couple. Naturally she assisted them after frantic telegrams had reached her. Helena begged her not to give Serge Von Shevitch money. "He spends it all on the girls!" What an ending! Meredith could have written a still more tragic coda to his story if he had known it. I am now making amends to his clairvoyance, and for presumptuously challenging his intuitions. But I was young, and believed what women told me; and was she not the Red Countess! What childlike faith a clever woman can arouse when she plays the rôle of the misunderstood; especially when she confides her "misery" to a young fool!

The fascination of a story set to music, sung by men and women in a picturesque setting, is as ancient as the immemorial hills. In America our passion for opera is divided by our love of baseball; yet we are a musical nation. (I preach this when optimists deny it after hearing so much "canned music.") And in music we are neutral (I am writing of pre-war times.) No particular nationality may claim exclusive dominion in the tone-art, though roughly set down the order of historical precedence is this: Italian, German, French, English and the rest somewhere in the field. I have heard opera in Yiddish, in Czech, and doubtless opera in some sort of volapük will be sung some day. I mention these various tongues as the tide of fashion has again set towards Italy. In my youth it was Italy. Then for a period came Germany; then Italian and French, followed by German, and now Italian. All of which proves nothing or everything. (When in doubt consult Brother Krehbiel's Chapters in Operas.) I do not always follow my own advice and occasionally come to grief, for I am not a date-monger. The impresarios in my early days were Max Maretzek, the Strakosch brothers, Maurice and Max —one of them married Amalia Patti, but don't ask me which—Maurice was an accompanist of merit. I heard him at the keyboard supporting the rich voice of Parepa-Rosa. Elsewhere (in Unicorns) I have spoken of Vieuxtemps, fat Brignoli, Rubinstein and Wieniawski. Opera has been going to the "demnition bow-wows" since Noah criticised the tone-production of the first soiled dove in the ark. And from Mount Ararat to Broadway there has been one prolonged wail of protest against "prevailing methods" in contemporary opera; in a phrase, from Genesis to Giulio Gatti-Casazza. My father, a half century ago, informed me that opera was heading for the dogs; that Brignoli—who sang like an angel and looked like a macaroni baker—was nothing compared to—who

was it? Some by-gone operatic Johnnie. Oh, yes,
Mario. I never saw a better actor-tenor than Campanini, though I've seen as good acting by voiceless
tenors. (No names, please!)

But opera was a mixed affair then. It still bore the
circus stamp of the seventies. Before he could play in
symphony in one evening's programme, Theodore
Thomas was forced to placate his audiences with dance
tunes, single movements from Haydn, Mozart, and
Beethoven, or arrangements of piano pieces, such as
Schumann's "Träumerei." In opera the cheap spec-
tacular ruled. Singers were advertised like freaks, and
managers always a half step from ruin. That manager
is become an extinct type. Only the pen of Charles
Dickens could have characterised the late Henry Mapleson, the Colonel, as he was affectionately named. Compared with him the florid personality of Sir "Gus" Harris
was a silhouette. A perfect flowering was Colonel Mapleson, bluff or tactful, roaring or ingratiating, as occasion
demanded. He was the most successful lion-tamer—
vocal lions—I ever encountered. He could make a
blank cheque sing with potential wealth. A prima
donna, rage in her heart and a horse-whip under her coat,
has been seen to leave him placated, hopeful, even smiling.
The particular artistic ointment used by the Colonel as
a cure-all for irritated "artistic" vanity was antique
flattery. If promises were rejected he applied, and with
astonishing results, the unguent of fat praise; he literally
smeared his singers. Then, conscious that another night
had been saved, that Signorina Pugnetto or Signor Niente
were conquered, the Colonel would exclaim in that prodigious voice of his: "My boy! I say! What about a
cold bottle?" (His nephew, Lionel Mapleson, is libra-

rian of the Metropolitan Opera House, a post he has held for over thirty years.) The truth is that clumsy methods were to blame in those antediluvian days. Opera from the financial view-point was as much a fly-by-night affair as the veriest theatrical barnstormer before the perfecting of the managerial machine by Frohman and Hayman. Now, when opera production is safely standardised we are confronted by the undeniable fact that the grand manner in singing has vanished, and that few plays are worth the paper on which they are typewritten.

Nor is this a dyspeptic opinion. So true is it that managerial foresight, abetted by shrewd composers, discounted long ago the possibility. It is an age of mediocrity the world over. As first-class singers are rare, the operatic mills grind out something that demands neither superlative vocal art nor superior acting; just that flying-fish known as a singing-actress, or singing-actor. For one Olive Fremstad, one Matzenauer, we are given a flock of young men and women who neither act nor sing convincingly. Instead of the glorious voices we heard at the Academy or Metropolitan Opera, we are offered more placid entertainment; a better ensemble, better stage productions, the splendor and variety of the scene-painter's art; and at least some compensation—a larger, more balanced orchestra, and greater conductors. There were no Seidls, no Toscaninis in the long ago. Signor Arditi, bald, rotund, self-complaisant, waved his white gloved hand and Adelina Patti sang the wooing measures of his "Il Bacio." As for the stage management it was the abomination of desolation. Because a gauze curtain misses at the opera now, there are columns of protest in the newspapers. What would our captious young scribes have written during the mighty régime when Seidl conducted, and Lilli Lehmann, Marianne Brandt, Niémann, Fischer, Robinson, and Alvary were in the company; when the singing was interrupted by refractory scenery; when the Rheingold was like a natatorium of frogs' legs; when that great artist and instinctive housewife, Brandt, stooped to pick up the potion vial as she sang Brangaene—it had rolled under the couch of the Irish Princess—and with Isolde and Tristan writhing in ecstasy hard by? Yet the stage manager, Theodore Hablemann made an envious reputation. The truth is that grand opera is like a table-d'hôte dinner. The public expects each course to be a miracle, but ends by accepting the good, bad, and indifferent. It's a cheap meal at any price, with music thrown in. Vogue la galère!

I am not particularly interested in the evolution of the operatic machine, but I do remember the golden days— they were usually leaden ones for the singers and managers. Both the Pattis I heard, Ilma di Murska, called by her manager the Hungarian Nightingale; Parepa-Rosa, Brignoli, Campanini. What Carmen performances were given: Minnie Hauk, Del Puente, Campanini and Clara Louise Kellogg-Strakosch, Anna Louise Cary-Raymond, Galassi, starry-voiced Christine Nilsson—it would need libraries to house stories of those artists. Adelina Patti when I last heard her in Albert Hall, London, was a youngish old lady with a blonde wig, her voice with an occasional strand of gold in it, and it was one of the most beautiful organs since Catalani (why drag in Catty? Because she is always mentioned by some critical Struldbrug in connection with Aunt Adelina; like Dean Swift's horrid old man of Laputa, music-critics never die; they dry up and blow away.) Brignoli ate too much and died. Ilma di

Murska married too much and died; and to my surprise
her manager, Signor de Vivo died. But his ghost keeps
company with the spirit of Seïdl in the lobbies of the
Opera. De Vivo was a character. He had a memory
that stretched back to Gluck, or to the early Florentine
opera reformers. He could relate the most moving tales
of managerial mishaps. We christened him the Ancient
Mariner. He was a kindly soul, and for young reporters
of music a treasure-trove. At that time our night school
was held on the Thirty-ninth Street side of the Opera
House. The critical chain-gang were not so comfortably
situated as now. Maurice Grau had recognised that
music-critics are almost human and his press-room became an institution, instead of a bleak barn; I say bleak
because in the old days critical comment was mostly
written in noisy cafés. With the advent of the press-
room and messenger service, criticism was put on a reasonable basis.

The picturesque character of the old-time operatic
manager was missing in the firm of Abbey, Schoeffel &
Grau. Those business men were devoid of the free-
booter spirit. Maurice Grau had experimented with
French opera of the lighter variety. He had served his
apprenticeship under the watchful eye of his uncle, Jacob
Grau. With Henry E. Abbey I seldom came in contact.
He was not musical, though a managerial Czar. I believe he admired Lillian Russell more than any of his
imported prima donnas, with the exception of Nellie
Melba. Mr. Krehbiel has told us of Abbey's belief that
Melba would outshine Calvé; but Maurice Grau knew
better. Maurice, I found charming, companionable, and
willing to judge a case fairly. We met in the old Hotel

St. James, at the corner of Broadway and Twenty-seventh Street, in company with the Dorvals, Joly, Steinberg, and Julian Story. Now all dead except the two Dorvals, who manage the park Casino. Walter Damrosch with Charles A. Ellis gave a season of German opera which proved its recrudescence. Like his father, Leopold Damrosch, he brought back Wagner to a city sick with musical frivolities and futilities (as Sir Thomas Beecham is doing now at Drury Lane, London). He also permitted us to hear Materna, Klafsky—who looked like a cook but sang like one of the choirs of Cherubim—and Gadski. Materna, Wincklemann and Scaria we had heard and seen—they were palpable, physically speaking—in concert at the beginning of the eighties. Shrewd as they were, Abbey, Schoeffel & Grau were more than once confronted by bankruptcy. No wonder. What company before or after could boast such a lyric firmament? Think of the names—a "galaxy," a "constellation," as the "passionate press-agent" —Philip Hale's phrase—wrote in those "halcyon" days. Imperious Lilli Lehmann, who had come over from the Stanton forces for a period; the greatest dramatic soprano, in Italian as well as German rôles, of them all; Jean and Edouard de Reszke, Scalchi—she had four distinct tone-productions—Melba, beautiful Emma Eames, Nordica, Calvé, Victor Maurel, Plançon, Lassalle and in one season! My brain positively goes giddy at the sight of "Les Huguenots" all stars programme. Luigi Mancinelli, among other conductors, held his own.

The consulship of Heinrich Conried was not during my critical bailiwick. He will go down in musical history as the man who defied the fulminations of Baireuth and produced "Parsifal" for the first time outside the sacred precincts of the Thuringian Graal. His "Salome"

production, with Alfred Hertz conducting—and he is a
sympathetic conductor of Richard Strauss—would have
been a musical event of importance had it not been for
the notoriety of the affair. Our music-critics, all sober,
God-fearing men, with imaginations devoid of the morbid or salacious, were thrown into a tumult by Philip
Hale, who called their attention to the fact that Salome
was a degenerate, suffering from a rare and "beautiful
case"—as the diagnosticians say—of necrophilia. No
one ever heard of the disease except madhouse doctors
or readers of Kraft-Ebbing and the poetry of Maurice
Rollinat. The conjunction of Oscar Wilde's name completed the havoc. A scandal ensued. Unhappy Olive
Fremstad never sang so overwhelmingly as at that Sunday morning's full-dress rehearsal. Her apostrophe to
the papier-mâché head of John the Baptist, on a "property" charger, set moralists gloating. Here was a chance
to get back at haughty Richard Strauss, who had dared
to flout local criticism. The opera was withdrawn.
Anne Morgan, the daughter of J. Pierpont Morgan, was
shouldered with the responsibility, although she has frequently disavowed the soft impeachment, always going
to hear "Salome" when Oscar Hammerstein revived it
with wonderful Mary Garden as the sweet-scented heroine. Philip Hale must have smiled more than once at
the effect on our unsophisticated souls of his verbal firebrand. There is no more "degeneracy" in the magnificent outburst of savage exultation and poignant passion
of Salome over the head of the Baptist than in Isolde's
loving lament over Tristan—his, too, is a dead skull.
The real neurotic in the sloppy little play—a parody of
Flaubert's "Hérodiade"—is the King. Since then Salome has become a commonplace. But that last song

is the most intense in all musical literature. When he wrote it—not without the aid of Richard Wagner—Strauss was a genius.

I came to New York in 1886 and found the American Opera Company in full swing, with Jeannette M. Thurber on the managerial side-saddle and Theodore Thomas at the musical helm. And that is history, a history full of heart-burnings, bankers, Charles E. Locke, and other "bobos" inseparable from operatic infancy. That Theodore Thomas, by all odds the most satisfying conductor of symphony that America then had, and our supreme educational force, was at his happiest in opera I can't say. Like Toscanini, he was a martinet with his forces, but unlike the great Italian conductor, he was too rigid in his beat for the singers. My darling recollection of the Metropolitan Opera House is that of the first "Tristan and Isolde." I pawned my winter overcoat to buy a seat in the top gallery—it was the first seat, first row, to the right. But it was worth a hundred coats to hear Lehmann, with Seidl conducting. When I told Maurice Egan, our Ambassador to Denmark for many years, then an editor, always a poet, of the episode, he was in despair, saying that people don't do such things even for art's sake. At his home I met Henry George, and played for him a "Single Tax March" on the theme of his then celebrated book (with the assistance of Chopin; it was a funeral march). Earlier at the opera I had heard Patti in "Carmen"—not any worse than Lehmann's gypsy—and Signor Perugini, Johnny Chatterton in private life, as Alfredo in "Traviata," his solitary appearance, I believe. With the advent of German opera the now familiar head of Victor Herbert popped up among the violoncelli in the

orchestra; he was then the husband of Theresa Herbert-
Foerster, a handsome Viennese woman, who sang with a
sumptuous voice in Goldmark's "Queen of Sheba."
Marcella Sembrich I had first heard in Paris and afterwards in Philadelphia about 1884. She belongs to the
great and almost vanished generation of vocal goddesses.
Milka Ternina, an Isolde and Brunhilde without parallel,
has left the lyric stage. Calvé still sings. I heard her
in vaudeville. I swear that my eyes were wet. There
were holes in her voice, but the "magnetism" as of old.
What a night was that first Carmen of hers! She chucked
tradition to the winds, also her lingerie. Some of the
elder critics are still blushing. I recall a certain hot
morning in August, 1892, when I was hurriedly summoned by Manager Edmund C. Stanton to the Metropolitan—rather to an eruption of fire, for the stage and
the rear of the house were burning. Otto Weil, now
with the present management, stood with Rudolph and
Albert Aronson on the roof of the Casino and watched
the flare-up. I was luckier. After the worst had passed
I stood in a parterre-box with Mr. Stanton and looked
at the blazing pit which had been the stage. Tongues of
flame, yellowish-red, still licked the edges of the prosce-
nium, and I expected to hear the magic fire-music of the
Valkyries. Wotan was fire chief, but Loki had fairly
vanquished him. Where the Knickerbocker Theatre
now is was Luehr's Café, and with a few of the house-
staff, Thomas Bull among the rest, we discussed the depressing outlook for the forthcoming operatic season.
There was none; 1892–1893 was a closed season, not the
first that had gone up in smoke. The Luehr's hostelry
saw many musical faces during the Stanton régime.

Report hath it that Isolde Lehmann "rushed the growler" from the hotel across the street; I think she was then the wife of the tenor, Paul Kalisch.

I was Mr. Stanton's private secretary at the National Conservatory of Music, where he was Mrs. Thurber's Secretary (I spelled my job with a small "s") and as two hired men we hit it off capitally. He was first and last the typical clubman. Tall, distinguished in bearing, he never lost his equilibrium even when verbally assaulted by irate lyrical ladies. Once, at a rehearsal, after Lehmann had protested in an eloquent manner about the dusty stage, and said that it was like a latrine, he calmly replied in his homespun German: "Frau Lehmann, Sie sind nicht sehr lady-like." This drove her to fury and her retort froze my blood. It was both an invitation and a menace. Stanton never winced. Saluting the prima donna, he left the auditorium. Even the imperturbable Seidl smiled. But Stanton was not the man to lead a forlorn operatic hope. If Abbey, Schoeffel & Grau couldn't, who could? Certainly not Conried. Gatti-Casazza seems to have solved the problem. But he has subventions and Caruso. He also had Arturo Toscanini, who, I am sorry to say, is in Italy. He belongs to the Brahmin conductors; to the company of Richter, Levi, Seidl, Mottl, Mahler. A more poetically intense "Tristan" than his reading with the lovely Olive Fremstad as the impassioned Isolde, I have seldom heard. Toscanini is a superman. In that frail frame of his there is enough dynamic energy with which to capture Gehenna. He is all spirit. He does not always achieve the ultimate heights as did Seidl, as does Arthur Nikisch. While his interpretation of "Tristan" is a wonderfully worked-out musical picture, yet the elemen-

Meinem lieben verehrten Freunde
James Huneker zur Erinnerung
Marcella Sembrich

New York Febr. 3. 1909

MARCELLA SEMBRICH

tal ground-swell, which Anton Seidl summoned from the vasty deep, is missing. But what ravishing tone-colours Toscanini mixed on his orchestral palette!

I saw much of Seidl. His profile was sculptural. So was his manner. But a volcano beneath. He was a taciturn man. He smoked to distraction. I've often seen him with Antonin Dvorak, the Bohemian composer, at the old Vienna Bakery Café, next to Grace Church. There the coffee and pastry were the best in town. The conductor and composer would sit for hours without speaking. It was Seidl who introduced the New World Symphony by Dvorak. Nahan Franko told me that Seidl's hair was originally red till he dyed it; and Fred Schwab asserted that he was a Jew. I only know that Seidl's hair was iron-grey, and that he had studied for the priesthood at Budapest. His expression was eminently ecclesiastical. He never seemed a happy man to me. His wife in the eighties was pretty and fresh-coloured, a Teutonic blonde, also an admirable singer. As Seidl-Krauss she was a member of the Metropolitan Opera House and I recall her Eva in "The Mastersingers" with pleasure. It was rumoured that the great Hungarian conductor had been in love with an equally celebrated Wagnerian singer in the Neumann company years before. His Gothic head I've seen in mediæval tryptichs, as a donator at Bruges or Ghent or else among the portraits of Holbein. His shell was difficult to pierce, but once penetrated his friends found a very warm-hearted human.

Of Rafael Joseffy I can only say this: I loved the man as well as the artist. He was that rara avis, a fair-minded musician. He never abused a rival, but for pre-

sumptuous mediocrity he had a special set of needles
steeped in ironic acid. Pst! A phrase and the victim
collapsed, the wind escaping from his pretensions like a
pricked toy-balloon. His touch, his manner of attack on
the keyboard spiritualised its wiry timbre; the harsh,
inelastic, unmalleable metallic tone, inseparable from the
music made by conventional pianists, became under his
magic fingers floating, transparent, evanescent. His
plastic passage-work—so different from Liszt's wrought-
iron figuration, or the sonorous golden blasts of Rubinstein—his atmospheric pedalling and gossamer arabesques
—you ask in desperation if Joseffy played the piano, what
instrument then did his contemporaries play? With a
few exceptions he made the others seem a trifle obvious.
De Pachmann, Godowsky, Paderewski were his favourite
artists. To him alone may they be compared. Chopin's
style must have been, according to reports, like the
pianissimist Vladimir de Pachmann's. That Russian was
extraordinary, though his playing never had the intellect
nor the brilliancy of Joseffy's. Ah! the beauty of Joseffy's hands, with their beautiful weaving motions, those
curved birdlike flights symbolic of the music. One night
at Lüchow's, sitting with Ed Ziegler, August—Himself—
Joseffy and De Pachmann, an argument was started. De
Pachmann, who had been especially irritable, turned vicious and spitting out his rage—he was a feline person—he
called Joseffy an unprintable name. Before Joseffy could
answer the villainous attack, I, with a recklessness unusual for me, let the Chopinzee have the contents of my
glass full in the face. If I had been sitting closer I would
have slapped his mouth; as it was, the wetting might
cleanse it. Sputtering, he was led away by a waiter and
presently returned, smiling as if nothing had happened.
Joseffy was disgusted with me, as well he might be. It

was unpardonable, my conduct, and I promptly apologised. Then De Pachmann explained it was jealousy, as I had mentioned Joseffy's name seven times more—he gave the exact figure—than his in my Chopin book. It sounded childish but it dissolved the disagreeable business into laughter. After all had gone away except Ziegler, Joseffy turned to me and severely reproached me but ended his sermon thus: "And you, of all men, wasted such a lot of good beer!" I can recall the diabolic twinkle in his eye yet.

I always had a strong affection for the Poles and Poland. I fancy it was the Celtic streak in me which spells romantic. If Poland and Ireland and women were "free" what a dull world this would be (excuse the metre), although you may well ask—free for what? Jane Porter's sentimental hero, Thaddeus of Warsaw, was my first introduction to the Sarmatian theme, Chopin my next, and Joseph Conrad is the latest incarnation, though he seems less Polish than his compatriots because his fiction deals with exotic countries; yet rightfully understood he is au fond, as Polish as Mickiewiez or Paderewski. For a decade and more three Polish singers, Marcella Sembrich, the De Reszkes, a Polish actress, Modjeska, and a Polish piano virtuoso, Jan Ignace Paderewski, ruled here in their respective spheres. When Jean de Reszke left us his admirers believed he would never be replaced; nor has he been. There is but one Jean. Not being born with a tenor voice he, "midway in his mortal life," made himself one. He thought tenor as an indispensable proceeding in transforming his barytone into tenor. It was not merely an affair of altitudinous tones, but of timbre. To be an emerald the jewel must first think itself one. This is not Transcendental Mysticism—pardon the seeming tautology—but a trait

well understood in biology, for, while a man cannot add
one cubit to his stature, the giraffe elongated its neck to
get its daily nourishment, and with the will-power and
genius of a Jean de Reszke, a barytone might presumably
become a tenor. There was, naturally, material to work
upon. Jean had vocal wealth in his throat, though not a
multi-millionaire like Enrico Caruso, and he had vocal
brains, an artistic intellect. He, born a barytone with a
high range, will be remembered in operatic history as the
most fascinating tenor in French or German opera. As
voice, and little else, is demanded in the old-fashioned
Italian repertory, he did not shine with the same lustre,
but as Faust or Tristan, Romeo or Siegfried, Raoul, Jean
of Leyden, Don José, Romeo, Lohengrin, who has left
in the memories of his auditors such lovable images?
The nobility of his attitude towards art, his dramatic
assumption of the various rôles, his personal pulchritude,
these were important factors, but beyond all these was
the enigmatic, the magnetic fluid that envelops certain
men and women, an aura—one word is as useless as
another in explaining this—and also enveloping the auditorium. Jean de Reszke possessed the nameless quality
in such abundance that he had only to appear and—there
was light! His entrance in "Lohengrin," the arrested
attitude—and without opening his mouth he became the
Swan Knight in our imagination. There is the word;
Jean was the most imaginative operatic singer of our
times, poetically, tenderly, exquisitely imaginative. This
supersubtle Pole employed the entire battery of his forces;
he was not one of those distressing tenors who tickle the
ear of the groundlings. He invested a character with
all its attributes. Oh, yes! he could take a high C, he
often did in "Faust" and "Siegfried," but such tricks
did not appeal to him. Once, at the Albemarle Hotel, I

heard him sing in the trio from "William Tell" with his brother, Edouard, and Jean Lassalle. Jean sang a high C sharp from the chest without straining. I tell you, he "thought" C sharp, for singing, of all musical achievements, is primarily thought. He was one of the rare tenors who was both virile and musical.

Does Wagner write "vocally"? That question became superfluous after hearing the De Reszkes, Lehmann, Ternina, Fremstad, Fischer, Nordica, Eames, and Plançon. Wagner would have died of enthusiasm if he could have heard his essentially melodic line brought into high relief by these artists. The ancient Baireuth vocal tradition did not quite satisfy the composer, mighty as were its effects. Niemann, almost voiceless, was an incomparable Siegmund and Tristan; in Meyerbeer, despite his histrionic genius, he could not gloss over his vocal deficiencies. And there was a long list of large ladies, barrel-shaped, with iron lungs and a method of acting which consisted in waddling and brandishing aloft their pudgy fists, only that and nothing more. One, we remember, I christened the "Foghorn of Hoboken," because, if the wind was propitious, an easterly wind, and all's well! you could hear her in the heart of Hoboken. Her husband, too, had a Hoboken thirst. The last time I saw the unfortunate couple was at Baireuth. I asked Schumann-Heink the news of the husband-barytone. Madame Ernestine never minces her words: "Last night they were fished out of the gutter, fighting." It was true. The barytone once sang Hans Sachs at the Metropolitan to an obbligato of hiccups. Poor chap, he went down on a steamer off the Hook of Holland. He was doomed to a liquid death. I mention this particular case not as representative but as illustrative of certain characteristics in the old-fashioned Wagnerian school of

singing and acting. These singers had tradition, understanding, and musical ability, but they sang by main
strength, as the Irishman played the fiddle. Seldom
was there plangency in their tones. Lilli Lehmann had
first mastered Italian music; she had been a coloratura
soprano, singing in such rôles as the Queen in "Huguenots," or Filina in "Mignon." (We actually heard—
and saw—her as Filina.) So she brought to Wagner's
music vocal perfections, though she never altogether
cured herself of that glottis-stroke (coup de glotte) which,
however, she could at certain moments make so dramati-
cally effective; her imploring accents when on bended
knees Brunhilde asks her father, Wotan, if her disobedi-
ence is irrevocably unforgiven. This mannerism and a
certain hardness in style, are the only defects I can pick
out in the dazzling artistic cuirass of her career. She was
too stormy in the first act of "Tristan"—oh! that desperate invocation after the curtain rises, when Wagner steals
the thunder of Chopin's C minor, Revolutionary Etude—
and she was not voluptuously tender in Act II. But in
the last scene Lilli was glorious, precisely at the point
where Milka Ternina, her superior in the previous acts,
failed to reach the vocal summit. Fremstad's Isolde is
largely modelled after her teacher's, but it is more tender
and womanly, and in the garden more poetic and lovable. There was always a little of the remote goddess
Brunhilde in Lehmann's impersonation of Isolde, though,
curious to relate, her scene with Wotan in the third act
of "The Valkyrs" was most human, most moving. In-
consistencies are the very web of an artist's conception.

Max Alvary looked a Siegfried, but sang it in a harsh,
pinched voice. That didn't hinder him from becoming

a matinée idol, like Caruso to-day. There was a tug-of-war between mobs of girls when he left the Thirty-ninth Street door of the Opera House. The son of an Achenbach, one of the Düsseldorf school of glazed oil-cloth painters, he was personally a man of breeding, and handsome. But he could eat more at a sitting than Michael Cross, or the huge basso, Lablache, whose feats as a trencherman were Brobdignagian; yet Alvary kept his figure, though I don't doubt that his appetite caused the stomach cancer from which he died. Among the men of the Grau régime, Edouard de Reszke, Plançon, and Victor Maurel were pre-eminent. I don't suppose there is to be found in musical annals a versatility in aptitudes as that displayed by the French barytone, Victor Maurel. Or if this claim is lacking in historical perspective, then I shall put the question this way: Is there an actor on any stage to-day who can portray both the grossness of Falstaff and the subtlety of Iago? Making necessary allowance for the different art medium that the singing actor must work in, and despite the larger curves of pose and gesture, Maurel kept astonishingly close to the characters he assumed. His Falstaff was the most wonderful I ever saw; Billy Burton and the elder Hackett were not in my time. Tree's Falstaff was a Jack-pudding in an inflated life-saver. I think that Mr. Wenman's—he came here with Irving—Falstaff and Sir Toby Belch were the best assumptions, for I can't recall my old friend, George Giddens, in these parts, which he must play superlatively well. But Maurel—from what school or schools is he the crystallised product? His voice, worn and siccant, nevertheless could take on any dramatic colouring desired. In Verdi's "Falstaffo" it was bullying, blandishing, defiant, tender and gross; charged with an

impure suggestiveness, and as jolly as a boon companion's.   When he sang the scherzo, "Quand ero paggio del
duca di Norfolk," the lightness of touch brought back
boyish horizons.   And the soliloquy—what eloquence!

And this fat knight whose corpulence and lechery and
unction were conveyed to us not by such obvious symbols as padding or leering, or belching, but were in the
very larynx of Maurel, would, without the wave of an
enchanter's wand, become overnight the sinuous, lean and
treacherous Iago.   The two most satisfying Iagos I
remember were Henry Irving's and Edwin Booth's—
and the first shall be last.   Victor Maurel's paralleled
them at every point.   Admitted that the singing height-
ens the impression, but in reality weakens the characterisation, yet Maurel's Iago never betrayed a tendency
towards the melodramatic; he held a middle course, as
difficult as treading on eggs without crushing them, and
was both a picture and a dramatic happening.   Malignant he was, that is the "fat" of the part; but he underlined the reason for his sinister actions.   Iago is beginning to be less the "spirit that denies" than a human
with a sound motive for revenge.   I know you will remind me that critical "whitewashing" is become the
fashion, that Nero, Simon Magus, Judas Iscariot, Bene-
dict Arnold are only getting their just dues at the hands
of various apologists.   De Quincey, you remember, said
that without Judas the drama of Jesus crucified would
not have occurred; Nero was a much abused monster,
though Renan believes him to be the Beast mentioned
in the Apocalypse—it seems now there were no "atroci-
ties" during the fabulous persecutions of the Jews and
Christians; and Arnold—well, he was of British descent;
that may have accounted for much.   But in the case of

Iago there is something to be said. A pure devil, as we conceive devils to be, he was not. A rough, hard-drinking soldier he admits he is, and to call his "put money in thy purse" cynical is to contravene all worldly wisdom. No, Othello had wronged him, and he hated him for it, hated his wife for her infidelity; therefore, his revenge is credible. It is its method that revolts; Iago is a Machiavelli in action, and Desdemona, perfectly innocent, is crushed between the upper and lower mill-stones of inexorable destiny. This is not meant to be an essay on the esoteric meanings of Shakespeare, but merely the result of studying Maurel's conception, who painted the portrait of Othello's Ancient not all black, but with many gradations and nuances. We used to make fun, Steinberg and I, of what was called the "psychological crook of Iago's left knee," yet not a movement but meant something. Maurel was economical in gesture. His was true objective characterization. His Don Giovanni was another finely painted character. He was the live, courtly, quick to take offense, amorous, intriguing, brave, cruel, and superstitious. His drinking song was vocal virtuosity in its best estate. And there is a catalogue of other rôles, such as De Nevers, Amonasro, which need not detain us. Suffice to say that Verdi entrusted to him the task of originating such widely sundered rôles as Iago and Falstaff.

Tall, handsome, athletic, a boxer of skill, Maurel in private life was not unlike his Don Juan of the footlights. Innumerable are the anecdotes related of his conquests. Women in society deserted hearth and husband for him. If there were Elviras there were Annas and Zerlinas; also Merry Wives. Once these merry ladies plotted a surprise for Falstaff in St. Louis. Letters brimming with

passionate protestations were sent to the Fat Knight and
fairly drove him to distraction as they all made a rendezvous for the same hour, though in different parts of
the city. He drove from spot to spot, but the merry
wives failed to keep their appointments. They saw
him. They were in ambush and their laugh was longer
than at Herne's Oak. But the Knight never roared,
nor betrayed a sign of defeat. Perhaps he knew. Had
Eames, Scalchi, Melba, or Calvé hatched the conspiracy
against his happiness? I'll never tell. One thing I do
know—Maurel interested women, even those who de-
claimed loudest against his philandering. I saw a pho-
tographic nude of him posed as a boxer. It was as
Greek as if the figure had been modelled by some classical
sculptor. A picturesque figure of a man. In his best
years, Maurel was an inspiring swell. On Fifth Avenue
of a fine day he was to be seen with his retinue. He
swaggered. He was the Great Lover to the life. Surrounded by his secretaries, his pugilist, his fencing-master,
his pianist, and a lot of singers he was an event on the
Avenue. One could have said some fantastic Italian
Prince of the Renaissance who had strayed into the nineteenth century. To-day at three score and ten, he is
still the Grand Seigneur, and seldom misses a first night
at the Metropolitan.

A friend of mine, a young American painter, first saw
the object encircling the robust throat of Victor Maurel
at the opera. Standing in the auditorium during the
entr'acte, talking to the French portraitist, Théobald
Chartrain, the great singer faced the audience. He wore
evening clothes, did Maurel, like any other private
citizen. It was his collar that riveted the glance of my
friend, the painter. Such a collar! Such a shape;

archaic, mediæval, exotic, altogether fascinating for students of costumes of historic periods. It was a low turnover collar, the points close, its height inconsiderable; indeed, so low that the throat of the singer was exposed. Nearer, the observer noted that two gold pins were carelessly thrust into either side of the linen. These pins evoked Byzantine luxury. Puzzled by the odd architecture, yet fearful of appearing rude, the painter devoured this collar with hungry eyes. Then retreating to the lobby he made a pencilled sketch from memory, upon his cuff. But he questioned his memory. Where had he seen just such a cryptic pattern? From what storehouse of pictures had the barytone drawn his model? The Prado, the National Gallery? The Louvre? And from whom? There is a Bronzino there—a warrior in black armour over the hauberk of which flows a point lace creation. No, not Bronzino. Botticelli, Da Vinci, Velasquez? Aha! He had it. A Hyacinthe Rigaud, also the simulacrum of an armoured warrior, from whose neck peeps a low, reversed collar, with close points, two jewelled stick pins speared through the sides. He had his Maurel now. He, too, could command his phœnix among collars. And he did. He continued commanding for years. He spent his inheritance on shirt-makers. He dissipated the considerable legacy of an aunt. He went abroad. He became known to London haberdashers. In Paris he was called "M. le Col." He was the King of Collars. But his pursuit of the infinite was in vain. Though he dragged an artist, skilled in the facture of collars before the Rigaud portrait at the Louvre, yet did he fail to extort from his plastic genius the desired perfection. The collar! The collar! Almost beggared he dragged his weary soul back to New York. His brush for want of practice had lost its cunning and he was forced to earn a living by photography. One day he saw M. Maurel on the Avenue. With a rapidly beating heart the painter feverishly stared at the neck of the Frenchman. He fled, despair counselling suicide. The singer was wearing a high-standing monstrosity, with flaring points. No gold stick pins. A life had been wasted in search of an impossible ideal. The tragedy is all the more poignant because the unhappy young fanatic for "significant form" did not know that whenever Maurel changed the style of his neck linen he was traversing a new psychic emotional tempest, the symbol of which he bravely displayed to curious impertinents. Ah! the collar, the very subtle collar, of M. Maurel.

IV

THE DE RESZKES AND PADEREWSKI

Edouard de Reszke was a splendid man, yet not the finished vocal artist that was Pol Plançon. That Frenchman, despite his mincing gait and meticulous methods, could melt the heart of a wooden Indian; naturally he was best in French and Italian rôles, though it was a pleasure to hear him deliver with faultless finish the music of Wagner. He, like the De Reszkes, was an imposing figure on and off the boards. But virility was absent, though in "La Navarraise," that noisy little piece of Massenet and in company with Emma Calvé, he was a soldier every inch of him. And his Mephistos, Gounod's and Boito's, were masterpieces of characterisation. Edouard, however, had dramatic temperament. With what sonorous abandon he sang the "Veau d'or" or the "Piff-Paff." The first night of "Romeo and Juliet" he was the Friar Laurence, Eames, with Jean de Reszke, as the lovers. The music is sentimental pastry—the French from Voltaire to Gounod have never grasped Shakespeare —but with such singers even the sloppy music did not veil the poetry and pathos of the interpretation. Jean often sang the rôle with Nellie Melba as the Juliet, yet, for me, Eames seemed the ideal Juliet. Edouard was a big, good-natured Mephisto, and a satisfying King Mark. When the brothers lived at the old Gilsey House, I occasionally visited them and witnessed some performances of Edouard in the eternal Italian opera called "Spaghetti."

Living as they did so many years in Italy their favourite
cuisine was the Italian. "Why should I fill up on soup?"
Edouard would ask. "A dinner should begin with a
pasta," and his always did. Eating nothing before they
sang, their midnight meal was a spectacle that would
have driven a dyspeptic frantic. The spaghetti was literally wheeled into the room and disappeared like snow
under the rays of a mellow sun. Years later at Warsaw,
I met their brother, Victor de Reszke, who owned one
of the principal hotels in the Polish city. He boasted
a genuine tenor voice, a lyric tenor, and, being a De
Reszke, also a musical temperament. He told me, inter
alia, that a singer should not eat much, but, he added,
they always do. He meant Edouard; even Jean became
too stout; when he abandoned opera his voice was far
from being worn. He could have lasted ten years—but
that spaghetti! In Paris, I heard Josephine de Reszke,
his sister, at the opera. She sang with consummate
taste.

The advent of Paderewski was the most sensational
since Joseffy's and Rubinstein's. He took the town by
storm. His first rehearsal occurred one afternoon in
1891 at Carnegie Hall. He was slender, orchidaceous,
and resembled the drawing by Edward Burne-Jones. He
was the very flowering of the type beloved of the Pre-
raphaelite painter. He played with orchestra the C
minor concerto of Saint-Saëns' musically empty work,
but a favourite warhorse of Leschetizky pupils, why, I
can't say; the G minor concerto is of more musical value.
I attended that rehearsal, not only because I was curious
to hear the young Polish virtuoso, but for the reason that
I had to write two criticisms of the concert, which was to
take place the evening of the next day; one for *The*

EDOUARD DE RESZKE   JEAN DE RESZKE

Reproduced by courtesy Frida Ashforth

Musical Courier, the other for the New York *Recorder,* a
new-born daily newspaper, of which I was musical editor.
Of course, I raved over "Paddy" and wrote a prose-
poem, A Study in Old Gold, or some such affected
title. I was suffering from "preciousness" and a rush
rhapsody to the pen. I was earnest, however, in my
admiration of Jan Ignace, who painted with a golden
romantic brush, whose style was poetic, manly, musical.
In Paris he had, unannounced, made a deep impression
with the Schumann concerto. He had "substituted"
for his friend and preceptor, Annette Essipova, one of
Leschetizky's wives, and a pianist of the first rank. She
was indisposed—quite conveniently—and the unknown
youth had his first hearing and pleased a critical audience. His subsequent triumphs are history. I may add
that as a man, artist, and patriot, Premier Jan Ignace
Paderewski is altogether remarkable. His general culture is wide, his modesty most engaging, and he has heart
enough to free Poland, if heart alone counted. Not
witty in the sense that Rosenthal or Joseffy were witty,
his is the profoundest nature of the three. The "magnetism" which overflows the auditorium when he plays
is the same in his impassioned appeals for the succour of
his unhappy land. He is the reincarnation of Thaddeus
of Warsaw, or the "Pan Tadeusz" of Mickiewicz. In
certain Chopin compositions, I have never heard his
peer notably in the F minor concerto; but then he
plays all schools with amazing versatility. But Schumann and Chopin are his favourites. I have preserved
a telegram he sent me bearing the date February 19,
1900, and from Memphis, Tenn. It reads: "Will you
kindly do me the favour to act as judge in prize competi-
tion for American composers in April? Please reply to

Vendome Theatre, Nashville." I accepted, and that
was the last I heard of the matter, evidently he hadn't
apprised the other judges—I've forgotten who they were
—and I've also forgotten the winners of the prize. I
fancy my connection with *The Musical Courier* did not
please the members of the jury, and I confess I wasn't
sorry. Such competitions seldom bring forth fruit;
nevertheless, I told Paderewski, but he only smiled—in
Polish. At one period I saw much of him, heard him
play fragments from his unpublished Polish Fantasy for
piano, and he made me the proposal for me to edit a
projected musical journal in London. He was to furnish
the capital. I refused. I was too much enamoured of
New York, in 1892, and its multitudinous attractions.
This refusal I now regret. I asked Paderewski about the
Burne-Jones sketch. He said that when he first visited
London, probably in 1889 or 1890, he was riding in a
'bus and facing him was an elderly artistic-looking man,
who stared at him in a most embarrassing fashion. When
the pianist alighted the other followed and, asking his
pardon, gave him a card. It was Sir Edward Burne-
Jones, then celebrated, and Paderewski with his accustomed amiability accepted the invitation of the painter
to pose for him. It is the one head of his that I like.
The flaming locks, the intense spiritual life that marked
the mask of the Pole, must have been an inspiration to
the Englishman, who has in a large composition shown us
Vivien and Merlin, and, for the enchanter, enchanted
by the "woven paces" of the siren, he took Liszt as the
model. Paderewski's head fascinated him.

IGNACE PADEREWSKI
From a crayon drawing by Burne-Jones

V

NORDICA AND FREMSTAD

Nordica never impressed me as a genius, as did Lehmann, Ternina, and Fremstad. She had not much emotional draught. She was not temperamental in their
sense. Her voice, too, sweet as it was, never thrilled.
She was not a Brunhilde born nor could she sound all
the notes of Isolde's tragic octave. But she had charm,
and before she entered the Felia Litvinne class of operatic
heavy-weights, she was pleasant to gaze upon; towards
the end of her career she looked like a large, heavily
upholstered couch. She was a "slow study" but stub-
bornly industrious, and underwent the torture of one
thousand piano rehearsals before she ventured to sing
Isolde. At the last one her faithful accompanist became
so enthusiastic over her singing that he expressed it in
unmistakable masculine style. A furious chase ensued
and Nordica, after dodging her adorer, finally slipped out
of the room. She told me the story with such realism
that I asked her why she troubled herself about such a
little thing as a kiss, and her reply was truly feminine:
"He had been eating garlic." And "he" was not an
Italian nor a Frenchman. Of Olive Fremstad I may
only say that whatever critical reservations one may
make as to her performance of Isolde or Brunhilde, her
Brangaene and Sieglinde were the most satisfying to the
eye and ear I ever experienced. Her Brangaene was a
dazzling young witch, and not the plain maid-of-all-work

we usually see and hear; her Sieglinde was a creature
compact of love and pathos and vocally wonderful.
When Fremstad as a girl sang in a Valkyrs chorus, led
by Seidl at a concert hall, Madison Avenue, corner
Fifty-ninth Street—about 1890—she was very pretty and
her blonde hair an aureole; you recalled the exclamation
of that Pope, who, on seeing some English youth, pris-
oners, said: "Non Angli, sed Angeli." At Baireuth the
American girl was one of the Rhine Daughters, this was
1896; and in 1901, a developed artist, she sang Brangaene
to Nordica's Isolde at the inauguration of the Prince
Regent's Opera House, and she is my only agreeable
artistic memory in a performance that was enlivened by
the Isolde, Nordica, falling across the Tristan in the garden
scene, and as both were corpulent, there was a silent
scramble watched with immense sympathy by a corpulent
audience. Madame Fremstad's artistic career has been
all her early critics prophesied.

I spoke a moment ago of Felia Litvinne. She was the
sister of Edouard de Reszke's wife, a Canadian born, I
believe; and the sister of Willy Schutz. Madame
Litvinne was an excellent operatic soprano. She sang
Isolde to Jean de Reszke's Tristan. She was also blonde,
and very stout. Edouard said that it was mere turn of
the wrist for her to eat a two-pound box of sweetmeats
at a single sitting. He remonstrated with her, so did
her women friends, but to no avail. Her brother, Willy,
was indignant when he related his struggles with her.
She always swallowed the chocolates before he could
grab them; she said that he wanted them for himself.
It may have been so. Willy was a joyous character.
He would have made the ideal prima donna's husband,

OLIVE FREMSTAD
At Baireuth, 1896

the kind that hunts the Metropolitan lobby during en'tr
actes, who, conducting you to a corner, whispers: "Hein!
Now what you think! My wife she knocks fifty hells
out of that stupid Museria!" The stupid one is the
rival prima donna, of course. If you cheerfully acquiesce
you are immediately piloted across the street to the chop-
house. On account of such husbands of prima donnas
both Max Hirsh and William J. Guard acquired their
grey hair. Willy Schutz never attempted to conceal his
admiration and love for Nordica. He must have proposed to her at least twice a week. I was in his company
on the terrace of the Monferino Café, Paris, when the
startling news reached us that Nordica had married the
Hungarian, Zoltan Doeme—whose real name is Solomon
Teitlbaum. He sang Parsifal at Baireuth only once. I
was present. So was Nordica. Yet she married him.
This marriage proved almost fatal to Willy. He had
fetched from New York the pet French poodle of Madame
Nordica. It was a fetish for Willy. He and the dog disappeared for a week, after the news from America, and
when next he turned up, the pup, which had been snow
white, was dyed black, and around its woolly neck it
wore a huge crêpe bow. On its tail another emblem. It
was the palpable expression of Willy's sorrow. The
cocottes on the terrace set up a wail of commiseration:
"Oh! la belle Toutou, he has lost his maman!" The
history was pretty well canvassed and with the sentimental sympathy of their class. That night Willy Schutz
was a hero who had been jilted by a heartless coquette.
He positively sobbed as he looked at the canine in mourn-
ing; but the dog didn't seem to mind it. Poor Willy, he
was not very strong above the eyes, but he was tender-
hearted and he meant well, but his waistcoat was so

heavily paved with good intentions that he waddled. His dog, Nordica's forsaken animal, reminds me of the epitaph I made for a Mexican hairless pup, one of those shivering tiny brutes that yaps and snarls at every stranger. It was prized by Adelina Patti, who forced her visitors to kiss its snout. When it passed away during some ineffable indigestion I wrote this for its tombstone: "Requiesdog in Patti." Henderson, then of *The Times*, said my Latin was faulty, but you can't write "requiescat" when it's a dog, can you?

VI

OSCAR HAMMERSTEIN

Well I remember the first day that the late Oscar Hammerstein entered *The Musical Courier* office and introduced himself. He told Marc Blumenberg that he was worth a million dollars, made by some patent cigar-cutting machine. He was also the editor of a trade-journal devoted to the tobacco industry. Blumenberg looked at me and shook his head. "Meshugah! You think I am," said the future impresario; "I'll show you I'm not crazy." He produced proofs. A millionaire he certainly was, and Marc became interested. Who wouldn't? Oscar was dreaming of opera in English. The failures of the American opera had only blazed the trail for him. He saw that cheap prices and good singing in our native language would solve the problem. There was much pow-wowing which didn't intrigue me as the less I understand of operatic speech the more I enjoy the music. Yet, as Harry B. Smith has truthfully remarked: "When the opera is a success the composer gets the credit, when a failure, the blame is inevitably saddled on the librettist." As the librettist of "Robin Hood" and a string of De Koven successes, Mr. Smith knew what he was talking about. W. S. Gilbert was in the same rocking boat with Arthur Sullivan. Later, Oscar Hammerstein was to settle the question by writing the words and music of his opera "The Kohinoor." But at first he was rather timid. I don't believe he took Blumenberg's advice, or the advice

of anyone. Opera at the Harlem Opera House followed.
It was not enlivening. I recall the burning mountain
in Auber's "Masaniello—or the Dumb Girl of Portici!"
—and the various burning thirsts of 125th Street.
Naught else. But Oscar was not a man easily discour-
aged. He played the game with energy and recklessness.
Strictly speaking, he was a gambler born. Organising
opera companies, vaudeville shows—at the old Victoria,
for example—erecting opera houses in New York and
Philadelphia and London, playing with men and millions,
what were the achievements of Henry E. Abbey or Col.
Jack Haverly compared with this shrewd, ever witty,
good-tempered Hebrew, who was as prodigal with his own
money as the others were with the capital of strangers!

Hammerstein's original operetta was as celebrated as
the Hammerstein hat. It was the result of a wager
made between Oscar and Gustave Kerker, the composer
of "The Belles of New York," "Castles in the Air," and
a dozen popular operettas. "Gus," an excellent musician,
was skeptical concerning the ability of Hammerstein.
At a table in the café of the old Gilsey House sat Hammerstein, Kerker, the late Charles Alfred Byrne—dramatic
critic of *The Journal* and librettist of "Castles in the Air,"
which employed the talents of De Wolf Hopper, Tom Sea-
brooke, and Della Fox—Henry Neagle, dramatic editor
of *The Recorder*, and myself. Oscar, becoming excited,
offered to compose an opera, words and music, in forty-
eight hours. Kerker took him up. The thing became
serious. Rooms were engaged on the top floor of the
Gilsey, an upright piano installed, and, cut off from the
outer world, Hammerstein began fingering out his tunes,
writing words, putting them all on paper. I forgot to
add that Gus Kerker agreed to arrange the music for

orchestra. We had lots of fun. Louis Harrison engaged a relay of hand-organs to play under the composer's windows, but Oscar never winced; plates of sinister ham sandwiches were sent to his room accompanied by cocktails. And the tray was returned empty with many thanks. I've forgotten all the pranks we played to no purpose. Complaints were made by sundry guests at the office that a wild man was howling and thumping the keyboard; again uselessly, for, barricaded, the stubborn composer refused to give up the fort. Exhausted, but still smiling, he invited the jury on awards to listen to his music. It proved a tuneful hodge-podge, as might have been expected, and Kerker threw up the sponge. The opera was actually produced at the New York Theatre a few months later, reinforced by extra numbers and considerably edited, and it met with success. That first night of "The Kohinoor" was a notorious one; also side-splitting. The audience, of the true Tenderloin variety, laughed themselves blue in the face. I remember that the opening chorus consumed a third of the first act. Oscar knew the art of camouflage before the word was invented. Two comic Jews, alternately for a half-hour sang: "Good morning, Mr. Morgenstern, Good morning, Mr. Isaacstein," while the orchestra shifted the harmonies so as to avoid too much monotony; I fancy that was a Kerker device. Oscar "composed" a second operetta, but it never achieved the popularity of the first.

During a certain period the Hammerstein hat was without a duplicate except that worn by William M. Chase, the painter. However, the Hammerstein hat was unique, not alone for the grey matter it covered, but because of its atmospheric quality. It was a temperamental barometer. When the glass had set fair the tilt of the hat was unmistakable. If storm-clouds gathered on the vocal horizon the hat felt the mood and righted itself like a buoy in agitated waters. Its brim settled over the eyes of the impresario. His people scurried into anonymous corners. Or the hat was pushed off his forehead; unbuttoned then his soul. You could approach and ask for seats. A weather gauge was Oscar's hat. What a brim! Oh! the breadth and flatness thereof. How glossy its nap, in height, how amiable. To have described Hammerstein without his hat would be to give the ring without Wotan. Shorn of it the owner would have been like Alberich sans tarnhelm. As an Irishman would say: his hat was his heel of Achilles. He was said to wear it while sleeping, if he ever slept. Inside was stencilled the wisdom of Candide: "Il faut cultiver notre Jardin" (Mary, of course). Many painters have yearned to portray that hat on Oscar's dome of action. The Impressionists would paint its complementary tones: the late William M. Chase would have transformed it into a shiny still-life; George Luks would make it a jest of Hades; while Arthur B. Davies would turn it into a symbol—the old Hebraic chant, Kol Nidrei, might be heard echoing about its curved surfaces, as echoes the Banshee on a funereal night in Tipperary. It was a hat, cosmopolitan, joyous, alert, both reticent and expansive. It caused a lot of people sleepless nights, this sawed-off stovepipe with its operatic airs. Why did Oscar Hammerstein wear it? For the same reason that the miller wore his hat, and not for tribal or other reasons.

VII

ANTONIN DVORAK

It was Rafael Joseffy who introduced me to Mrs. Jeannette M. Thurber. This energetic and public-spirited lady, who accomplished more by her failures than other people's successes, met with an enormous amount of critical opposition when she started the American opera movement. Some of her opponents would have liked to mount the "band wagon," and, failing, abused her audacity. But she had the right idea which was the French one. She first founded a National Conservatory in 1881, where musical talent was welcomed and tuition free. There was a "théâtre d'application," with Emy Fursch-Madi, Victor Capoul, Emil Fischer, M. Dufriche, Jacques Bouhy, and other famous opera singers and teachers, wherein the rudiments of acting and vocal delivery could be mastered. What a list of artists the faculty comprised! Antonin Dvorak, the great Bohemian composer, in his prime, was musical director; Rafael Joseffy and Adele Margulies—a fine pianist and founder of the Margulies Trio—headed the piano department; Camilla Urso, greatest of women violinists, Victor Herbert, then a leading solo violoncellist, Leopold Lichtenberg, formerly of the Boston Symphony Orchestra, and one of the most brilliant American talents I recall— although John F. Rhodes, of Philadelphia, had an immense technical gift—Anton Seidl, Otto Oesterle, the flutist of the Thomas Orchestra and the Philharmonic

Society, conductor Frank Van der Stucken, Emil Paur, C. P. Warren, organist, Bruno Oscar Klein, Horatio Parker, Wassili Safanoff, Gustav Hinrichs, John Cheshire, the harpist, Sapio, Fritz Geise, great Dutch cellist of the Kneisel Quartet, Leo Schulz, first cellist of the Philharmonic, Julia Wyman, all these and others were teachers at this institution, which was then located on Seventeenth Street, east of Irving Place. Well I remember the day that I begged Harry Rowe Shelley, the Brooklyn organist, to submit his compositions to Dvorak; later he became one of the pupils of that master; some of the others were Rubin Goldmark, nephew of the famous composer, himself one of the most gifted among our younger Americans. Harvey W. Loomis, Henry Waller, Harry T. Burleigh, the popular coloured barytone, now a composer of repute, and William Arms Fisher. Henry T. Finck, the faithful, still lectures in the National Conservatory at its new building on the West Side. I taught piano classes twice weekly for ten years, and in addition was the press representative of the Conservatory and secretary to the Secretary, Mr. Stanton, and after he died, I was a secretary to Mrs. Thurber, my chief duty being a daily visit at her residence, where I sat for an hour and admired her good looks. She was a picturesque woman, Gallic in her "allures," but more Spanish than French in features. She spoke French like a Parisian, and after thirty years I confess that her fine, dark, eloquent eyes troubled my peace more than once. But I only took it out in staring. Curiously to relate, Mrs. Thurber has changed but little, a grey lock or two, which only makes her more picturesque than ever.

Old Borax, as Dvorak was affectionately called, was handed over to me by Madame Thurber when he arrived.

He was a fervent Roman Catholic, and I hunted a Bohemian church for him as he began his day with an early Mass. Rather too jauntily I invited him to taste the American drink called a whisky cocktail. He nodded his head, that of an angry-looking bulldog with a beard. He scared one at first with his fierce Slavonic eyes, but was as mild a mannered man as ever scuttled a pupil's counterpoint. I always spoke of him as a boned pirate. But I made a mistake in believing that American strong waters would upset his Czech nerves. We began at Goerwitz, then described a huge circle, through the great thirst belt of central New York. At each place Doc Borax took a cocktail. Now, alcohol I abhor, so I stuck to my guns, the usual three-voiced invention, hops, malt, and spring water. We spoke in German and I was happy to meet a man whose accent and grammar were worse than my own. Yet we got along swimmingly—an appropriate enough image, for the weather was wet, though not squally. He told me of Brahms and that composer's admiration for Dvorak. I agreed with Brahms. Dvorak had a fresh, vigorous talent, was a born Impressionist, and possessed a happy colour sense in his orchestration. His early music was the best; he was an imitator of Schubert and Wagner, and never used quotation marks. But the American theory of native music never appealed to me. He did, and dexterously, use some negro, or alleged negro, tunes in his "New World Symphony," and in one of his string quartets; but if we are to have true American music it will not stem from "darky" roots, especially as the most original music of that kind thus far written is by Stephen Foster, a white man. The influence of Dvorak's American music has been evil; ragtime is the popular pabulum now. I need hardly add that the negro is not the original race of our country. And ragtime is only rhythmic motion, not music. The Indian has more pretensions musically as E. A. MacDowell has shown in his Suite for Orchestra. This statement does not impeach the charm of the African music made by Harry Burleigh; I only wish to emphasise my disbelief in the fine-spun theories of certain folk-lorists. MacDowell is our most truly native composer, as an Alsatian-born is now our most potent American composer. His name is Charles Martin Loeffler, and he shared the first desk of the violins in the Boston Symphony Orchestra with Franz Kneisel, a noble artist. I mention Loeffler lest we forget.

But Borax! I left him swallowing his nineteenth cocktail. "Master," I said, rather thickly, "don't you think it's time we ate something?" He gazed at me through those awful whiskers which met his tumbled hair half-way: "Eat. No. I no eat. We go to a Houston Street restaurant. You go, hein? We drink the Slivavitch. It warms you after so much beer." I didn't go that evening to the East Houston Street Bohemian café with Dr. Antonin Dvorak. I never went with him. Such a man is as dangerous to a moderate drinker as a false beacon is to a shipwrecked sailor. And he could drink as much spirits as I could the amber brew. No, I assured Mrs. Thurber that I was through with piloting him. When I met Old Borax again at Sokel Hall, the Bohemian resort on the East Side, I deliberately dodged him. I taught one class which was nicknamed "in darkest Africa" because all the pupils were coloured. I confess a liking for negroes, possibly because of my childhood days spent in Maryland. They are very human, very musical, their rhythmic sense remarkable. I had a talented pupil named Paul Bolin, who also studied organ with Heinroth; and another, Henry Guy, whose piano talent was not to be denied. I had the pleasure of hearing this pupil play Mendelssohn's "Cappriccio Brillante" in B minor with an orchestra conducted by Gustav Hinrichs, well known to Philadelphians for his pioneer work there in opera. Both these young men are now professionals, and like the many hundreds educated at the National Conservatory, are earning their living in a dignified manner. What Mrs. Thurber has done for the negro alone will, I hope, be credited to her account in any history of the coloured race. Her musical activities are still unabated. In 1891, Congress granted her school a charter, and the privilege of conferring the degree of musical doctorship. With the war over, the National Conservatory should by right of precedent, and by reason of the vast good accomplished in the musical world since 1881, be made a national institution. So mote it be.

VIII

STEINWAY HALL

Old Steinway Hall on East Fourteenth Street, where it is at present, was my favourite rendezvous. It was the musical centre of the city. William Steinway, high in political councils, was a genuine philanthropist. He assisted struggling talent. He had his hand, a charitable one, in every enterprise of musical moment. A generous, hearty, forthright man. His chief aid was Charles F. Tretbar, in charge of the artistic section of the hall. Mr. Tretbar managed visiting pianists, and helped to organise such orchestral concerts as those given by Theodore Thomas and the Boston Symphony Orchestra. It was in Steinway Hall that I first heard the band from Boston, Gericke, conductor, and Kneisel, concert-master. I was fresh from the orchestra of the Paris Conservatoire, but it couldn't hold a candle to Boston's pride. One rival it had, still has, the Vienna Philharmonic, which I last heard in 1913 under Felix Weingartner. As for piano recitals, they rained on you; even in those days everybody played the piano well, as Felix Leifels has truthfully observed. It was there I heard Karl Klindworth play Chopin, but I preferred his masterly edition of the master's music to his personal performance. A giant then was Edmund Neupert, the Norwegian, to whom Edvard Grieg dedicated his A minor concerto, because it is said Neupert composed for it that massive cadenza in the first movement. Certainly no one before or since interpreted the work as did Neupert, and I heard Grieg himself in London. Neupert's eyes were so large, liquid, and luminous that Madame Alice Garrigue-Mott hinted a summer chalet might have been built on their edge. (Come on in, the water's fine!) He had an orchestral style, and he was to be found nightly at Maurer's or the Hotel Liszt. Think of a Liszt Hotel on Fourteenth Street! Truly a musical neighbourhood. Later it reminded me of the hotels and apartment houses in the vicinity of the Hispanic Museum in Audubon Park, founded by Archer M. Huntington. At every turn you read such names as Velasquez, Goya, Murillo or El Greco.

Steinway Hall was once the resort of our crowd composed of Harry Rowe Shelley, Harry Orville Brown, Henry Junge, John Kuehl, Joseffy, Friedheim, Max Bendix, Victor Herbert, and, when in town, the witty Moriz Rosenthal. It was in Steinway Hall, at a Thomas concert, I heard Joseffy strike a false note for the first and only time in my life, and of all concertos the E minor was the one he played the best. The arpeggio after the opening chords, he rolled to the top, but didn't strike the E. I remember Theodore Thomas staring at the back of the little virtuoso as if he thought him insane. If burning glances could have slain, Joseffy would have died on the stage that afternoon. But it didn't disturb him. I heard Rubinstein make a slip at one of his historical concerts, but with magnificent nonchalance he took as a point of departure the false note at the top and rolled down the keyboard, only to roll up again in the correct tonality. But he wasn't playing with orchestra.

IX

A PRIMA DONNA'S FAMILY

About 1888 the general character of New York began to change. The foreign influx had become accelerated. Barn-like structures invaded the residential section; along the Avenue strange tribes crowded the native off the sidewalk. And that was thirty years ago! To-day we are living in an Asiatic metropolis; New Cosmopolis I have called it. As the "old Knickerbocker families" have sold, still are selling, their birthright no fault need be found with the present conquerors. The melting-pot, which doesn't always melt, is rapidly dimming hopes. Irving Place at that time was not the street of tall buildings it now is; rows of modest three-story dwellings from Fifteenth Street to Gramercy Park were occupied, for the most part, by their owners, and interspersed with comfortable lodging or boarding houses. The only thing that hasn't suffered a change is the sky-line at either end of the street; the park on the upper side, and the familiar façade of the restaurant at Fourteenth Street are still there. Unchanged, too, is Washington Irving's pretty cottage at the corner of Seventeenth Street. A block away is Union Square. Old Moretti gave you perfect spaghetti in his original home on Fourteenth Street, and Italian opera was heard at the Academy of Music. The golden age of the cuisine, music, art, and letters in the old town are gone, never to return. For daily exercise I usually walked around Union Square; the park railings had been removed, but the square was not yet spoiled by tramps or disfigured by shanties. There were trees, shady seats, and the sound of fountains. Gloomy business lofts did not hem in this park, and on summer evenings it was a favoured promenade for residents in the vicinity. Several seasons I had noticed a ponderous dame of certain years, and fantastically attired, escorted by a tall elderly man with a grizzled beard, and had been informed that the lady was a well-known singing-teacher, Madame Miramelli, or to give her full title, Miramelli-Mario. The soldierly looking man was M. Mario, ex-barytone, and the manager of his wife's affairs. She had a studio on Irving Place, one flight up; the basement was a Turkish bath. On the two door-plates you read the rather confusing legend: "Miramelli: Vocal Instruction"; and "Baths: Turkish and Russian. Downstairs." However, the numerous singing pupils that streamed in from eight A. M. to six P. M. didn't seem to mind this jumbling of music and manners, and "Madame" was too busy to bother about it. Curiously enough, whenever I passed the house her husband was either entering or emerging. He was a busy man. I did not meet him personally till later at the old Beldevere House, Fourth Avenue and Eighteenth Street—now only a pleasant memory. It was during luncheon, and, as we shared the same table, I spoke to him about the excellent coffee. He elevated his shoulders, and in his reply I found less of the Italian and more of the Slav than I had expected from one of his appearance. He explained to me that he had spent twenty years at the Royal Opera, Petrograd.

We slipped into an easy-going acquaintance, and met, now at Riccadonna's on the Square, or at Morelli's on Fifth Avenue, also at Lienau's and Maurer's; at the last named resort for the sake of the excellent wines. The taste of M. Mario was cosmopolitan. But no matter his whereabouts, at seven o'clock every evening he could be seen piloting his heavy wife around Union Square; she, fatigued, though voluble, he taciturn and melancholy. They did not create the impression of a well-mated couple. One day, when I had occasion to call upon him, the little maid who opened the door shrewishly, responded to my question "Is M. Mario at home?" with "You mean the husband of Madame?" That threw some light on their domestic relations, and when I saw him shovelling snow, carrying bundles and market baskets, or running errands, I realised his subaltern position in the artistic partnership. I was then a music-critic, and possibly the friendly advances made by M. Mario were prompted by professional reasons. Yet he never hinted that his wife gave annually a concert at which her pupils were supposed to distinguish themselves. He possessed tact, was educated, and a linguist. His clothes, while not of a fashionable cut, were neat and clean. Perhaps M. Mario did take a drop too much and too often, though I vow I never saw him the worse for it. He seldom appeared at any of his daily posts after seven o'clock, so I set him down as an early bird, till one night returning late from the opera I saw him sitting on a Union Square bench, his face buried in his hands. It was moonlight. I hesitated, fearing he did not wish to be disturbed. Then I suddenly changed my mind. I called out: "Hello, my friend! What are you doing up so late?" He instantly arose and I saw that he had been weeping, but was sober. I joked and invited him to Lüchow's. He gravely refused. "It is this way," he said in his strangely streaked accent. "I was warm

and didn't sleep. I sometimes worry. I"— he stopped,
hesitated a moment, then asked: "Couldn't you come to
Madame's to-morrow morning, say about noontime? I
promise you a surprise. A young voice, bell-like, with
velvet added to the crystalline quality"—he was strangely
excited, as are all artists when a rare talent is discovered.
I promised, though I dislike hearing novices, especially
when the affair smacks of réclame. But the agitation of
M. Mario was unmistakable, his interest sincere, and,
thinking that there had been a family row, and I could
do him a favour, I said yes, and at noon the next day I
passed the office of the Turkish bath on the first floor
and reached the studio of Madame Miramelli.

She was at her piano, a battered instrument still ser-
viceable, and she only inclined her head on my entrance.
Evidently I was not too welcome. In the middle of the
room stood a young girl of seventeen or eighteen. She
was blonde of complexion and dressed her hair in foreign
fashion. She was indifferently clad. To tell the truth,
I was taken by her face, not so pretty as attractive. Her
features were irregular, her nose snub, but her large blue
eyes—the clear eyes of a congenital liar—blazed with
intense feeling and her mouth quivered. No wonder.
Madame Miramelli had been scolding her. "Lyda," she
screamed—a long name followed, Slavic in sound, beginning with the letter Z—"Lyda, you sing like five pigs!
If you sing thus to the gentleman, I believe a critic"—
she lifted her savage old eyebrows sardonically—"you
will drive him away. As for my beloved husband"—
more pantomime—"he thinks you are to become a second
Gerster or Nilsson. Don't disappoint him, for he is the
greatest living ex-barytone and a wonderful judge." She
would have continued this nasty railing tone if M. Mario

hadn't entered and seated himself near the girl. His
wife stared at him and his eyes fell. Shrugging her fat
shoulders she cried: "Again! Skip the introduction,
begin at the aria." She struck a chord. The girl
looked entreatingly at the husband, who literally trembled; his expression was one of mingled fear and admiration. His eyes blazed, too; he folded his arms and
his whole being was concentrated in his hearing.

The girl sang. He had not boasted, her voice was like
a velvet bell. She sang with facility, though her musical
conception was immature, as might have been expected.
Without doubt a promising talent. When she finished
M. Mario shook her by the hand, which limply fell as
he released it; he led her to a seat and to my pity and
astonishment, I saw that she was lame, sadly lame, her
gait was waddling, almost ludicrous, so distorted was the
hip movement. My gaze collided with the eyes of the
old woman at the keyboard, and if there is such a thing
as infernal malice blended with hateful jealousy, it was
expressed by her face. She held her silence and feeling
the unbearable tension, I said some pleasant, conventional words to the timid girl, bowed to Madame, and
left the room. M. Mario accompanied me to the street,
but did not ask for further criticism, though thanking
me for my kindness in giving so much of my "valuable
time." I cut him short and escaped, not without notic-
ing the tears in his eyes. Decidedly an emotional man
—or an old fool, too easily affected by a pretty voice.
But the lameness! maybe that had aroused his interest;
also disgusted him with his wife's sharp tongue and un-
amiable demeanour towards the poor girl. Ah! these
ancient prima donnas and the tyrannical airs they as-
sume for the benefit of their pupils and their superflu-

ous husbands. The husband of Madame! It was a tragi-comedy, his; yet, why should he become so tearful over the lame girl with the lovely voice and plaintive eyes? Madame was jealous and the girl wouldn't be treated any too well because the husband was sentimental.

The musical season had set in, and on the wings of song and symphony I was whirled away from memories of Irving Place and the pupils of Madame Miramelli-Mario. But as the winter modulated into spring, I occasionally thought of these people, though one warbler in the present is worth a dozen in the future. It was May before I again saw M. Mario. He pretended not to know me; at least, it looked so. I was offended. I knew his odd habits. In the evenings I resumed my old walks about the square, more as an appetiser than a diversion. Precisely at seven o'clock the musical couple slowly moved through the park. I avoided them. They seemed, as ever, bored, and I noted that Madame was no longer loquacious. These walks continued for a month, when one afternoon I found M. Mario at the fountain gazing at the water. I saluted him and was shocked by his altered exterior. He had thinned, was neglected looking, his linen not too new, and he had a desperate air. In a stately style he bowed, and to my inquiry as to his health he did not reply. "Come and have a drink," I bade him, "it will cheer you." We went across to Brubacher's café, where they played chess in those times, and I asked M. Mario: "And that girl with the splendid soprano—is she improving?" His eyes filled. "She is no longer with us," he answered. "Too bad," I commented. "She had talent, though I fancy her lameness would hurt her career; still, there was

Carlotta Patti"—he raised his hands with a gesture of supplication. "No," he whispered, "she was driven out-of-doors by Madame Mario." I was utterly taken aback. Driven away because of petty jealousy. Then the humorous side struck me. "I fear you are a Don Juan, my friend. Can you blame your good wife? Such a handsome chap as you, and still dangerous, you know"— He stopped me. "Say no more, caro amico, the subject touches me too closely. Yes, Madame Mario is jealous. That girl—that girl—how shall I say it? My first love, she is dead. She was a great dramatic soprano, a Russian, and that girl—she is my daughter, she . . ." I was tremendously excited. "Your daughter! Now I see it all." "You see nothing," he tersely replied. I persisted. "But does your wife know the girl is yours?" He shook his head and took a sip of wine. I was puzzled. After all, it was not polite to put such personal questions. "Pardon me, M. Mario, but I can't help feeling interested." He pressed my hand. We sat in silence, then he exclaimed: "I was crazy to bring the girl to her, I hoped for a magnificent artistic future. No, Madame Mario doesn't know; she shall never know. She is jealous of the girl's youth, jealous of me, of my own daughter—" I hastily interposed. "Well, why didn't you tell her?" "Why? Why? Because the girl doesn't know it herself. Because I am a miserable coward, afraid of my old she devil. Because . . ." He went away without saying good-by, leaving me in a stupefying fog of conjecture. That evening for the first time the husband of Madame did not keep company with her in their promenade around old Union Square.

I possess an indifferent sense of time; the years pass and leave little impress on my spirit. Nevertheless, I'm

sure I felt older when on a certain evening at Carnegie
Hall I awaited without undue impatience the début of a
much advertised Russian soprano, Zelocca, or some such
name. It was to be one of those tiresome mixed concerts in which a mediocre pianist, violinist, or tenor with
bleating voice, or an impossible buffo-basso, participate.
The only missing element of horror on the bill of fare
was a flute virtuoso; but flutists and harps as solo instruments were no longer in mode. However, as a seasoned
veteran I settled in my seat prepared for the worst. It
came in the shape of a young woman who gave her audience a dislocated version of the Chopin Ballade in the
ingratiating key of A flat. I regret to add that she was
applauded, but concerts of this sort are the joy of the
encore fiends, who were out in force that evening. The
tenor sobbed his aria, and then came the bright star of
the entertainment. A blonde woman of some distinction, at least twenty-eight years old, hobbled over the
stage, leaning on the arm of her accompanist. It was
Madame Zelocca, "the greatest living exponent of coloratura singing." I confess I was neither intrigued by
this managerial proclamation, nor by the personality of
the singer. What did interest me, however, was the idea
that perhaps Carlotta Patti might have a successor.
Zelocca sang the Bell Song from "Lakmé," a mild, pre-
paratory exercise to "warm" her fluty tones. Yes, it
was a marvellous voice, wide in range, of extraordinary
agility, and the timbre was of a fruity richness. And she
sang as only an accomplished artist can sing. When she
limped away, after applause hearty enough to awaken
even the critics, a compartment in my memory flew open
and out popped the past—Irving Place, and the white,
hard light of a shabby music-room, a lame girl singing in

the middle of the room, a sour-faced foreign woman accompanying her; and the most vivid impression—a middle-aged man devouring the girl with a gaze in which was equally mixed pride and humility. It was the protégé of Madame Miramelli-Mario. Why had I not immediately recognised this lame singer? And what was the use of my musical memory if I couldn't recall the colour of this brilliant voice. But a decade and more had passed since I first heard the girl Lyda, now Madame, or was it Signorina Zelocca? Much music had filtered through the porches of my ears since then. Was I to blame for my short memory—hush! here she is once more.

For her second number Zelocca sang, and with astounding bravura, the famous aria from "The Magic Flute," followed it with Rossinian fireworks, and threw in "The Last Rose of Summer," and "Home, Sweet Home" as crumbs of consolation for a now frantic audience—in a word, she played at ease with the whole bag of prima donna tricks. It needed no prophet to tell us that she was not only a great singer, but also a money-maker of superlative possibilities. Pardon my cynical way of putting things. The practice, year in, year out, of musical criticism doesn't make a man an idealist. This young woman, with the opulent figure, lark-like voice, and homely, though intelligent face, would surely prove the successor of Carlotta Patti, Ilma di Murska, and other song-birds with gold-mines in their throats. But only in the concert room; in opera her lameness would be deplorable; she floundered rather than walked. Yet, such was the magnetism of her voice. . . .

I pushed my way to the corridors, leaving a mob of lunatics clustered about the stage clamouring for more,

like true daughters of the horse-leech. As the front of
the house was impassable, I tried to go out by the Fifty-
sixth Street artists' entrance, but before I reached the
door, I was in a midst of babbling humanity. Some
sinister magic must lurk in music that can thus transform sensible men and women into irresponsible beings.
It is called temperament, but I think it is our quotidian
sensual souls out of the loose. Pushed and shoved as I
was, I felt my arm grabbed. I turned. It was Mario,
but aged a quarter of a century, so it seemed to me; perhaps it was the uncertain light, the excitement of the
moment, perhaps because I hadn't seen him for years.
His face was full of gnarled lines, his hair and beard
white; his large, dark eyes alone hinted at their former
vitality. They burned with a sombre fire, and if ever a
man looked as if he was standing on the very hub of hell
it was poor old Mario. Why hadn't I thought of him
earlier in the evening as the father of Zelocca? I whispered vague congratulations. He didn't hear me, his
face was that of a gambler who has played his last and
lost. Gradually I fought my way through a phalanx of
half-crazy humans, Mario tugging at my arm. We found
ourselves on Fifty-sixth Street, and I hastened to tell
him the pleasure I had experienced, adding: "And you,
aren't you proud to be her father?" "Yes, I am proud."
His toneless voice surprised me. I continued: "What
did she say when she saw you, for you were her first inspiration?" "I was her first inspiration." This echo
annoyed me. Was the poor chap too feeble to realise
the triumph of his daughter? "Wasn't she glad to see
you?" I persisted. He stopped under an electric light
and gave me a bewildered look. Then more explicitly:
"No, she wasn't glad. I went in after her first aria,

which Madame Miramelli-Mario, God rest her soul"—he piously crossed himself—"taught her, and"—"Well, well?" I impatiently interposed. "Well, she didn't know me, that's all." His voice trailed into ghostly silence. I became indignant. Such abominable ingratitude! "I tell you the truth," he reiterated. "She had forgotten me, my face, my name, and, as she never knew I was her father . . ." He paused. To the heavens I whistled my rage and incredulity. "Much must have happened to her in ten years. She forgot, she forgot, she is not to blame—only she forgot me. . . ." He slowly moved down Broadway, this débris of a great artist, this forgotten father of a famous singer, with a convenient memory. That night, at the office, I wrote a critical notice about his daughter, Zelocca, which bristled with technical terms, and was bejewelled with adjectives. Was she not the only living successor of Carlotta Patti! I moaned as I thought of the "inside" story, of the newspaper "beat" I had burning at the tip of my tongue. But I had to play fair and write about her singing, not of her wretched behaviour to the man who had forwarded her on her career. The Welsh rabbit I ate at the Arena later did not console my palate. I went to bed in a wretched humour.

To go or not to go? For hours I argued the case before I decided to accept the prettily worded invitation of La Zelocca to visit her some afternoon, or, to be precise, the afternoon following the arrival of her note. I dislike informal little calls upon prima donnas at hotels, where you usually find a chain of adorers, managers, press-agents, and anonymous parasites. Nevertheless, I went up to the Plaza, the Lord only knows why. Per-

haps my curiosity, now aflame, would be gratified, perhaps the young woman might make an excuse for her
cold-blooded behaviour to her abandoned father. Who
knows? Some such idea was in my mind when, after
the pompous preluding of my presence, I knocked at the
door of her suite in the hotel. She was sitting in a comfortable room and gazing upon the still green park. I
begged of her not to derange herself as she made a feint
of rising, and saluted her with the conventional kiss on
the hand—I'm bound to acknowledge a finely articulated,
well-kept hand—and in return was warmly welcomed.
At close range, Zelocca was handsomer than on the stage.
Her robust figure was set off in a well-fitting street costume, and her shapely head had evidently been handled
by a discriminating hair-dresser. We conversed of the
weather, of the newspaper criticisms (mine in particular)
and I ventured to ask her about the box-office. Yes, it
had pleased her, better still, it had pleased her manager
—a jewel of a man, be it understood. She spoke in a
silvery voice, with the cool assurance of a woman who
fully recognised her financial worth. We drank tea in
Russian fashion. I saw my opening. "So you were in
Russia before taking the western world by storm?"
"Ah, yes, cher maître" (I always bristle with importance
when thus addressed). "I studied hard in Petrograd,
and benefited by my intimacy with the great Zelocca."
(I was puzzled.) "I am a relative of hers, you know.
I took her name by her kind permission. My mother
gave me a letter to her when I left New York. She was
a friend of an early friend of my mother's husband."
Her mother! Who the deuce is her mother? I asked
myself. My face must have betrayed me, for she looked
at me pensively (her eyes were truly glorious with their

deceptive frankness) and murmured: "Of course, M. Mario must have told you of mother's death." I understood. She meant old Miramelli-Mario, and should have said stepmother. I nodded as sympathetically as I could—music-critics are sometimes better actors than the singers they criticise—and replied: "Yes, yes, M. Mario told me. But you say Zelocca still lives. He said to me, if I remember aright, that she was dead years ago." She seemed startled at this news. "He told you —that! Ah! the miserable!" I jumped at the chance. "But, my dear lady, he is, after all, your father, and if I guess the truth, your mother in Russia has proved your best friend. I mean your real mother."

She harshly interrupted: "My real mother was a she devil." This sounded like the daughter of Mario. "And," she angrily pursued, "she treated me as if I were a kitchen-maid." The dramatic manner in which this speech was delivered left no doubt as to its sincerity. Again I was at sea. She poured a torrent of words into my ears. "My father, that old drunken beast my father? If you only knew the truth. How an artiste must suffer before she drags herself out of the mire! It was a vile swamp, that home of mine on—on—" She paused for want of the name. "On Irving Place," I interposed. "Yes, Irving Place. That Mario was not my father, he was only the husband of Madame—and she—she was, I'm ashamed to say it, my true mother." La Bella Zelocca covered her face with her eloquent hands, while her shoulders sobbed if her throat did not. I was flabbergasted by this unexpected, this absurd, revelation. What sort of a devil's dance had I been led, what kind of a sinister impasse had I reached? She continued, her face still hidden: "A cruel, unnatural mother, a still crueller stepfather . . . he never ceased his persecutions. . . . And I was too young, too timid, too much in fear of my jealous mother—who soon found out what was going on. That's why she was so disagreeable the day you called. She got rid of me soon after that —I was packed off to Russia, to her sister. Oh! didn't I tell you that the other Zelocca is my aunt? No? She is, and a kinder woman than was my mother. Now you know why I wouldn't see the old rascal—who expected to live on me as he had lived on the bounty of two sisters —why—why—"

But I felt that my presence was becoming indecorous in this close atmosphere of family scandal. I arose, seized my hat. She sat bolt upright, stiff as a votive candle; her expression was one of annoyed astonishment. "Surely you are not going so soon, and not going without a word of sympathy! You, I feel, are one of my oldest and truest friends"—at these doleful words my tongue clove to the roof of my mouth—"and to whom should I appeal but you?" I wriggled but saw no way of escape. Then I burst forth. "In God's name, Madame, what can I say, what can I do for you? This is the third time I've seen you in my life. I only knew that venerable scamp, Mario, superficially. Your mother, great heavens! your mother I've seen often enough—too often." She beamed on me and became so excited that she, too, got on her feet, supporting herself with a gold-topped stick. "Ah!" she triumphantly cried, "I knew it, I knew it. You are the man I thought you were. You hated my mother. You despised her husband and you will, I'm sure, help me in my search, my search—"

The room began to spin slowly around; the grand piano seemed to tilt my way. Possibly Zelocca saw the hunted look in my eyes, a man and a critic at bay, for she exploded the question: "You will look for him, find him, bring him to me?" I wavered in my walk towards the door, fearing heat apoplexy, yet I contrived to stammer: "Find—find—whom shall I find for you?" "My real father," she fairly chanted, and her face was as the shining face of an ardent neophyte at a tremendously mystical ceremony. As I left the room on a dead run, I swear that an aureole was foaming about her lovely head. I didn't stop sprinting till I reached the ground floor, ran across Fifty-ninth Street into the park, and, finally, at the Casino I threw myself into a seat and called for —oh! it wasn't water; after such a display of drab family linen one doesn't drink water. Any experienced social washerwoman will tell you that. By Jove! I was positively nervous with their crazy-quilt relationships. I pondered the situation. Was Zelocca an artistic liar, a wonderful actress, or simply a warm-hearted woman, too enthusiastic, in search of a father? I couldn't make up my mind. I haven't yet. She may have suspected that my critical notice of her forthcoming second concert might not be so fervid as the first because of Mario's tale regarding her cruelty. I've known singers to tell worse lies for a smaller reason. But then, she had won her press and public; her next appearance was bound to be a repetition of the première, as far as success went. No, I give it up. I knew I should go to all her concerts and write sweet words about her distinguished art. And I did. (Later she married her manager and ever afterwards lived unhappily.) I'm beginning to regret I left her so hurriedly that afternoon. Perhaps she might have given me a clue. What a liar she was! Or a crazy woman! Her father, I believe, was M. Mario, the husband of Madame, and her aunt— Oh! hang her Russian aunt.

X

NEWSPAPER EXPERIENCES

The daily newspapers I worked for while in New York City were not many. In 1891 *The Recorder* was started with heavy financial backing, and it ran a half-dozen years, losing much money for its sponsors. In a way it was a pioneer journal, late-comer as it was. Novelties were to be found in its columns, which nowadays are part of the equipment of every newspaper. A woman's page, a children's page, a daily column devoted to theatre and music and art criticism of a human sort; the "Cholly Knickerbocker" column in which fashionable folk were written about—John W. Keller wrote it—and, last but not least, old Joe Howard's column of gossip and comment, ranging in subject from a dog-fight to the personality of the President. These three columns were to be found on the editorial page. General Howard Carroll was editor-in-chief, John W. Keller managing editor. My first Sunday editor was Julius Chambers, formerly of *The Herald* and now with *The Brooklyn Eagle;* my second was Winfield Scott Moody, later the editor of *The Lamp,* a literary monthly published by Charles Scribner's Sons. Mr. Moody, who is now in the editorial department of *The Evening Sun,* is the husband of that pioneer in women's journalism, Helen Watterson Moody, author of The Unquiet Sex (gorgeous title). At the suggestion of W. J. Henderson, John W. Keller engaged me as music-critic on the newly founded journal. Then I became chums with Harry Neagle, dramatic editor, who planned and conducted the daily column to which I contributed. Neagle roved about the theatre district and captured the good stories. I did much of the writing. The department was called "The Prompter." It was not the first of its kind, for Alan Dale wrote a daily column in *The Evening World;* but "The Prompter" was full of life and made readers. Those were the flush times of theatrical weeklies. Editors punched each other, wrote terrific insults, and started libel suits, which usually ended before the bar—but not of justice. Charles Alfred Byrne, after an exciting career as editor of *The Dramatic News* and *Truth*, was dramatic critic of *The Morning Journal*, then edited, and ably, by Joseph I. C. Clarke, Irish poet and patriot. Byrne had a positive genius for getting in and out of scrapes with men and women. He was a picturesque Irishman, who had been educated in Belgium, and his knowledge of the French language and dramatic literature enabled him to "import" some ideas for his productions. Dion Boucicault turned the same trick more profitably; indeed, some of that remarkable man's "adaptations" were as good, if not better, than the originals. Byrne was a born fighter. The up-town *Recorder* dramatic office was next to Daly's Theatre, and Byrne and Neagle had desks in the same room. Thither I repaired every afternoon from *The Musical Courier*, then at No. 19 Union Square.

One day Byrne and Joe Arthur, the playwright, quarrelled, and agreed to fight to the finish; but I'm not certain as to the battle-field, as I wasn't present. I think that Harry Neagle was bottleholder. Byrne returned to the office in a bad condition, both eyes black and blinking, but his Celtic spirit was undaunted. "You ought to see poor Joe," he cried to me. Arthur looked all right when I saw him the next day; he made the usual formal call of condolence. There was no bad blood between the men, though Byrne had been badly whipped in the encounter. Leander Richardson was another militant editor. He is said to have knocked out the irresistible John L. Sullivan in a bar-room brawl, though Sullivan must have been under the alcoholic weather. Richardson was a powerful man, a bruiser, and would have proved a formidable opponent at any time. He edited *The Dramatic News*, and his editorial notes were racy. I saw him attack John T. Sullivan in the lobby of the old Madison Square Theatre, then managed by Frank McKee for Charles Hoyt, the playwright. Sullivan, an amiable actor, was the husband of Rose Coghlan. That same night Leander Richardson, who was looking for trouble, found it in the person of Louis Massen and was thrashed in the café of the Knickerbocker Theatre, then called Abbey's. But he was about next day, alert and smiling. Harrison Grey Fiske, husband of Minnie Maddern, vivacious in soubrette rôles, later the serious Mrs. Fiske of Ibsen fame, was editor and proprietor of *The Dramatic Mirror*. I mention all this to show you that in the theatrical world conditions were worse than in the musical. Ugly phrases, such as "blackmail" and "revolver-press" were freely used. Not edifying, these rows, but typical.

Vance Thompson was dramatic and literary critic on *The Commercial Advertiser*, and he introduced me to Foster Coates, the editor. As *The Recorder* had gone the way of all mishandled enterprises I was glad to become dramatic and music-critic of *The Morning Advertiser* at what seemed a fabulous salary, $75 a week; this, with my stipendium from *The Musical Courier*, enabled me to live luxuriously and work like a dog. Many were the sentimental abysses into which I peered, many the angry, tearful partings—why angry, why tearful, I can't say now. Why young people take such things seriously, I wonder. I also wondered why *The Morning Advertiser*, which was in a palpably decrepit condition, paid me such a high salary. To be sure, I was working double-tides, driving two or three horses abreast, as Daniel Frohman said to me. I was both dramatic and musical critic and still found time to write for *Town Topics, Vanity Fair,* and *The Courier.* No bed-spring-chicken I, but a hustler. I had to be. There were other mouths to feed, and to use the expression of Vance Thompson, the mortgages were so tame that they fed from my hand. And a tame mortgage is more dangerous than a wild; it gets too familiar by half. And then a man must pay alimony to his divorced ideals. "Ain't it fatuous," as the old lady said when she first saw a hippopotamus. I was fatuous in my belief that I could succeed where others fail, just as later it took the writing of fifteen books, not only to get my hand in—Balzac's phrase—but also to get my hand out. One day the office 'phoned me; good old Major Clowes it was who told me that I needn't come down-town, there was no longer a *Morning Advertiser.* Mr. Hearst had bought it for the Associated Press franchise and paid, so it was said, $600,000 for the privilege. That accounted for the altitude of my salary. Behold me, with only two or three positions to fill. I filled them, yet longed for new worlds to conquer. On *The Recorder* the work had been severe, on *The Advertiser* much lighter. I didn't care. Scribbling came easy, and as I had no solemn "message" to deliver to an expectant world, I sunned myself on the right side of the street and took little heed of the future.

George Washington Turner, the manager of *The Recorder*, was a versatile man. His energy drove the machine of his frail little body at too high a pressure. Chockful of ideas, he made the wheels of his newspaper hum for a while. I shall not forget the afternoon when, in company with Edward A. MacDowell, the composer, and brilliant pianist, I went to the Everett House on Union Square—a delightful hostelry kept by old Mr. Bates, and where it stood is now an ugly fortress of brick. G. W. Turner showed us a complicated invention of his, all spools and ribbons and wires, a rudimentary forerunner of the self-playing piano, one of those diabolic unmusical machines that lend a new terror to life. Why didn't Turner gain millions from his idea—and it was one of many? A Yankee genius, his, but he succeeded in nothing but failures—to make an Irish bull.

While on *The Recorder* staff I was asked by Editor Keller if I should like to interview Annie Besant, theosophist, radical agitator, and at one time associate of Charles Bradlaugh. She had arrived from London that morning and was at the house of friends. Fortunately, her friends were my friends: Mr. and Mrs. August Neresheimer, cultivated and musical folk with whom I became acquainted through Max Heinrich. Mr. Neresheimer sang Schumann and Brahms with taste and intelligence, and was interested in the New Paths. A hardheaded man of business and a mystic. The conjunction is not uncommon. I had taken a dive into that shining pool, whose waters are so deceptively clear and deep. I knew Helena Blavatsky in the flesh, and I had read

some of the effusions of Mrs. Besant. I related these
facts to Mr. Keller. "Good!" he cried, and away I
went to the faraway region of Lenox Avenue—there were
no subways, and north of 125th Street seemed the country. When I reached the Neresheimer residence, I found
myself in company with a dozen other reporters, one of
whom quickly informed me that he also represented
The Recorder I was surprised. So was he when I told
him that Mr. Keller had sent me. "But there mustn't
be two stories!" he expostulated. "There won't be,"
I replied. "I'm not going to pump Mrs. Besant as to her
political rows." She had experienced trouble with the
British authorities over birth-control pamphlets, and
Bradlaugh's religious opinions were hardly orthodox,
though now they seem as innocuous as Bob Ingersoll's.
My friend pricked up his ears and suddenly became confidential. "Say," he whispered, "does she read your
palm? Cross the gypsy's hand with silver, eh?" After
that I didn't bother with him, and presently Mrs. Neresheimer beckoned to me. I followed her, and in the
morning room I met a little lady with a shy manner,
her soul concentrated in her eyes. Such latent energy!
She had just gone over, or was going, to Roman
Catholicism, but of this she said little. She had broken
several years before with Madame Blavatsky, but was
interested in what I had to say of that extraordinary
lady.

I came away with mixed impressions of Mrs. Besant.
Like Helena Blavatsky she was one of those reservoirs
of spiritual forces that nature creates from time to time.
She was almost spirit, a strange soul shone from her
eyes. In her various incarnations—in the earthly plane,
as our theosophical friends say—she had wavered from

faith to faith as wavers a candle in the wind. That she would not long abide in any house of the flesh was written on her candid brow. She soon seceded from Mother Church as she had earlier fled from the raw agnosticism of Charles Bradlaugh. She is now, I hear, a petticoated Grand Panjandrum in India irradiating the wisdom of the ages. She never possessed the profound animal magnetism of Blavatsky—it is the only phrase that describes her—nor her intellect, nor yet the firm grasp on affairs displayed by the "Purple Mother," shrewd Katherine Tingley, of Point Loma, California. There, I think, the Neresheimers are, having renounced the world and all its pomps to follow the Inner Light. When I had finished the interview so graciously accorded me by Annie Besant, I found a grumbling gang, my associates, impatient, and blaming me for blocking their plan; it was to be a joint interview, cried the chap from *The Recorder* with a taste for palmistry. I didn't explain. Why should I have done so? If not an Adept, was I not a Neophyte? Shoo! I said, and to the office I went and wrote an article on Theosophy and the claims of the Ideal—I capitalised every other word—and ended with a glowing description of soulful eyes. It was duly printed. But my more practical colleague had succeeded in coaxing the lady into definite statements, and Mr. Keller liked his interview better than mine. When I explained that Mrs. Besant had told me many things in confidence the mighty John—he was a giant—roared: "Then why the blankety blank didn't you print them? It's the strictly confidential confessions that the public likes." It was a lesson in the art of interviewing that I never forgot. Nowadays I print everything.

The public, as the late Mr. Barnum insinuated, is fond

of mystification. Phineas knew. I never read modern mystics without some such feeling. Just as the mob always demands "miracles" so a certain class of readers must be fed with oracular phrases, else perish from spiritual inanition. I had read, not without considerable misgivings, Isis Unveiled—what a title to whet the appetite of the curious!—and the Key to Theosophy, by Helena Blavatsky; indeed, these books are still in my library ranged next to the Koran and the Revelations of the Mormon Apostle, Joseph Smith. Yet compared with Science and Health, I prefer the dark sayings of the Russian woman. She, at least, had a great literature to tap, Eastern philosophy; and she tapped it to good purpose. When I went to New York the Theosophical movement was in full blast. Like the dilettante philosophy of the subtle Bergson in our day, the doctrines of Blavatsky and her disciples were a fashionable diversion. Madame Blavatsky held seances in which participated society people and "literati," the mild and hairy authors of that epoch—James L. Ford called them the "Century School"—and avowed mystics. William Q. Judge, Col. Olcott, the Munroes, and other luminaries were much mentioned in the newspapers, and we spoke of Karma as if it were a breakfast food. I knew Edwin Bjeeregaard, Swedish mystic and librarian at the Astor Library, then on Lafayette Place (now Lafayette Street), and he introduced me to the writings of the Theosophists. I swallowed them all, but I confess I found little new or stimulating in them. My reading in the Eastern wisdom had been extensive and these restatements and attenuations, modulations, and modern transpositions, cleverly as they were fashioned, did not impress me as the "Real Thing." Why not take the Zend-Avesta, or the

Triple Baskets, unadulterated by Russian mysticism? The trail of Helena Blavatsky was over the crystal-pure precepts of the ancients. But the woman herself! That was another thing. I visited her one rainy afternoon at a house not far from Astor Place. Never mind how I secured my invitation, except to say that it was not easy to get one. She was only for the elect. I have met many outlandish, eccentric, and many interesting people; anarchs of art, society, literature, but Blavatsky left the profoundest image of all in my memory. I say, profound, advisedly. Dostoievsky or Joseph Conrad, would have fathomed her and painted a deathless portrait of her in prose; but at twenty-five I was gullible, and my brain whirled with her cryptic and sonorous phrases—more sound than sense, I suspect—and I was but another bird lured by the pipe of this fowler. She was a short, fat woman, with sensual lips, without personal distinction, and as she wore a turban, I couldn't make out plainly her head. Her eyes! The eyes! The eyes! cried Bill Sykes. If Bill had ever seen the eyes of Helena Blavatsky he would have abandoned burglary and gone into retreat at Simla, India, there to await his next Karma. I think now of what Joseph Conrad did with the Princess in Under Western Eyes. From Blavatsky he would have carved another masterpiece.

I have never but once seen such a pair of orbs in a human's head, and those belong to Margaret Matzenauer, the opera-singer. The eyes of Blavatsky were not so radiantly electric as Matzenauer's, but they had the same hypnotic effect. They were slightly glazed as if drugged by dreams of smoky enchantments. They englobed you in their slow, wide gaze. I felt like a rabbit in the jaws of a boa-constrictor. I literally was.

Fascinated, I watched the oracle on her tripod blow circles of cigarette smoke through her flattened Kalmuck nostrils. The room was dim. There were divans. Too many. Exotic odours pervaded the lifeless air. Queen Helena—"she who must be obeyed"—murmured wisdom which I gulped without a word. An idol enthroned. She was amiable. She asked me if I wrote, and if I were a believer. I swear that I could have believed anything then, only to escape the aura of intolerable suspense in the atmosphere. What was it? The celebrated mesmerism must have been at work, else how account for my rapidly oozing vital force! I once attended a Black Mass in Paris, a blasphemous travesty, stupid, obscene, yet I did not feel as enervated as when I kissed the pudgy and not too white hand of Blavatsky, and got into the open under God's blue roof. Pouf! I inhaled huge breezes, and tried to forget the Isis I had seen Unveiled. If I remember my Oriental studies the wisdom of the East is not tainted with sex; sexuality, the keystone of our world, is purified. It becomes Idea. But Oriental wisdom when passed through the sieve of the Occident, takes on a more earthly aspect; it is even fleshy. I had expected astral messages, showers of roses from the ceiling, the mango and rope-ladder miracles, perhaps levitations. But nothing happened except that Helena Blavatsky gazed at me with her sombre, fanatical gaze, and my foot slipped at the edge of her optical pool and I fell into the crystal-clear lake of wisdom, which was Nirvana, and I lived a trillion æons until the Greek Kalends, and, the great bell of destiny sounding through the Corridor of Time, I awoke on Astor Place, rubbing my eyes and wondering whether it hadn't been a nightmare. Maya! The Mother of Illusion! But her eyes,

the eyes of this prophetess of esoteric tidings! What of
her eyes? They weren't dreamed! Whenever I smell
a Russian cigarette I recall her eyes. She smoked day
and night and I can't remember a word she said to me.
I should make a grand theosophist, shouldn't I?

XI

MONTSALVAT

A few years later another strange adventure befell me. It's a queer yarn, but it's true. As it is in the same key of the pseudo-mystic, I'll tell it now. We were sitting, my friend and I, in the smoking-room of the old Vienna Café. The long apartment was almost deserted; it was too late for luncheon, too early for tea. In a corner were Anton Seidl and Dr. Antonin Dvorak, their heads bent over a manuscript score; the Slavic conductor was showing the Hungarian conductor the music of his "New World Symphony." Happy folk! thought I. They have an interest in life, while here is Oswald, one of the greatest violinists, an unhappy, sulking wretch, and for no possible reason that I could discover. When he had reached the age of seven, his passion for the violin was so strong that he was allowed to have his way, and the schooling the lad received was mostly on four strings. Five years later he attracted the attention of some wealthy amateurs and was sent abroad. Another five years and Oswald had become the favourite pupil of Joachim, and was hailed as the successor to Wieniawski. Never had there been such brilliant, daring talent, seldom such an interesting personality. In his play there was the tenderness of woman, and the fire of hell. His technique was supreme, and when he returned to New York, his audiences went mad over him. I say mad, because I saw the madness. It was Paderewskian. It was Jascha Heifetzian. I was an old friend and his handsome face glowed when I

99

called at his hotel in my capacity of music reporter.
Oswald was a man who never drank. His one dissipation was coffee. He smoked cigarettes, but not furiously.
The women who sought him were treated with distinguished courtesy, but he contrived to evade entangle-
ments. I don't think he was ever in love. Then came
the change. At first I noticed it in his playing. At the
last Boston Symphony Concert in Steinway Hall he had
interpreted the Brahms Concerto in a listless, tepid manner, and his phrasing was not faultless. It was the absence of the inner spirit, the fire, that set buzzing critics
and public. What ailed the man? Was he worn out
by the labours of a strenuous musical season? I suspected a reason more dangerous. After months of de-
spondencies and disappearances, I had caught him at the
Vienna Café, and put the question to him.

He impatiently pushed aside his coffee. "Of course,
if you will insist on preaching, I must leave you. It's a
new rôle for you." "Oswald, you needn't take me up
that way. I'm not preaching, I'm playing the part of a
friend in a case of this kind, and—" "The only kind
you can play," he interrupted. "That's right, my boy.
Flaunt your virtuosity under my nose. I'm not a bull
when I see red." "Go on," he answered in a resigned
manner, reconsidering his rejected coffee. "What's the
matter with you, Oswald? Come, be frank with me!
You haven't touched your fiddle for months. You don't
show yourself to your friends. Are you in debt, are you
in trouble, are you in love? Stop a moment—" for he
had begun to scowl—"I don't wish to pry into your private affairs, but you owe your most intimate friend some
sort of explanation as to your odd behaviour, besides,
old man, you are looking very bad. Your skin is like

the Yellow Book, and your expression suggests Aubrey Beardsley's most morbid manner." I stopped for want of breath. Oswald smiled, rather contemptuously, at my stale similes, but held his peace and drank his coffee, ordered a fresh one, and over the third cup he brightened and slowly rolled a cigarette. I watched him. His face looked worn and wan, his colour was leaden, and his eyes lacked intensity. His handsome nose, purely Greek in line, was pinched, his mop of curls disordered. Evidently he had been having a hard time; but his was no common form of dissipation. At last, rousing himself, he gazed at me, almost piteously. It was the silent cry of a man going under, the cry of a man whom none could save. Involuntarily I caught at his arm; so unpremeditated was it, and he so easily read the meaning of the gesture that he turned away his head. For some minutes the silence lay thickly upon us, then I spoke to the stricken man: "Your face recalls to me one of those damned souls that Dante, the dreamer of accurst visions, met midway in his mortal life." "And I am a damned, irrevocably lost soul, and because of my own perverse temperament. Why does music lead us into such black alleys—My God! Why?" He was keyed up to a dangerous pitch, I forebore further questioning. We aimlessly drifted out of the café and, I going towards theatre-land, we separated for the night.

Naturally, I thought much about Oswald. Evil he was not. There was no love-affair. The idea of hypnotic obsession suggested itself, but was at once dismissed. The curious part of the affair was his refusal to play either in private or in public. He never went to concerts and had an absolute horror of music. Long absences from his house alarmed me. I made up my mind that some one was leading him astray. I determined to find out. Several months after our meeting at the café I met him again. He was gaunt, yellow, almost shabby. Another solution of the problem presented itself; perhaps, like other ardent temperaments, he had tasted of that deadly drug admired of the Chinese. A drug eater! I taxed him with it. As we slowly walked down-town we had stopped under an electric light; it was a dismal November night, a night of mists and shadows. Oswald spoke, faintly: "You accuse me of the opium habit. If I were a victim, I would be a thrice-blessed man. Alas! It is much worse."

Completely mystified, I took the arm of the unfortunate violinist in mine, for he seemed feeble, and asked him if he had eaten that day. He nodded. I did not believe him. We left Union Square behind us and soon reached Astor Place. I clung to him and only when we turned down the long, dark street, where the library then stood, did I notice our whereabouts. My companion moved with the air of a man to whom things corporeal no longer had meaning. When we arrived at the lower end of the ill-lighted avenue, I called his attention to the fact that we were drifting into strange quarters. He gave me a sharp glance, seized my elbow and guided me up the steps of a low building in semi-obscurity. He did not ring, but rapped with something metallic; at once the door was opened, and I saw a hallway filled with the violent rays of a lamp. I experienced a repugnance to the place. I would have gone away but Oswald barred the passage, regarding me with such sad eyes that I seemed to be dealing with a deranged man. "Welcome!" he said, "welcome to Montsalvat." Then I noticed over the door an incomprehensible musical motto, which I did not

at first recognise.   But I followed my friend into a comfortable library warmed by a fireplace, in which hissed
and crumbled huge lumps of cannel coal.   In all faith, I
had to confess that the apartment was homelike, though
the tragic expression of Oswald recalled to me that
I might discover his tormenting secret.   "And what,"
said I, sitting down and lighting a cigar, "is Montsalvat?
And what in the name of all that's fantastic means the
fearsome motto over the door?   Is this a suicide club,
or is it some new-fangled æsthetic organisation where
intense young men say sweet things about art?   Or is it
a singing society, or"—and here the humour of the situation broke in on me—"mayhap it is a secret college of
organists wherein pedal practice may be continued during late hours, without arousing refractory neighbours?"
Oswald, with his glance of anxious rectitude, did not smile
at my foolish speech.   "Montsalvat is not any of those
things," he softly replied.   "True, it is a club which occasionally meets, but not for recreation or discussion.
You have read the poet, Baudelaire, have you not, dear
friend?   Then you may remember those profound lines
beginning: 'J'ai vu parfois au fond d'un théâtre banal . . .
une fée allumer dans un ciel infernal. . . .'"   "It sounds
like Poe done into French," said I, wondering at Oswald's
suppressed excitement; "like a more malign Poe.   John
Martin, the English mezzotinter, could have translated
this poem of sombre bronze into his art of black and white
—you, yourself, Oswald, remind me of that artist's vision, 'Sadak Seeking the Waters of Oblivion.'"   I felt
I was talking for effect.   His actions puzzled me.   Why
in this lonely house should he become emotional over a
verse of Baudelaire?   Why should the Redemption theme
from "Parsifal" be placed across the door-top?   (I had

recognised the music.) Suddenly voices aroused him, and he started up, crying: "They are here!"

Folding doors, heavily draped by black velvet, were pushed asunder, and I found myself staring about me in a large chamber with a low ceiling. There were no pictures, two busts were in a recess and seemed to regard with malevolent expression the assemblage. I noticed that they were plaster heads of Arthur Schopenhauer and Richard Wagner. Conversation was languidly progressing. We sat, Oswald and I, in a corner. No one paid attention to us. I studied the people about me. They were the faces of cultured men, a few dissipated, but the majority were those of dreamers, men for whom the world had proved too strong, men who were striving to forget. I saw several musicians, one poet, a half-dozen painters. No evidence of opium was to be seen, no one drank, all smoked. As we entered Chopin's name had been mentioned, and a big, lazy, blond fellow said: "Oh! Chopin. We are, I hope, beyond Chopin or Poe. Debussy is our music-maker now—as Browning did not say." "Why?" asked a pianist. "Why have we got beyond Chopin? For me the Pole has an invincible charm." "That's because you are a pianist," came the retort. "You know I never play any more," was the sulky rejoinder. For a time the conversation halted. "What does it all mean?" I whispered. Oswald shook his head.

"Montsalvat, my friends," said a grave, measured voice, "is the ultimate refuge for souls resolved to abjure the illusion of happiness. Our illustrious masters and inspirers, Schopenhauer and Wagner, declared that only the saint and the artist may attain to Nirvana in this

life. But we hold that the artist is ever the victim of
the Life-Lie, of the World-Illusion. Wagner, when he
wrote 'Parsifal,' revealed his hatred of art, of the very
root of life. Full well he knew the evils brought into this
world by music, by sex. Immobility, the supreme ab-
negation of the will, the absolute suppression of the pas-
sions—better, the state of non-existence—are they not
worthy of attainment? To live in the Idea! Ah! my
friends, I fear that we are still too worldly, that we will
stamp with too much vehemence on our inner nature;
renounce thou shalt, shalt renounce! Surely by this
time we should have attained psychic freedom. Oh! for
a cenobite's life. Oh! for a crust and a hut in some vast
wilderness! The blood burns hotly in cities, life thrusts
its multi-coloured grin upon you there; you cannot escape it. To live on one tone, yourself to be the pedal-
point over which life's jangling harmonies pass your
soul-suspension—to do this is to live, not play, music;
to do as did the Knights of Montsalvat—that is existence.
Wagner knew it when he created his 'Parsifal,' for all
Time a perfect mirror of the souls of pure men who re-
volted at the banality of quotidian life. A new monastic ideal is our Modern Montsalvat." In wonder I
gazed at the speaker, not a hoary-headed Pundit, but a
youth of perhaps twenty-five summers. His strained
expression, his sunken cheeks, lent him a detached, even
fantastic appearance. In what manner of company
was I? What the aims of this strange crew? Men in
the heat and prime of their youth discoursing Schopenhauer, Wagner, Chopin, Verlaine, as if the last keen joy
were a denial of self almost depraved. I was bewildered.
The voice of Oswald broke in: "J'aime les nuages . . .
les merveilleux nuages." "There you go again with

your Baudelaire!" cried some one. "Oswald, I fear that
you still love life. It's consuming you. You delight in
reciting verses beginning: 'J'aime.' You have no right
to love anything, not even dream-tipped Baudelairian
clouds. I suspect that you still yearn for your fiddle, and
read that apostle of damnable Titanism, Nietzsche."
At the name of the arch-heretic of brutal force, of bar-
baric energy, the others shuddered.

Oswald seemed crushed. The voice of the new speaker
was toneless and depressing. I felt mentally nauseated.
What club of hopeless wretches had I encountered?
Robert Louis Stevenson, when he invented his Suicide
Club, had apparently reached the bottom of the vicious.
But here was something more infernal, a darker nuance
of pain, a club of moral suicides living, yet dead; slaugh-
terers of their own souls; men who deliberately withdrew
from all commerce with the world; men who abandoned
their ambitions, successes, friends, families, to plunge
beyond hope of redemption into a Satanic apathy, a
slavery worse than drugs; yet gleaning a fearful and exquisite joy in the abstention from joys; an intellectual
debasement, a slow strangling of the will, coupled with
the sadistic delight that comes in dallying on the for-
bidden edge of pain and pleasure. Morose delectation
is the precise name given to this lustless lust by wise
Mother Church, greatest of psychologists. Surely Bud-
dhism in its birthplace, cannot work such evil as I saw
before me. These men had not the absorbed air of de-
voutness and interior exaltation I have caught on the
faces of certain East Indians. Nor were they lotus-
eaters. Eastern mysticism grafted on Western faiths
may result unfavourably. In the weary faces around me,
in the agonised eyes of Oswald I saw the hopelessness of

such moral transplanting. Oswald was dying by infinitesimal degrees, dying withal. His violin was his life. His music was dammed up in him. The struggle against his deepest instincts was an unequal one; he must go mad, or perish. And these men enjoyed the spectacle of his ruin. To their jaded brains his pitiable condition was as absinthe. They were Manicheans. They worshipped Satan; saying, Evil be thou my Good! Oswald with his youth, his genius, his once brilliant career, had been drawn into this maelstrom of Nothingness. "His life," I thought, "his life has not yet been lived, he is not ruined in body, his soul is not yet a thing of dust and darkness like the others. What a sacrifice is his!" My face must have been an index of my agitation, for the same voice sardonically continued:—

"Oswald, I fear, has a Philistine with him to-night. Oswald cannot break from earthly ties. My dear violinist, you had better return to your Bohemia, with its laughter, its wine, its silly women, and to your fiddle, with its four mewing strings. Such toys are for boys, the illusion of love, women's soft bodies, and other gross nudities. Return, Oswald, with your friend to your old life. Make empty, useless noises, call them art, and forget the lofty heights of serene speculation, the pure, ravishing vision of a will subdued. Go, Oswald, and do not remember the Life Contemplative or Montsalvat and its Knights in search of the Holy Grail of Renunciation. Instead, go join the modulating crowd." The voice grew more silvery, but it pleaded as it menaced. In the hazy atmosphere I saw with apprehension the altered expression of my poor friend. His eyes closed, accentuating the violet bruises beneath them, his body became rigid. A living corpse, he only obeyed the will

of the Master. With an effort he roused himself, and
taking me by the arm, muttered: "Come!" Silently
we walked through the library and into the hall. The
busts were more malevolent than before. The street
door was opened for us, but I alone went into the mist
and darkness.

"The waters of the river have a saffron and a sickly
hue; and they flow not onward to the sea, but palpitate
forever and forever beneath the red eye of the sun with
a tumultuous and convulsive motion. For many miles
on either side of the river's oozy bed is a pale desert of
gigantic water-lilies. They sigh one unto the other in
that solitude, and stretch towards the heaven their long
and ghastly necks, and nod to and fro their everlasting
heads. And there is an indistinct murmur which cometh
out from among them like the rushing of subterrene
water. And they sigh one unto the other." Edgar Poe
wrote that in his "Silence." Poe, too, had tarried in the
House of the Ineffectual. Oswald, I never saw again.
His case is an image of the sinister consequences of universal egoism, so powerfully expressed in the lines of the
French poet, Alfred de Vigny: "Bientôt, se retirant dans
un hideux royaume, la femme aura Gomorrhe et l'homme
aura Sodome; Et se jetant de loin un regard irrité, les
deux sexes mourront chacun de leur côté . . ."

XII

I AM A FREE-LANCE

It was at the invitation of Paul Dana that I joined the staff of the New York *Sun* in 1900. There was no music-critic, and Mr. Chester S. Lord had read my Chopin, hence the engagement. The great race of editors was a thing of the past, Charles A. Dana, the noblest Roman of them all, was dead about three years when I had the luck to become an humble member of the institution created by him. I remained with *The Sun* fifteen years, writing for it until April, 1917, when our entrance into the war automatically stopped discussion of æsthetics. I was away several years in Europe, so I can claim a connection of fifteen years. For the columns I wrote musical, dramatic, art, and literary criticism. I wrote editorials, and for years I was on the much envied editorial page with articles principally on art, but often every other subject under the heavens save politics. I fenced with William James at the time pragmatism was spelled with a capital "P." He did me the honour of writing me most interesting letters on the subject, which letters are now in the possession of his son, Henry James, and probably will be published when Mr. James has the leisure to give us his long-expected study on his great father. I also attacked single-handed that subtle sophist, Henri Bergson, who was called by me "The Playboy of the Western World." But my proudest day on *The Sun* was when I had five columns in one day on its editorial page. That was a "stunt." If I may recall them, they were devoted to a study of Botticelli seen with modern eyes, a story of the Emma Bovary, the real name of the unhappy heroine and her village being given, and the sources from which Flaubert drew his immortal portrait; finally a column devoted to the genius of Rodin, the French sculptor. When Franklin Fyles, for years dramatic editor, became ill, I took his position, and not without misgivings. But my first assignment was the reappearance of Eleanora Duse in the D'Annunzio plays, "La Gioconda," "Francesca da Rimini," and "La Città Morta," and as I had already made a study of her and knew the plays in the original, I came off creditably enough; and then my six years of laborious theatrical apprenticeship counted for something.

But somebody always was after my job on *The Sun*. And I was too amiable. I went to Europe, wrote about theatres from London to Budapest, via Paris, Rome, Vienna. When William M. Laffan bought the newspaper I relinquished my position as dramatic editor to John Corbin. I began writing of art and succeeded in pleasing Mr. Laffan, himself an art critic, an authority on porcelains and a collector. At his suggestion I went to Spain for five months and saw the Velasquez pictures at the Prado, Madrid, and lived to write a book about him and other "moderns"—Velasquez is still the most modern of all painters. A man of force and enamelled with prejudices, Mr. Laffan had his likes and dislikes, usually violent. After a study of George Woodward Wickersham had appeared on the editorial page—I think I called it a cabinet picture because Mr. Wickersham had just become Attorney-General in President Taft's Cabinet—Mr. Laffan sent for me and I expected a raking,

ELEANORA DUSE

but it was quite otherwise. While in Paris I wrote for him a review of an Independent Salon, and a few months later on my return a notice of the Comparative Exhibition at the Academy of the Fine Arts. These articles led to my writing art criticism till 1917, with the exception of the years of my absence.

Thanks to the editor-in-chief, Edward Page Mitchell, I wrote signed and unsigned book reviews on the page made famous by Hazeltine. Edward P. Mitchell is an editor in a thousand. To work with him is a privilege and a pleasure. He always gets the best from a man. Sympathy is the keynote of his character. Chester S. Lord, for so many years managing editor, I knew before I wrote for *The Sun*. We had foregathered with Edward A. Dithmar, dramatic critic of *The Times*, and Montgomery Schuyler, Lawrence Reamer, and other prime spirits in Perry's old drug store. Not without warrant was Mr. Lord rechristened the "Easy Boss." Beloved by his "young men," as he called them, though some were grey, he also had the disagreeable task of lopping-off heads, which task he accomplished in a humane manner. I lost my "official" head once—some friction between the upper and nether millstones in which I was ground to powder—and no executioner could have been more "easy"; besides, he knew I would return. I was always returning to *The Sun*. It is a superstition. Just to encourage struggling "journalistic" talent, I may tell out of school that I was paid the highest salary in town as a dramatic critic, $125 a week, and I still cherish the little pay envelope on which I wrote as Finis, "The last of the Mohicans." This was in 1904. But I earned much more when later I wrote art criticisms, editorials, book reviews, and travel-notes for Mr. Mitchell.

Those were the palmy days when the handy all-round
man had his innings. Now each department is "standardised." Newspapers have lost their personal flavour.
Huge syndicates have taken the colour and character and
quality from daily journalism. I am quite sure that if
ever a comprehensive history of *The Sun* is written my
name will be absent simply because I would be considered a myth, the figment of a fantastic imagination.
Much of my *Sun* work appeared, duly expanded, in
Iconoclasts, Egoists, and Promenades.

I have told you how I interviewed Pope Pius X, and
visited Calabria after the earthquake for the New York
Herald. That was in 1905. A year later, and for the
same newspaper, I made little journeys to certain eastern
watering-places, from Bar Harbor to Cape May, not
forgetting Newport, Long Branch, and Atlantic City.
As I had often visited Ostend, Brighton, Scheveningen,
Blankenberghe, Zandvoort, Trouville, and a dozen other
European vacation beaches, I had opportunities to make
comparisons. I made them, wondering why, despite the
millions annually spent "over here," we have so little to
show for them that is substantial. Atlantic City is an
honourable exception. I have yet to see its duplicate.
But the solid stone of the Brighton and Ostend and
Scheveningen sea promenades we have not. And our
cuisine. And the absurd prohibition. Europe is our
master in the art of making life pleasant at summer resorts. I wrote music criticism for *Town Topics* when
such men as C. M. S. McLellan, Percival Pollard, Charles
Frederic Nirdlinger were making its columns attractive.
When Nathan Strauss, Jr., bought *Puck* with the idea of
transforming it from a barber-shop comic weekly to an
artistic revue, I conducted a page, "The Seven Arts,"

17-19250

PERSONAL RECOLLECTIONS

OF

JOAN OF ARC

BY

THE SIEUR LOUIS DE CONTE

(HER PAGE AND SECRETARY)

FREELY TRANSLATED
OUT OF THE ANCIENT FRENCH INTO MODERN ENGLISH
FROM THE ORIGINAL UNPUBLISHED MANUSCRIPT
IN THE NATIONAL ARCHIVES OF FRANCE

BY

JEAN FRANÇOIS ALDEN

ILLUSTRATED

FROM ORIGINAL DRAWINGS BY

F. V. DU MOND

*AND FROM REPRODUCTIONS OF
OLD PAINTINGS AND STATUES*

NEW YORK AND LONDON
HARPER & BROTHERS PUBLISHERS

but the times were not propitious. War was the only
interest, and the arts could go hang. They did. Despite
the money spent on illustrations, *Puck* did not fulfil its
new mission, and was sold to Mr. Hearst in 1917, and is
now non-existent. For the New York *Times* I wrote much
in 1912 from European cities. A mania for travel set in.
I lived in London, Paris, Berlin, Brussels, Bruges, Vienna;
I ate spaghetti in Milan, drank dark beer in Munich.
I saw midnight suns and daughters of the dawn. I
loved Prague in Bohemia, deeming it a fit companion
for Toledo, Spain; one of the most fascinating cities on
the globe. I loved Rome. Who doesn't? And found
Venice too florid and operatic. But my beloved Holland
and Belgium came first; especially Bruges. The Lowlands always appealed. Rodin spoke of the "slow"
landscapes of the Dutch country. It is an illuminating
phrase. The grandeur of the Alps left me rather un-
touched. I quite appreciate their frosty sublimities,
also feel their lack of human interest, The flatlands of
Holland with their processional poplars, their silvery
shining network of canals, the groups of patient cattle,
egotistic windmills, and the low friendly skies—all these
went to my heart like a rich warming cordial. The homelike life, the treasure houses of art at Amsterdam, The
Hague, and Haarlem, win the imagination, and there is
an abundance of good music. The Concertgebouw in
Amsterdam listens to symphonic music and the best of
European singers and players with Willem Mengelberg
as conductor, and a brilliant one he is. I had settled in
1914 at Utrecht for the remainder of my days I thought;
but destiny had something to say, and I found myself
once more in Manhattan. In the quaint Dutch town I
vainly sought for the peace of Utrecht, which is purely

historic, as it is for its size as noisy as Naples. Rug-beating there is raised to the dignity of a peace treaty.

I heard under Conductor Mengelberg compositions by three Dutchwomen, Cornelia Van Oosterzee, Anna Lasu-brecht Vos, and Elizabeth Kuypers, that gave me pleasure. Miss Van Oosterzee's symphony is an "important" work. With such a world-renowned genius as Hugo De Vries at Amsterdam, and such a profound neurologist as Doctor C. U. Ariens Kappers, of the Central Institute of Brain Research at Amsterdam, or Professor Dubois, who discovered in Java the "missing link"—Pithecanthropus Erectus—at Amsterdam, Holland, is not soon likely to fall out of the fighting line in science. I saw our remote and distinguished collateral at the Amsterdam Museum. He has been reconstructed by Dubois and I confess I've encountered far more repulsive specimens among his human cousins, but the Piltown skull dug up in England in 1912 is more in the key of Homo Sapiens. Thanks to the courtesy of Doctor Kappers, I met Hugo De Vries in his own "experimental garden" at the Amsterdam Botanical Garden ("Hortus Siccus" is the legend over the gates). Professor De Vries—he is a professor at the University of Amsterdam—looked very well after his long visit to the United States, where in New York he was invited by President Butler to join the faculty of Columbia College. He wisely declined the honour, notwithstanding the horticultural temptations of Bronx Park; but, a canny Dutchman, he hammered this offer into the heads of the Dutch Government and was given a new and more commodious building in which to work out his famous doctrine of plant and flower mutation. He admires Luther Burbank, and thus summed up the difference in their respective experiments: "Burbank crosses species, I seek to create new ones." He does create new species, does this benevolent-looking Klingsor, with the flowers of his magic garden. But his is white, not black, magic. He lets nature follow her capricious way, giving her from time to time a hint. A sort of floral eugenics. I saw eight-leaved clovers and was told that many more leaves would bud, as originally the clover was a stalk full of buds. For the superstitiously inclined there are three, four, five, six, and seven-leaved varieties. The evening primrose (Æonthera lamarckiana) was then the object of the De Vries experiments. Certainly this yellow flower means more to him than it did to Wordsworth's Peter. The professor ties up its petals in tiny bags, and thus protected from marauding birds and bees, and no doubt bored by solitude (though pistil and stamen remain), the flower begins to put forth a new species. I witnessed the "miracle" of a half-dozen flowers coming into the world that were not in existence the season before. It reminded me of Professor Jacques Loeb and his "creative evolution" with sea-urchins.

That is "creating" life, and even Sir Oliver Lodge would give his assent to the statement. But when I spoke later in London to Sir E. Ray Lankester, a distinguished disciple of Huxley, and a hardened Darwinian, he rather pooh-poohed the De Vries experiments. And now Professor Henry Fairfield Osborn, president of the American Museum of Natural History, is inclined to minimise, not so much the value of the De Vries discoveries, but their philosophical inferences. He writes in his magisterial volume, The Origin and Evolution of Life, that "the essential feature of De Vries' observations . . . is that discontinuous saltations in directions that are entirely fortuitous . . . a theoretic principle which agreeing closely with Darwin . . . such mutations are attributable to sudden alterations of molecular and atomic constitution in the heredity chromatin, or the altered forms of energy supplied to the chromatin during development." (Chromatin is another term for the germ-plasm of Weismann.) But, according to De Vries, his discovery is the reverse of Darwin's theory that evolution is slow, orderly, progressive, and without jumps; nature never leaps, there are no sudden miracles. De Vries proves the opposite; the miracle takes place overnight in his experiments; nature strikes out blindly, swiftly, apparently without selection. The new flower is a "constant," though it struggles to revert to its old pupillaceous state. I was shown what he calls a rosette, a green plantlike production, a new birth of the commonplace primrose. In Alabama, Professor De Vries gathered his parent flower. He was interested when I told him that I had seen Leidy and Cope at the Academy of Natural Sciences, Philadelphia, and he praised their genius. He tramped Fairmount Park and knows the Bronx Botanical Garden. His American travels and experiments are published in a big volume, but I balk at Dutch, notwithstanding its relationships to the German and English languages. His great work on Mutation is translated. The author speaks and writes English fluently and idiomatically. I was loath to leave this man, who, in the Indian summer of his life, looks like a bard and philosopher, summoning strange and beautiful flowers from the "vasty deep" of nature. He is an exalted member of the most honourable profession in the world— a gentle gardener of genius. Hugo De Vries is one of

the few significant figures in the history of science since
Darwin.

A brief connection with another journal gave me much
satisfaction, though less cash than kudos. It was *The
Weekly Critical Review*, devoted to literature, music, and
the fine arts, and was published at Paris. Founded and
edited by Arthur Bles, a young Englishman of Dutch
descent (his grandfather was a Dutch genre-painter,
David Bles, but whether of the Herri Met de Bles stock,
the old-time painter with the white lock sported Whistler
fashion, I know not) and far-ranging in his ambition.
The Review was bi-lingual, and boasted such contributors as Paul Bourget, Jules Claretie, François Coppée,
Gustave Larroumet, Jules Lefebvre; Henri Roujon, director of the Beaux-Arts; Alfred Capus, dramatist; Camille Chevillard, conductor; Remy de Gourmont, J.-K.
Huysmans, Hugues Imbert, Vincent d'Indy, composer;
Charles Malherbe, Catulle Mendès, Auguste Rodin,
Tony Robert-Fleury, J. H. Rosny, Havelock Ellis, Theodore Watts-Dunton, Laurence Housman, Ernest New-
man, John F. Runciman, Arthur Symons, and W. B.
Yeats. In this list my name "also ran," and next to
that of Huysmans'. Was I flattered! As I have already said, there are no modest authors. Mine was the
Higher Snobbery, and I'm not in the least ashamed to
admit it. You, if you wrote, would be proud in such
company, and I felt "some pumpkins" and exclaimed:
"Lawks, how these apples do swim!" after Huysmans
had addressed me as "confrère." Arthur Bles translated
part of my book on Chopin and it appeared in the columns of *The Review* as Chopin: l'Homme et sa Musique,
dedicated to Jules Claretie, director of the Théâtre
Français. I was specially "featured" and my study of

Maeterlinck's play, "Joyzelle," brought me letters from
the poet and from Huysmans and De Gourmont. This
was in June, 1903. Joris-Karel Huysmans—his bap-
tismal names were George Charles, but as a pen-name
he used their Dutch equivalent—was a disagreeable
man to interview if you were not fortified with letters of
introduction; even then he proved a "difficult" man of
gusty humours. He was, however, amiable to me after I
told him I was a Roman Catholic, but frowned when I
said that I was not particularly pious. "Mais, mon
cher confrère," he groaned, "vous êtes un imbécile.
Quoi?" No half-way epithet for him. I admitted my
imbecility and shifted the subject to Rops, the etcher of
Satanism. He contemptuously waved the artist away.
With Maurice Maeterlinck it was different; for the Belgian he had a predilection, yet that poet is not particularly pious. I sometimes suspect the piety of Huysmans, unhappy man who died a horrible death—cancer
in the throat. But I never suspect his sincerity, which,
as Abbé Mugnier wrote, is a form of his genius. William James abominated the writings of Huysmans, especially En Route, and in one of his letters to me distinctly
doubted the sincerity of the Frenchman's conversion;
but when I pointed out to him that Huysmans, strictly
speaking, was not "converted," but had only returned
to the faith in which he had been baptised, and when I
assured him that not even St. Augustine or John Bun-
yan, the saintly tinker, were more sincere, then Professor James, with his accustomed charity to all variations of religious belief, acknowledged that the array
of arguments almost persuaded him. But the erotic
prepossessions of Huysmans had evidently set his teeth
on edge. In the summer of 1896 I attended the funeral

of Edmond de Goncourt, the last of the famous brothers. I saw contemporary men of letters, painters, and musicians at the church, but I did not see Paul Verlaine, the maker of music as exquisite, as ethereal as Chopin's or Shelley's; also Paul Verlaine, the poetic "souse" and lyric deadbeat. He had died in January of the same year, 1896. I had often gone to Leon Vanier's bookshop on the Quai de Notre Dame, with the hope of meeting the most extraordinary poetic apparition since Baudelaire, but without success. Unsuccessful, too, were my visits to the Café François Premier on Boulevard St. Michel (usually called by pasteboard Bohemians of Greenwich Village and Washington Square "Boul' Miche," because they never were near the establishment). I saw, but not there, some of the younger group of French poets, also the Americans who wrote beautiful poetry in that language; Vielé-Griffin, and Stuart Merrill —who occasionally wrote me from Forest, near Brussels, till a few years before his death. But I never met Paul Verlaine. Indeed, I may boast that I am the only living writer who didn't lend money to that poet.

Maeterlinck's "Joyzelle" was produced at the Gymnase—temporarily renamed, Theatre Maeterlinck—in May, 1903. This "Conte d'Amour" had as heroine Georgette Leblanc. Veiling her temperament, this singer of songs of Isolde, of Mélisande, became gentle, naïve, poetic; but she was also feline and passionate. A curious artiste, at times a woman who seems to step from a page of Georges Rodenbach, that exquisite Belgian poet, the poet laureate, one might say, of Bruges—have you read his "Bruges-la-Morte," with its Poe-like legend of the dear, dead woman, and her golden strangling hair?—

and then she is metamorphosed into the double of the
old-time Sarah of the siren voice. Oddly enough, this
earlier wife of Maeterlinck is the sister of Maurice Leblanc, the fabricator of the "thrilling" tale of "Arsène
Lupin." In his admirably designed cabinet Maeterlinck
gave Arthur Bles and myself a welcome. He then lived
on the Rue Reynouard, in a house the garden of which
overlooks the Seine from the moderate heights of Passy.
To reach his apartment we had to traverse a twisted
courtyard, several mysterious staircases built on the
corkscrew model, and finally we were ushered into an
antechamber full of fans, screens, old engravings, orna-
mental brass, and reproductions from pictures by Man-
tegna, Rossetti, Burne-Jones, and symbolistic painters.
Symbolism was going out, Cubism coming in. (The King
is dead, damn the Pretender!) But we were not allowed
to abide there. A maid with doubting eyes piloted us
across a narrow hallway, through a room where sat a
tirewoman altering theatrical costumes, and at last we
were in the presence of Maurice Maeterlinck? Not yet.
Down another courtyard where he loomed up in cycling
costume, handsome, grave, cordial, with big Flemish
bones, a round head, with wavy hair dappling at the
temples. Past forty, a pensive man, he didn't look like
his present photograph, for his mustaches were un-
shaved. He was older, more vigorous than I had pictured him. His head was that of a thinker, his eyes
those of a dreamer. Grey-blue, with hints of green, they
were melancholy eyes, with long, dark lashes. He was
modest, even diffident, but touch on a favourite theme
and he readily reacts. He would not speak English,
though he has all English literature stored in his skull.
His general race characteristics are Flemish. He also

M. Maeterlinck
26 Mai 1903.

suggests the solid Belgian beef and beer. Like some mystics he believes in the things that cheer and nourish.

He told me that in composing "Monna Vanna" he read Sismondi for a year to get historical colour. He was frank as to the conception of the play: "I wrote it for Madame Maeterlinck," he said, which disposed of my theory that the piece was written to prove he knew how to make a drama on conventional lines. "Naturally I read Browning; who does not? 'Luria' I have known for a long time, but it is not a stage play." He spoke of Shakespeare as other men speak of their deity. I was interested in what he thought of "The Tempest," for he had been accused by some critics of studying that immortal fantasy before he wrote "Joyzelle." "Certainly I did. I simply used Shakespeare as a point of departure. Could I do better? And, then, how can any one speak of plagiarism, who has read 'The Tempest' and has seen my little piece?" M. Maeterlinck is open-minded. We spoke of other things, of Poe's vague, troubled beauty; of Emerson, upon whose aphoristic philosophy he sets a great store, and of the contemporary theatre. Fearful of tiring the poet, we went away, again across courtyards, down spiral staircases. Seemingly a recluse, Maeterlinck is the most active of men. His translation of "Macbeth" into French is the best I have read. Later I may quote from some of his letters to me.

XIII

CRITICISM

For at least five years in London, 1890–1895, I wrote for the London *Musical Courier*, a page or two weekly entitled the "Raconteur." It was signed. Through it I came to know many musical and literary people there. I was slowly discovering that to become successful, a critic can't wait for masterpieces, but must coddle mediocrity. Otherwise, an idle pen. Big talents are rare, so you must, to hold your job, praise conventional patterns. And that way leads to the stifling of critical values. Everyone criticises. You do, the flower that reacts to the sun, your butcher, the policeman on the block, all criticise. It is a beloved prerogative. The difference between your criticism and mine is that I am paid for mine and you must pay for yours after you hear music or see the play. In his invaluable studies, Criticism and Standards, William Crary Brownell does not hold with the Brunetière nor with the Anatole France opposing schools of criticism He detects the doctrinaire and pedagogue in Brunetière, and he rightly enough fears the tendency towards loose thinking in the camp of impressionistic criticism, of which Anatole France is the recognised head. Mr. Brownell believes in central authority. Yet, he is not a pontiff. He allows the needful scope for a writer's individuality. It's all very well to describe the boating of your soul among the masterpieces if you possess a soul comparable to the soul of Anatole France, but yours may be a mean little soul dwelling up some back-alley, and your pen a lean, dull one. Will your critical adventures be worth relating? The epicurean test of the impressionist is not a standard, says Mr. Brownell, "since what gives pleasure to some, gives none to others. And some standard is a necessary postulate, not only of criticism, but of all discussion, or even discourse." He asserts that criticism is an art. "One of Sainte-Beuve's studies is as definitely a portrait as one of Holbein's." The "creative critic" of Wilde is hardly a reality. There are no super-critics. Only men, cultured and clairvoyant. Sainte-Beuve, Taine, Nietzsche, Arnold, Pater, Benedetto Croce, Georg Brandes—and this Dane is the most cosmopolitan of all—are thinkers and literary artists. It is perilously easy to imitate their mannerisms, as it is to parody the unpoetic parodies of Whitman, but it ends there. A little humility in a critic is a wise attitude. Humbly to follow and register his emotions aroused by the masterpiece is his function. There must be standards, but the two greatest are sympathy and its half-sister, sincerity. The schoolmaster rule of thumb is ridiculous; ridiculous, too, is any man setting up an effigy of himself and boasting of his "objectivity." The happy mean between swashbuckling criticism and the pompous academic attitude, dull but dignified, seems difficult of attainment. But it exists. To use the personal pronoun in criticism doesn't always mean "subjectivity." I don't believe in schools, movements, or schematologies, or any one method of seeing and writing. Be charitable, be broad —in a word, be cosmopolitan. He is a hobby of mine, this citizen of the world. A novelist may be provincial, parochial as the town pump, that is his picture; but a critic must not be narrow in his outlook on the world.

He need not be so catholic as to admire both Cézanne and Cabanel, for they are mutually exclusive, but he should be cosmopolitan in his sympathies, else his standards are insufficient. The truth is, criticism is a full-sized man's job. I was amused some years ago to read the edict of some young Johnny who writes hogwash fiction for bone-heads, in which he proclaimed that essay writing and criticism were for women. I don't deny they are, but our uncritical hero—whose name I've forgotten, but who probably turns out five thousand words a day on a type-writer—meant the statement in a derogatory sense. The literature that can show such a virile essayist as Hazlitt, as exquisite as Lamb and Alice Meynell, to mention only three, is hardly a literature that needs justification. And what of Coleridge, De Quincey, and Ruskin?

I wrote for the London *Saturday Review*. But I was growing tired of music and drama from the critical standpoint. Books, too, were getting on my nerves. There is a lot of nonsense written about the evil that a book may accomplish. Books never kill, even their vaunted influence is limited; else what vases of iniquity would be the reviewers. I confess I even doubt the value of so-called "constructive criticism." Interpreters of music, drama, paint, marble poetry and prose write nice little letters to critics, assuring them that such and such a critique changed their conception of such and such a work. I am sceptical. You tickle an artist in print and he flatters you in private. (I have known of prima donnas that send flowers to the wives of critics, but that is too obvious a proceeding, also too expensive.) The reason I don't believe artists of the theatre, opera, or the plastic arts ever alter artist's schemes of interpretation is because they couldn't do it if they tried. I don't mean that he or she doesn't broaden with experience; polish comes with practice; but I doubt those radical changes which some critics pretend to have brought about with their omniscient pens. In the case of no-bodies or mediocrities, who never make up their mind to a definite conception, it may be different. Great artists are secretly contemptuous of what amateurs—meaning critics—may say of them, no matter the thickness of the butter they spread on the critic's bread. A book review didn't kill John Keats. Criticism is an inverted form of love. The chief thing to the public performer—whether in the pulpit or politics—is neither blame nor praise, but the mention of their names in print. The mud or the treacle is soon forgotten. The name sticks. There is a large element of charlatanism in everyone who earns his living before the footlights of life. Ah! the Art of Pub-licity.

In his peculiarly amiable manner, George Bernard Shaw once reproached me with being a hero-worshipper of the sort who, not finding his idol precisely as he had pictured him, promptly tweaks, pagan-wise, his sacred nose. George probably thought of me as a pie-eyed youth who was all roses and raptures, one who couldn't see through the exceedingly large rift in the Shavian mill-stone. He changed his mind later. But I am a hero-worshipper. I have a large fund of admiration for the achievements of men and women, and I can admire Mr. Shaw simply because he so admires his own bright, par-ticular deity, Himself. But I can't go off half-trigger if the target is not to my taste. Many times I have been dragged to the well and couldn't be made to drink; not because of the water therein, but that I wasn't thirsty. I have with all my boasted cosmopolitanism many "blind" spots, many little Dr. Fells, the reason why I cannot tell. It was with difficulty I read Arnold Bennett, notwithstanding the joy he gave me in Buried Alive, yet I couldn't swallow Old Wives' Tales—the hissing lengths of s's—nor that dull epic, Clayhanger. Mr. Bennett, whose touch is Gallic, who is first and last a trained newspaper man, is out of his depth in the artistic territory of Tolstoy and Hardy. He is not a literary artist like George Moore or John Galsworthy. But Mr. Bennett enthralled me with his The Pretty Lady, an evocation, artistically evoked. So thus I had to reverse a too hasty judgment upon Arnold Bennett, whose resources are evidently not exhausted. When Mr. Wells writes a new book, I always take down one of his earlier ones. I can't believe in those silhouettes that he projects across his pages with the velocity of moving-pictures. They are not altogether human, those men and women who talk a jumble of Meredithese and social science. But how the wheels whiz round! I don't believe in them, I don't believe in Machiavel, or Tono-Bungay, or Mr. Britling, or that absurd Bishop; above all, I don't believe in the god—with a lower-case "g"—of Mr. Wells. A vest-pocket god, a god to be put in a microbe phial and worshipped, while sniffed through the nostrils. As prophet Herbert Wells touches the imagination. He foresaw many things, and if his heat-ray invented by his Martians could be realised, war would be forever banished from the solar cinder we inhabit and disgrace with our antics. The Wells of The First Man in the Moon, of The Isle of Dr. Moreau, of The Star, what prodigies of invention! His lunar insects are more vital than the machine-made humans of his newer fiction. No one, not even his artistic progenitor, Jules Verne, is comparable to him when his fancy is let loose. One living writer only is his match, J. H. Rosny, Sr. The Frenchman, a member of the Goncourt Academy, has recently written The Enigma of Givreuse, a war story which deals with a dissociated personality, physically double, and remarkable for its skill and fantasy. His Death of the Earth should be translated because it is a literary masterpiece. Mankind dies when water vanishes from our planet, and a ferro-magnetic organism follows him as master. We know nothing about the twist life may take to-morrow or a trillion years hence, so it is useless to predict that, with mankind, the most ferocious devastator of life—man mystically worships the shedding of blood, he is sadistic at his roots, murder is a condition of life—the creation of other vital forms will cease. Quinton, the French physicist, declares that birds followed man in the zoological series. Perhaps he means birdmen.

XIV

WITH JOSEPH CONRAD

One afternoon, years ago, Stephen Crane sat in the Everett House dining-room. We looked out on Union Square. The author of The Red Badge of Courage asked me if I had read anything by Joseph Conrad, a friend of his, a Polish sea-captain, who was writing the most wonderful things in English. That was the first time I heard Conrad's name. When I went to see him in England I found a photograph of Stephen Crane on his desk. The Conrads loved the American writer, who had often visited them. I thought of Crane when I left London one foggy morning to go down to Kent, invited by Conrad, and I also thought of Mr. Shaw, for Joseph Conrad had become the object of my hero-worship; nor has the worship waned with the years; quite the contrary. His "royal command" to visit him stirred my imagination. The mirror of the sea, master of prose, though writing in a foreign language; possessing a style large, sonorous, picture-evoking, as microscopic in his analysis as Paul Bourget, as exotic as Pierre Loti, without the egotism of that essentially feminine soul; withal a Slav when he most seems an Englishman, Joseph Conrad is the unique weaver of magic variations on that most tremendous theme, the sea.

I was summoned, as I say, to his country home in Kent and in the most cordial fashion. I had not expected a typhoon blast in the form of an invitation, nevertheless

from the writer of The Nigger of the Narcissus, I had
looked for something more nautical, something like this:
"What ho! luff-to and run your miserable little writing
yawl into my harbour, and don't be slow about it, blast
your buttons!" But I had forgotten that I was about
to visit Joseph Conrad, and not the merry Mr. Jacobs
and his many cargoes. Kent is charming. Kent is
hospitable. But it consumed all of two hours to reach
a remote station called Hamstreet, after changing at
Ashford. A motor-car met me. I thought again of
Mr. Shaw. If it had been a hydro-airplane or a steam
launch, I shouldn't have been surprised, but a motor-
car and Conrad didn't modulate; which proves the folly
of preconceived notions. I had seen protographs of
Mr. Conrad, mature, bearded, with commanding eyes,
a master-mariner as well as a master-psychologist.
Would he resemble his portraits? Of course not, and I
prepared for the worst. I was delightfully disappointed.
At the door of his "farmhouse," as he calls it, I met a
man of the world, neither sailor nor novelist, just a simple-
mannered gentleman, whose welcome was sincere, whose
glance was veiled, at times far-away, whose ways were
French, Polish, anything but "literary," bluff, or English.
He is not as tall as he seems. He is restless. He paces
an imaginary quarter-deck, occasionally peers through
the windows as if searching the horizon for news of the
weather. A caged sea-lion. His shoulder-shrug and
play of hands are Gallic or Polish, as you will, and his
eyes, clouded or shining, are not of the Anglo-Saxon race;
they are Slavic, even the slightly muffled voice is Slavic.
One of the most beautiful sounding of languages is Polish
—the French of the North. When Mr. Conrad speaks
English, which he does swiftly and with clearness of enun-

ciation, you may hear, rather overhear, the foreign
cadence; the soft slurring of sibilants characteristic of
Polish speech. He is more "foreign" looking than I
had expected. He fluently speaks French, and he often
lapsed into it during our conversation. And like other
big men he asked more questions than he answered,
supersubtle Sarmatian that he is. But his curiosity is
prompted by boundless sympathy for things human.

He is, as you must have surmised, the most lovable of
men. He takes an interest in everything, save bad art,
which moves him to vibrating indignation, and he is
sympathetic when speaking of the work of his contemporaries. What a lesson for critics with a barbed-wire
method would be the opinions of Mr. Conrad on art and
artists. Naturally, he has his gods, his half-gods, his
major detestations. The Bible and Flaubert were his
companions throughout the years he voyaged in southern
seas; from holy writ he absorbed his racy, idiomatic and
diapasonic English; from the sonorous, shining prose of
the great French writer he learned the art of writing sentences, their comely shape and varied rhythmic gait, their
sound, colour, perfume; the passionate music of words,
their hateful and harmonic power. He studied other
masters; Balzac and the Russians. Henry James has
written of the effect produced on his French fellow-
craftsmen by Ivan Turgenev. His Gallic side, a side
frequently shown by Russians, they appreciated; his
philosophical German training they understood; but the
vast mysterious reservoir of his Slavic temperament was
for them non-existent. So close a friend as Flaubert
was unresponsive to the rarest in Turgenev. At this
juncture I can't help thinking of Conrad. No prophet
has been more envied out of his own country. His fellow-

artists, Hardy, Kipling, Galsworthy, Arthur Symons, the late Henry James, and the younger choir, were and are his admirers. His critics are sometimes extravagant in their praise of his art; yet, I haven't thus far read a critique that gives me a sense of finality. They miss his Slavic side, else are repelled by it. And irony . . . an unforgivable offence. Mr. Shaw found out that fact early in the game, and always uses a bludgeon; that is why he is called subtle in England—and America—when he is drawing blood with the blunt edge of his razor. Conrad is nothing if not ironical. His irony is an illuminating model for the elect, but it has not endeared him to the public and to certain critics. What havoc was wrought on the appearance of Under Western Eyes, which might have been written by Turgenev so far as its verbal artistry, and planned by Dostoievsky, because of its profound characterisation and mystic power; yet it is unlike any book by either of the two Russians. Its almost malign, ironical mode has been seldom noted; we were only informed by the pens of presumptuous young persons—principally in petticoats—that Under Western Eyes is a copy of The Crime and The Punishment, when it is the most searching arraignment of Russian tyranny, Russian bureaucracy—which is the same thing—ever written. But in the quiet inferential Conrad key. A Pole, he hates Russia, as hated its miserable Czar-crowned rule, Frederic Chopin. And like Chopin, Conrad buries his cannon in flowers. That is the clue to this great fiction—a Dostoievsky reversed, a contemner, not an apologist of the Russian Government. I have told you that I loved Polish art, and Joseph Conrad is another of my idols.

He is pre-eminently versatile, and in the back garden

of his culture, in the enormous storehouse of his experiences, there flits betimes an uneasy shadow, an ogre that threatens; it is his Slavic temperament. He would not be Polish and a man of genius if the Polish Zäl was not in his writings, in his gaze and speech; that half-desire, half-melancholy, that half-yearning, half-sorrow, a divine discontent, not to be expressed in a phrase, unless it be in the magical phrase of. his countryman, Chopin.

The existence of Conrad has been too close to the soil not to have heard the humming of the human heart and its overtones. The elemental things are his chief concern, not the doings of dolls. He is not a propagandist. He never tries to prove anything. He is the artist pure and simple. He has followed the ancient injunction to look into his heart and write—he the most objective of artists, with the clairvoyance of a seer. Nevertheless, his true happiness lies nearer the core of his nature—the love of his family. For certain young writers this human trait may seem banal. Any butcher or policeman can love his wife and children. Art is a jealous mistress, we are told by pale youths who wearily look down upon a stupid world from their ivory towers. It was the unhappy Marie Bashkirtseff who said that her washerwoman could breed children, so there was nothing to boast about maternity. Mr. Conrad thinks otherwise. He is not only a great writer, but a loving father and husband—that classic obituary phrase! There is no paradox here. It is because he is so human that helps him to be so masterful a writer. He can pluck the strings of pity, terror, irony, and humour, and draw resounding music from them. But if you speak of him as a "literary" man, he waves you an emphatic negative. He admires literary virtuosity but does not often indulge in it. He admires Anatole France, but in the practice of his own art he is the opposite of that velvety sophist. He takes pride in his profession, yet is free from vanity or self-seeking; indeed, he is far from being a practical man. This worries him more than it does his friends, and the fact that he is not a well man is another thorn in his flesh. For months at a time he is tortured by rheumatic gout, which illness keeps him from his desk; thereat much wrath and many regrets. However, the optimistic spirit of the great artist shines through the mists of his pessimism. In his reminiscences you will find a veracious account of his childhood and his early passion for the sea.

Later in the afternoon of my visit he astonished me by transforming himself into an Englishman. He sported a monocle and his expression was haughty as he drove his car over the smooth Kentish roads. The Slav had disappeared. He spoke no more of art, but dwelt on his gout, his poor man's gout, as he smilingly called it. Too soon, I was standing on the platform of Ashford station en route for London. Conrad is only one of his names, his family belongs to the Polish nobility, but the magnetism of the waters drew him to the sea in ships, and only accidentally did he become a writer. Accident! Chance! It is a leading motive of his fiction. One night sitting in a café in Ghent, Maurice Maeterlinck conversed with his friend, Charles Van Lerberghe, a Belgian writer of originality, and that same conversation proved a springboard for the art of the younger man. Van Lerberghe indicated; Maeterlinck developed. Chance, again, or divination! Joseph Conrad is of the company of Flaubert, Turgenev, and Dostoievsky. "Not yet is Poland vanquished."

XV

BRANDES IN NEW YORK

When I saw Dr. Georg Brandes at the Hotel Astor a few months before the outbreak of the war, I told him that he resembled the bust of him by Klinger. It was the first time that I had seen the famous Danish author to whom I dedicated Egoists. Past seventy then, as active as a youth, I saw no reason why he shouldn't live to be a centenarian. An active brain is lodged in his nimble body. I had made up my mind to ask him no questions about America. I found him in a rage over the manner in which he was misrepresented by his interviewers. It should be remembered that primarily he is a cosmopolitan. He writes in English, Danish, French, and German with equal ease. As to the provinciality of our country in the matter of art and literature he has definite opinions, but he was polite enough not to rub them in on me. He was accused by some rough-rider cub reporter of finding his favourite reading in the works of Jack London! That amused him. Poe, Emerson, and Whitman interested him, though not as pathfinders or iconoclasts. The originality of this trinity he failed to recognise; made-over Europeans, he called them; Emerson and German transcendental philosophy; Poe and E. T. W. Hoffman; Whitman and Ossian. Even Walt's rugged speech is a parody of MacPherson's—and Ossian himself is a windy parody of the Old Testament style. Brandes is an iconoclast, a radical, a born non-conformist, and oftener a No-Sayer than a Yes-Sayer. The many-headed

monster has no message for him. As he was the first
European critic to give us a true picture of Ibsen and
Nietzsche, I led him to speak of Nietzsche. Once at
Baireuth, where I went many times to hear the Wagner
music-drama at the fountainhead—and often muddy was
the music-making, I am sorry to say—I was shown the
house of Max Stirner by a friend, who said: "When the
name and music of Wagner is forgotten, Stirner's will
be in the mouth of the world." I pricked up my ears at
this. I knew Stirner's extraordinary book, The Ego and
His Own, knew his real name, Johann Kaspar Schmitt,
a poor school-master half-starved in Berlin, and in 1848
imprisoned by the Prussian Government. This intellectual anarch, rather call him nihilist—for compared
with his nihilism Bakunine's is revolutionary rhetoric—
was to become the mightiest force in civilisation! I
couldn't believe it. This was in 1896. But in 1919 I recall my friend's prophecy when I read of the Bolsheviki
in Russia. Not Nietzsche, but Max Stirner has been the
motor-force in the new revolution. No half-way house
of socialism for the Reds. That is the lesson of Artzi-
bachev's Sanine, which most critics missed, partially
because of an imperfect English translation—whole key-
note chapters suppressed—and also because they did not
note the significance of the new man, who, while continu-
ing the realistic tradition of Dostoievsky and Tolstoy,
was diametrically opposed to their sentimental Brother-
hood of Man humbug, and preached the fiercest individualism while repudiating Nietzsche and his aristocratic individualism.

Dr. Brandes sets more store by Nietzsche than Stirner,
and was the first to apply to Nietzsche the appellation of
"radical aristocrat." He did not think that Nietzsche

had access to Stirner's The Ego and His Own.   I believe
the opposite.   I know he had, and there is a brochure
published by a learned Swiss which proves the fact.
However, the man who called the Germans "the Chinese
of Europe" wasn't Stirner.   It was Nietzsche.   When
we switched to August Strindberg, of whom I wrote at
length in Iconoclasts, Dr. Brandes remarked: "Yes, he
was mad.   Once he visited me and related how he had
called at a lunatic asylum near Stockholm.   He rang
the bell and asked the physician if he (Strindberg) were
crazy, to which the doctor replied, 'My dear Mr. Strindberg, if you will only consent to stay with me for six
weeks and talk with me every day, I promise to answer
your question.'"   After that Brandes had no doubts.
And, then, Strindberg's wild ideas about Ibsen—he was
convinced that Ibsen had taken him for the model of
Ekdal, the erratic photographer in The Wild Duck.
Brandes considers Miss Julie the best play of Strindberg.
I amused him by telling how I had gone to Stockholm
sixteen years ago to interview the Swedish poet and
dramatist.   I saw him once, for two minutes.   It was
after midnight and he stood in his lighted window and
cursed me, cursed the lady with me, who had aroused
him by throwing gravel at his bedroom window, and
then he disappeared in a blue haze of profanity.   It was
gently explained to me that one reason for his bad
humour, and for the rift in the matrimonial lute—he had
three or four such lutes—was the knowledge that his
third wife had played Nora, in "A Doll's House," the
night I had called on him.   Which was unfortunate for me.
Strindberg hated Ibsen, which hatred was not returned;
quite the contrary; Ibsen is said to have admired Strindberg's versatility and bursts of dramatic power.

August Strindberg

Brandes is not alone the discoverer of Ibsen, Nietzsche, and Strindberg, but he is himself a re-valuer of old valuations. Therein lies his significance for this generation. He wrote to Nietzsche in 1888: "I have been the best hated man in the North for the past four years. The newspapers rave against me every day, especially since my last long feud with Björnson, in which all the 'Moral' German newspapers take sides against me. Perhaps you know Björnson's insipid drama, 'The Glove,' and have heard of his propaganda for the virginity of men, and his league with the women advocates who demand 'moral equality.' In Sweden the crazy young things have formed themselves into large societies promising to marry only virgin young men. I presume they will get them guaranteed like watches, but there will be no guaranteeing for the future." There, you have a specimen of the hitting out from the shoulder by this Dane. He believes in the vote for women, but dislikes the moral humbuggery and sentimental flimflam, which everywhere permeates the movement. He knows as all sensible women know, that the vote will not prove a panacea for the "wrongs" of their sex, the chief one seeming to be in their eyes the fact that they are born women, and not men; nor will it add one cubit to their physical or mental stature. Dr. Brandes is an uncompromising individualist. Men or women must work out their moral salvation, and "movements," "laws," "majorities" will not help, in fact, will impede personal development.

The affections of Brandes have always been bestowed on the literatures of England and France. Consider his Modern Spirits, studies of Renan, Flaubert, Turgenev, Goncourt, or his work on Shakespeare, or his Main Currents in the Literature of the Nineteenth Century, of

which a French critic, Maurice Bigeon, has said that
Brandes did for his century what Sainte-Beuve did for
the seventeenth century in his History of Port-Royal.
And how many flies, large and small, there are imbedded
in the amber of the Brandes style! He is of Jewish
origin, and like his parents, not orthodox. Christians
call him a Jew, while orthodox Jews will have none of
him. He little cares, no doubt crying a plague on both
their houses. But he fights for his race; he repeatedly
attacked Russia for its treatment of the Jew, and he has
always been disliked in Germany for his trenchant arraignment of the Schleswig-Holstein incident. He has
combated the eternal imbecility of mankind, fighting
like all independent thinkers on the losing side. The war
with Prussia in 1864 made a deep impression on the young
man. (He was born in 1842.) It opened his eyes to the
fact that the Latin genius was more akin to the Danish
than the Germanic. In 1866 he visited Paris, and fell
under the spell of French culture. When the war of
1870 began he went to London, later to Italy. At this
time his mind, mirror-like, reflected many characteristics
of contemporary thinkers. He had already met John
Stuart Mill, and translated him into Danish. The hard
positivism of the Englishman he was never wholly to
lose; luckily it was tempered by his acquaintance with
Taine and Renan. What is vital, what makes for progress, what has lasting influence in social life? he asks in
his Main Currents. With his Hebraic irony he stung the
intellectual sloth of Denmark to the quick. His life was
made unpleasant at the Copenhagen University, but he
had the younger generation behind him. He knew that
to write for the entrenched prejudiced class would be a
waste of ink. He exploded his bomb beneath the na-

tional ark and blew sky-high conservative ideals. He not only became a national figure, but a world-critic. Not the polished artistic writer that is Sainte-Beuve, not the possessor of such a synthetic intellect as Taine's, Georg Brandes is the cosmopolitan thinker par excellence, and on his shoulders their mantles have fallen. He will remain the archetype of cosmopolitan critics for future generations. It is of him I think when I preach breadth in criticism, and while he is not a specialist in art or music, his culture is broad enough to embrace their values. A humanist, the mind of Brandes is steel-coloured. When white-hot it is ductile, it flows like lava from an eruptive volcano, but always is it steel, whether rigid or liquefied. It is pre-eminently the fighting mind. He objected to being described as "brilliant." He must hate the word, as I'm sure Bernard Shaw does. When all other adjectives fail, then "brilliant" is lugged in to do duty at a funeral, or a marriage, and no doubt at "brilliant" obstetrical events. The model of Brandes as a portrait-painter of individuals and ideas is Velasquez, because "Velasquez is not brilliant but true." Yet he is brilliant and steel-like and lucid, whether writing of Lassalle or Shakespeare or Poland. His Impressions of Russia barred him from that country. If the powers that be had listened in 1914 to the denunciations and warnings of Brandes and Israel Zangwill, certain disasters might not have come to pass in Russia. An ardent upholder of Taine and the psychology of race, he contends that in the individual, not the mob, is the only hope for progress. He is all for the psychology of the individual. Like Carlyle he has the cult of the great man. The fundamental question is—can the well-being of the race, which is the end of all effort, be attained without great men? "I say no, and again, no!" he cries. He is a firm believer that every tub should stand on its own bottom, and in this earthly pasture where the sheep think and vote to order his lesson is writ clear: To thyself be true! the lesson set forth with double facets by Ibsen in Peer Gynt and Brand. And also by Emerson. For mob and mob-made laws Georg Brandes has a mighty hatred. He is a radical aristocrat, whose motto might be: "Blessed are the proud of spirit for they shall inherit the Kingdom of Earth!" Agitated as he is by the Great War—his letters to me were full of it—he was philosopher enough to plunge into philosophical work, and he has written since 1914 two profound works on such divergent themes as Goethe and Voltaire, both of which will be given an English garb when a more propitious period arrives.

XVI

THE COLONEL

I was not precisely "summoned" to Oyster Bay on election day early in November, 1915, but I took Colonel Roosevelt's invitation in the light of a "royal command" and went down in company with John Quinn, who had arranged the affair and Francis Heney, formerly public prosecutor in San Francisco. I had received several letters from the Colonel of Colonels, of which I recall two sentences. One was: "What a trump John Quinn is!"; the other: "I have just received New Cosmopolis; my son Kermit, whose special delight is New York, would probably appreciate it more than I do, for I am a countryman rather than a man of the pavements." Now I had always thought of Theodore Roosevelt as a "man of the pavements," despite his delight in rough-riding over Western prairies. Personally, I found him the reverse of either; a scholarly man, fond of the arts—he has a number of pictures by the late Marcius Simons, a young American painter, who had been influenced by Turner. He has an excellent library of Colonial literature and is fond of digging out pregnant sentences from early preachers and statesmen. He showed me some of the trophies he had acquired in Europe while on his Grand Tour. One was a photograph of the late Andrew Carnegie taken in Berlin during military manœuvres. Both Colonel Roosevelt and Mr. Carnegie were guests of Kaiser Wilhelm. On the photograph the Kaiser had politely scribbled: "That old fool, Andrew Carnegie," probably allud-

ing to the projected Peace Palace at The Hague. Young
Philip Roosevelt was visiting his uncle that day. I had
previously met him. War was discussed by the Colonel
with the zest he displayed to the last. I told him that I
had been present at the formal opening of the Peace
Palace in September, 1913, at The Hague, and that the
day was so hot that all Holland fled to the beach at
Scheveningen, adding that I believed the palace would
eventually be turned into the finest café in Europe. And
I printed this prophecy (?) in the New York *Times* in
my reporting of the hollow mockery. One question I
permitted myself: "Colonel, would the *Lusitania* have
been sunk if you had been in the White House?" Snap-
ping that formidable jaw of his he exclaimed: "I don't
think there would have been a Lusitania incident if I had
been President." I believed him.

John Quinn, to whom he referred, is, I need hardly tell
you, an art collector and a well-known barrister in New
York. His collection is rich in modern pictures, from
Puvis de Chavannes to Augustus John and Picasso. I
saw Henry Ward Beecher once on Fulton Street, near
the ferry. He had the mask of a tragic actor, the jowls
heavy, the eyes wonderful in expression. This virile
clergyman and patriot has a statue erected to his memory
in Brooklyn. Which is just. Setting aside his services
for the cause of liberty during the war of emancipation,
did he not enrich English speech with such racy phrases
as "nest-hiding," "on the ragged edge," and "the parox-
ysmal kiss"? With the solitary exception of Walt Whitman no man has come out of Brooklyn who could write
such powerful words. Henry James I only saw once,
and then as he stepped on the lift he saluted me as "Good-
by, Mr. Scribner!" It was at the publishing house of

From a photograph, copyright by Moffett Studio, Chicago

To James Huneker
with the best wishes of
Theodore Roosevelt
Nov 29 1915

Scribners, then on Fifth Avenue below Twenty-second Street. My shaven face and glasses must have deceived him. Still, for a poor devil of an author to be taken for one of his publishers was, after all, achieving something in literature. Another great man that I saw and only once was the poet, Swinburne. It was during a Channel-crossing. I had encountered Heinrich Conried, not then manager of our Opera House, in Dieppe, and he was so seasick that I was alarmed, fearing he would collapse. Swinburne did not look cheerful himself, and for a poet who so rapturously celebrates the sea, I fancied he felt rather seedy; certainly he hugged the rail. The water was very rough. I should like to have gone closer, to have touched his hand and cried, Thalassa! but his eyes were distraught, his locks dank, and, with a shawl around his slim shoulders, he was far from a heroic spectacle. Swinburne looked less like a poet than Arthur Symons, who in the old days was poetical in appearance.

XVII

DRAMATIC CRITICS

When I began writing about the theatre, the principal critics of the drama were William Winter, of *The Tribune ;* "Weeping Willie," as Charlie McLellan nicknamed him because of his lachrymose lyrical propensities; Edward A. Dithmar, of *The Times*, who literally made Richard Mansfield; "Nym Crinkle," of *The World*, in private life Andrew C. Wheeler, an able writer; "Alan Dale" (Alfred Cohen), of *The Evening World*, later with *The Morning Journal*, now *The American ;* Steinberg, of *The Herald ;* Franklin Fyles, of *The Sun;* Willy von Sachs, of *The Commercial Advertiser;* John Ranken Towse, then, as now, dramatic editor of *The Evening Post;* Charles Dillingham and Acton Davies, of *The Evening Sun.* Mr. Dillingham soon graduated into the managerial ranks. C. M. S. McLellan was the wittiest of all and his theatrical column in *Town Topics* was worth reading, though it stabbed some one in every sentence. I have told you of *The Recorder* and its fortunes. Lawrence Reamer, who has been with *The Sun* for a quarter of a century, wrote with equal ease musical and dramatic criticism. As I have already told you, I followed Mr. Fyles in 1902 as dramatic critic of *The Sun.* William Winter was the most poetic and erudite of critics. For years he wrote with unflagging vivacity English undefiled and musical to the ear. He was unfair to visiting artists unless of English origin. He nearly strangled Henry Irving—that worst of great actors—with undeserved praise. But if actresses came from the continent, such as Bernhardt, Duse, Réjane, Segond-Weber, Mr. Winter poured a volley of abuse into them, riddling their private life, ridiculing their art, altogether behaving like a "hen-minded" and "highly moral" man. His unfairness has had no equal before or since, notwithstanding his vast knowledge and experience. "Foreign strumpets" was no unusual expression to be found in his reviews. He notoriously overpraised Ada Rehan, who couldn't hold a candle to Helena Modjeska; not that he was unfair to that subtle and charming Polish actress, but that Augustin Daly and Miss Rehan had won his critical suffrage. He used to be called the House Poet of Daly's, not without warrant.

One morning he published a nasty attack on Maurice Barrymore, not because of his acting, but his morals. Maurice, who lived a Bohemian life, didn't see what his doing off the boards had to do with his artistic capacity. I was with him at the Arena when he wrote the following brief letter to Mr. Winter: "Sir, in your column of *The Tribune* this morning you allude to me as an immoral actor who should not be allowed to blister the gaze of the theatre-going public. Sir, I never kissed your daughter. Maurice Barrymore." I was aghast. "But, Herbie," I remonstrated, "people don't write such letters." He gave me one of his swift dagger glances and coolly rejoined: "But they do, Honey, they not only write them but they mail them," and he did mail the letter, and then turning to me he winked. "Of course, you know the old hedgehog has no daughter." (But he had.) "I shouldn't have written it if he had one." This was characteristic of Barrymore. Another of his bon-mots was made to me early one morning as we went up the steps of the Lambs' Club, then on Thirty-fifth Street, opposite the Garrick, formerly Harrigan and Hart's Theatre. We had been on the loose since the afternoon before, though not off the list of the living by a long shot. Barrymore had conceived the queer notion that a glass dog was following him, and being of a fanciful turn he speedily found a glass chain for the fragile animal. At Moulds', down on University Place, he explained the invisibility of the dog by the fact that light passed through it and cast no shadow. He fought one unfortunate man to a finish—Barry was a fighter of science, he had been successful in the prize-ring—and when he grabbed the doubter by the scruff of the neck he led him to the bar and bade him drink, adding: "Now, next time you'll know a glass dog when you see one!" The man assented. Well, we led the mythical canine to the Lambs, and there it occurred to me that dramatic critics were not admitted within its sacred enclosure. "Oh, come in, come in, you are not a dramatic critic," said Maurice. The witticism is ancient, but the instance was modern. I went in, the glass dog tinkling after us on crystal paws, and as we found Victor Herbert and Victor Harris, we didn't go home till breakfast. Dear old Barry! What an Apollo he was. Rather slack in his acting, a careless "study," he seemed the ideal Orlando and Benedick. I say "seemed" because he was not. Charles Coghlan was his superior at every point save virile beauty and personal fascination, though Coghlan had enough of both.

Alan Dale is still amusing us with his criticisms, in which always lurk kernels of truth despite his flippant manner. Nym Crinkle was more brilliant than safe, and after forty years I still find myself reading Mr. Towse in *The Evening Post*, and agreeing with him. Sane and scholarly he did not yield to the Ibsen or Shaw movement, but to his book, Sixty Years in the Theatre, I turn when I wish to learn something of an actor or actress, their act ing, their personalities, and not to Winter's more polished literary performances. Mr. Towse is the sounder critic of the two. We often wondered how Mr. Winter con- trived to turn out such a prodigious amount of "copy" in his morning columns. He would usually stay to the end of the play, then go to the Tribune Building and down-stairs in the public office would write standing at a desk; then he would go to his home on Staten Island. And for fifty years or more. It was puzzling till some one saw him working on his voluminous essays and the mystery was partly explained. So varied had been his experience, such a trained journalist was he, that he could write several thousand words about a play before the performance—especially Shakespeare's—leaving spaces for interlineations chiefly dealing with the acting. In the case of Daly's productions he attended rehearsals and had leisure to file his Augustan prose. A perilous example for a lesser talent. But what classics he wrote. When he and Henry Krehbiel—during the early Wagner seasons—and Royal Cortissoz were together on *The Trib- une* the combination was difficult to beat. In fact, it wasn't beaten. Mr. Cortissoz was literary editor in those days, and art writer, too. He is a ripe scholar and master of coloured prose.

I plodded. I did much reading in the Elizabethans, but I saw I could never hope to meet such a master as William Winter on equal terms; besides, I was interested in the moderns—Ibsen, Maeterlinck, Hauptmann, Suder- mann, Schnitzler, Strindberg, all the new Paris crowd, Henri Becque first, and also the nascent dramatic movement in England. For D'Annunzio I had a hearty admiration, though his poetic drama is not for this epoch in the theatre where vulgarity and frivolity rule. But as interpreted by that rarest of all contemporary actresses, Eleanora Duse, the works of the Italian are an æsthetic joy. Not only is D'Annunzio the greatest living poet, but as prose-master he has matched the rhythmic and "numerous" prose of Ruskin, Swinburne, and Pater. His "eroticism" barred all hope of fair critical judgment here and in England—which is piddling hypocrisy. But his themes, æsthetic and ever poetic, would have prevented him from the glaring badge of "popularity." The most virile poet of Italy since Carducci, Gabriele D'Annunzio, is uncrowned poet-laureate, but crowned by the love and admiration of his fellow-countrymen as patriot-poet. His most significant novel is not translated. It deals with aviation. It is magnificent, and is entitled Forse che Si Fors che No. (Perhaps Yes, Perhaps No.) How I did rave over Duse, when she called for reticence in criticism, the golden reticence of her mysterious and moving art! With Duse her first season was a remarkable actor, Flavio Ando.

The first play I saw in New York coincided with my first visit to the city, May, 1877. With my brother, John, I went to Wallack's Theatre, then at Broadway and Thirteenth Street, and enjoyed Lester Wallack in "My Awful Dad," not a prime work of dramatic art but amusing. Wallack was in his prime. Later I saw him in his repertory, "Rosedale" among the rest. But I admired Charles Coghlan the more. In "Diplomacy" with his sister, Rose Coghlan, you couldn't get anything better. John Brougham, John Gilbert, and Madame Ponisi had seen their best days. Edwin Booth enthralled me; Lawrence Barrett and John McCullough did not. William Thompson was beginning his versatile career, and Irving and Terry were considered the wonders of the world. The first night at Philadelphia of the English actors I was with my father. After Hamlet's entrance my father nudged me: "As cold as Macready, without the elocution"; which simply meant that like Macready, Henry Irving was cerebral; as for his speech and gait, they were distracting to ear and eye. It was a pity that Richard Mansfield went to London at a time when his style was unformed. He never outlived the mannerisms he borrowed from Irving, a deadly example for him. Mansfield was a dynamic actor. His German blood and breeding, his cosmopolitan culture made him totally un-American in his methods. He was born on the island of Heligoland when it was British. His mother, Madame Rudensdorff, I knew when she lived at the Belvidere House and smashed the furniture in her periodical rages. She had been a Wagner singer in her day. From her, Dick inherited his irritable temper, his megalomania, and from her he acquired his skill in music. His father? Gossip gave him several, Jordan in Boston, Mansfeldt and Signor Randegger, a fashionable singing-master in London. I saw Randegger in the Covent Garden Opera House one afternoon in 1901, when Hans Richter conducted "The Ring." I asked my friend: "Who does that old gentleman with the bald head, with his back to the orchestra, look like?" The answer promptly came: "Like Richard Mansfield's father." The resemblance was startling— but who shall say! With such artistic parents he was doomed to be either an actor or a singer; he was both. He could sing Schubert, Schumann, Brahms, with finish. Max Heinrich had coached him. His speaking voice was

resonant and varied.   Irving never had such range of vocal dynamics, apart from the fact that he was born with
an indifferent organ.   Richard Mansfield and voice! all
the rest was scowling and wire-drawn mimicry.   Yet he
possessed pathos, and was effective in a powerful cres-
cendo.   He reminded me of Friedrich Haase without that
excellent actor's range.   Nevertheless, Mansfield has not
yet been replaced in our theatre.

First heard in New York in 1897, and again in 1904,
we welcomed the Hamlet of Forbes-Robertson as a revelation.   Henry Irving's more intellectual reading was
almost forgotten, and comparisons with Mounet-Sully's
Gallic fanfaronades were out of the question.   The
Hamlet of Salvini had been magnificent, only it wasn't
the Prince.   Willard was too phlegmatic, Beerbohm
Tree too fantastic, and E. H. Sothern too staccato.
Edwin Booth's Hamlet alone outranked Robertson's;
finished as was the art of Rossi, his interpretation was
Italianate, not of the North.   However, for the younger
generation, which knew not Booth except as a ghost of
himself surrounded by a third-rate company, shabby
scenery, and costume, the performances of Mr. Robertson proved to be in the nature of a charm.   He was a
gentle Danish Prince, never truculent, seldom militant.
The swiftness and wholly modern quality did not conceal
the inexorable fact that no man has ever played in its
entirety the Prince that Shakespeare drew; that an experienced artist knowing this, is forced to compromise; that in the case of Robertson, temperamental bias led him into the only path for himself.   Of
the melancholic type, in facial expression sensitive, a
scholarly amiable man, perhaps by nature somewhat of

a pessimist—he was, above all, an actor endowed with imagination. These qualities pressed into service by a loving devotion to his art and an exalted sincerity of purpose lifted his work to a high plane. He had at his command a supple mechanism. And he was first the elocutionist, then the actor. Never electrifying his auditors, he managed his transitional passages smoothly, without robbing them of variety or emphasis. He modulated his effects without abruptness or violence. Sweetly morose, ever luminous, and in style largely moulded, never staccato nor colloquial, most musical, most melancholy, and of rare personal distinction, the Hamlet of Forbes-Robertson was the most appealing since the day of Booth. Mr. Robertson was not the mad Prince, not the histrionic maniac nor the pathologic case fit for the psychiatrist's clinic, which some players have made Hamlet. He was sane, so exquisitely sane, that while the rude buffets of a cruel and swirling fortune at times shook his spiritual nature to its centre, yet they never quite toppled it over. This Hamlet knew a hawk from a hernshaw. I may add that there is much nonsense in the statement that Hamlet cannot be altogether badly acted, that it is self-playing, when in reality it is the most abused character in the Shakespearean gallery. As for Kipling's sentimental "The Light That Failed," while Mr. Robertson exhibited technical skill and tender emotion, the rôle was beneath his powers. Yet in that and the sloppy Jerome play he made fame and fortune.

I have mentioned Kipling. I came up from Paris to Rouen one morning with him. I was about to pay a visit to the tomb of Saint Flaubert. When I alighted Mr. and Mrs. Kipling had taken their seats in the dining-car for the midday déjeuner. The window was open so

I said: "Mr. Kipling, you should have stopped at Rouen
and made a propitiatory pilgrimage to the tomb of
Flaubert in the Monumental Cemetery, if for nothing
else but to expiate your literary sins." Mrs. Kipling
smiled—her brother, Wolcott Balestier, was an old friend
of mine when he was on *The Sun*—but Rudyard of the
Clan Kipling, preserved a stony mask. The train moved.
No doubt he took me for a harmless lunatic, and perhaps
he was right. I tried to stir his artistic conscience, and
I knew of nothing more efficacious than a humble
prayer pronounced before the Flaubert commemoration
tablet in the Parc Solférino or at the grave of the Holy
Gustave. A trip down the Seine to Croisset, where is
the Flaubert Museum, would give the finishing touch.

In The Pathos of Distance I made a little study of the
Violas I had seen, beginning with Adelaide Neilson in
1877, down to Wynne Matthison. At the Arch Street
Theatre, Miss Neilson was supported by Eben Plympton,
the Sebastian; Walcot, Malvolio; McDonough, Sir Toby;
Howard, Sir Andrew; Hemple, the Clown; Miss Barbour,
the Maria. At the Fifth Avenue Theatre, Mr. Daly
revived "Twelfth Night" in 1877, with Miss Neilson as
Viola, Charles Fisher, Malvolio. Barton Hill, George
Clarke, Harry Dixey have played Malvolio, and can we
forget Irving? Charles Walcot was my first Malvolio.
The Violas were Mrs. Scott-Siddons, Ellen Terry, Fanny
Davenport, Ada Rehan, Marie Wainwright, Helena
Modjeska—most poetic, after Neilson's—Viola Allen
and Julia Marlowe. In her early days, Mrs. John Drew
played Viola. It was at a reading that I heard Mrs.
Scott-Siddon's Viola. She was beautiful to gaze upon.
Miss Marlowe was charming and Miss Matthison a Viola
in the mode minor. Her voice was noble, though not so

JULIA MARLOWE

caressing as the organ of rare Julia Marlowe. Ah! the pathos of distance.

Through the avenue of my memory there silently passes a throng of names. The members of the Union Square Stock Company, of Wallack's, of the Madison Square—during the auspicious reign of Daniel Frohman —of Daly's, of the Empire. I suppose the complaint of grumbling after forty is chronic with critics. The palmy days! we sigh, and some day the present generation will do the same—Ah! those were the palmy days of George Cohan, Sam Bernard and Louis Mann! When the Harrigan and Hart company dissolved, we thought no one could replace Annie Yeamans or Johnny Wild—and no one has. The Charles Hoyt régime set in, and it was amusing enough; after a lapse, George Cohan appeared on the scene, and seizing the Time-Spirit by the horns brought the beast to its knees. There is a divining sense given to a few lucky mortals, and clever George possesses it. The hour was ripe for vulgarity, and as there is nothing so catching as vulgarity, presently the theatrical world is wholly given over to it. The flim-flam film theatre completed the downfall of the drama. Yet, the theatre was as vulgar thirty or forty years ago, though the saving clause was the superior actors and actresses. The comic-opera stage, too; where are the Gilbert and Sullivan operas and their interpreters? Where the Bostonians? Think of "Robin Hood" in its pristine glory: Henry Clay Barnabee, Tom Karl—I remember him in opera during the early Pappenheim-Charles Adams days on Broad Street—McDonald, George Frothingham, one of the best low comedians in the country, Eugene Cowles, Jessie Bartlett Davis—she sang "Geneviève" at Opertis' Garden in 1876, and her admirers were Governor Bunn, and Will Holmes, the barytone. "Oh Promise Me" came later. Marie Stone-McDonald was a favourite. And let us not forget good old Sam Studley in the conductor's chair. Victor Herbert and his sparkling Gallic music is still with us. Yet we had great fun in the days of the McCaull Company with Della Fox, Camille D'Arville, Pauline Hall, Jeff De Angelis, De Wolf Hopper, Digby Bell, Laura Joyce, Mathilda Cotrelly, Marie Geistinger, and many others!

Mary Anderson never profoundly touched me. I recall Laura Burt, Mrs. John T. Raymond (Marie Gordon), Rose Wood, dainty Madeline Lucette, afterwards married to J. H. Ryley, and Nat Salsbury. Jacques Offenbach conducted his music at the Broad Street Garden. A genius! Did you hear Hughey Dougherty's story about inviting a friend over the telephone to a drink, and going down Eleventh Street, found the whole fire department in front of the bar? "If I had spoken louder," said Hughey, then the funniest "burnt cork artist," "I would have had to set 'em up for the entire City Government." Joe Emmet was on the rampage those days. The death of Miss Neilson at Paris made the world wonder. But it was not suicide, Edward Compton told us. A blood-vessel burst in her intestines. The iced-milk had nothing to do with the death. Dion Boucicault filled the papers with his plays and matrimonial adventure. Agnes Robertson left him and sued for divorce. Charles Backus, of Birch, Wambold and Backus, died in 1883. What a crowd he could draw! The Hanlon-Lees dazzled us. Minnie Palmer attracted us. Minnie Hauk painted her naked legs green, said Parisian newspapers, when she couldn't get tights to fit her. It was in Auber's "Carlo Broschi," and she had a male part. It's too bad to be true. Clara Morris had power, pathos, but a queer pronunciation. Caroline Richings Bernard and her opera company were much admired. Emma Abbott and her famous "kiss" did not impress me. Harry Richmond was a capital comedian. Maude Harrison, Charles Thorne, Frank Mayo, Lotta, Sara Jewett, Kate Claxton, Agnes Leonard, Frank Bangs, Estelle Clayton, Stella Boniface, Admiral Tom Thumb, and Commodore Nutt; (Lilliputians we call them now, then they were "dwarfs") Sadie Martinot, Katherine Lewis, Minnie Maddern, May (not Fay) Templeton, Marie Prescott, Harry Beckett, Jennie Hughes, Jeffreys-Lewis, Cora Tanner, Effie Ellsler, Louis and Alice Harrison in "Photos"—stop! I could go on for hours reeling off a litany of names. William Warren was a sterling comedian; Kate Castleton, Verona Jarbeau and the French group, Aimée, Judic, Rhéa, Théo, Paola Marié—sister to the celebrated Galli-Marié—Angèle and Victor Capoul—"Count Johannes" had just died. The star of Maurice Grau was ascending. Madame Frida Ashforth, in opera then, tells me that she was engaged to Antonio Barili, the singer and half-brother of Patti. She was a chum of Adelina from 1855 to 1860. The Barili-Patti household lived next door to Frida Ashforth on Broadway at Fourth Street. Caterina Barili, who had been celebrated in her day, led her daughters an unhappy dance. She was tyrannical and bad-tempered. Adelina, after missing her vocal practice, would be chased over the house into the back yard by the terrible old woman, and when she evaded her, Addie would wriggle derisive fingers, her

thumb at her nose. Charming idyll of childhood! Her
sister, Amelia Strakosch, was, according to the high vocal
authority I have quoted, not much of a singer.

On West Twenty-fifth Street there was a French
boarding-house kept by a couple, M. and Madame Félix.
The guests were mainly theatrical folk, with a sprinkling
of musicians and writers. The table was good, the wines
cheap, and always was there a little poker game in the
private apartment of M. Félix. I lived there for years.
It was in the heart of theatre-land, and thus I made
the acquaintance of David Belasco, who, with his
lovable family, occupied a suite on the same floor as I.
I verily believe that Balzac would have wished for nothing better to describe than the Maison Félix. The company was lively, there were pretty women, jolly men.
Occasionally—but not too often, or too openly—a basket
containing letters would be let down from an upper
story on a string. There were few ructions, nevertheless,
the atmosphere was worthy of De Maupassant. I got
into the habit of taking midnight walks with David
Belasco. He was stage producer then for the Frohmans,
and I was writing about the theatre. D. B., as we called
him, could think of nothing but the stage. As he drank
his milk he would urge me to play-making; but I hadn't
the vocation, and heeded him not. Have I written
poetry? Yes, waste-basket. Have I written plays?
Yes. Locked in the secrecy of my desk. However, Mr.
Belasco was right. One successful play and the author
is on Boulevard Easy. I have a half-dozen friends, old
newspaper men, who bother themselves with cutting
coupons, not producing "copy." Successful playwriters,
and sensible humans they are. A funny affair at the
Maison Félix was a farewell dinner given by his friends

to a singer about to launch himself into the perilous sea
of matrimony with a celebrated singing actress.   With
the exception of myself probably every man Jack at the
table had been on friendly terms with the bride.   Speeches
were made.   Toasts were drunk.   The bridegroom was
overwhelmed by emotion.   Did he guess the truth?   I
never made after-dinner speeches, but urged by strong
hands, I got on my legs and began: "Brothers, I
might say brothers-in-law"—I was ejected.   Luckily the
bridegroom was slightly deaf.   Talk about De Maupassant!   Plays and fiction have one gripping theme: Did
she?   It is the only theme that interests.   I was so impressed by the evening that I wrote a "prose-poem"
about it.   It makes me think of the two young women
in Paris who found themselves at a monkey cage in the
Zoo.   They were experienced members of a very ancient
profession, and as the agile and grotesque animals were
playing all sorts of silly tricks, one girl said to the other:
"Give them clothes with money in their pockets and they
would be real men."   Did I ever tell you the witticism
of Maurice Barrymore concerning a fiasco made by a
foreign-born actress of a certain reputation at the Manhattan Opera House?   Barry supported the lady, whose
voice was not powerful enough for the big auditorium.
I asked him how she succeeded—I was at another theatre.
"Obscene but not heard," he answered.   I have told you
that I knew Willie Wilde, Oscar's brother.   He was a
companionable pagan.   Every ten minutes he would
light a fresh cigarette, every fifteen ask for another
drink.   He invariably preluded with "I have a zoological
feeling that I may be thirsty."   Getting up at five in
the afternoon finally got on the nerves of his wife, Mrs.
Frank Leslie, and she divorced the poor chap, who did

hate to work. I saw much of Edward MacDowell, an admirable friend, and I wear on my watch-chain a medal of Franz Liszt, dated Weimar, 1880, and given to Edward by the master. After his death Mrs. MacDowell presented it to me.

XVIII

EARLY IBSEN

I have always detested propagandists while admitting their usefulness. I loathe "movements," cliques, cenacles, anarchs who don't "anarchise," but only bellow. I wrote about Nietzsche as early as 1888 and Ibsen still earlier, yet I was not an Ibsenite. The two Ibsen pioneers here were Professor H. H. Boyesen, of Columbia University, and William Morton Payne, then editor of *The Dial*. Mr. Payne translated and finished Jaeger's Life of Ibsen. In England, Edmund Gosse and William Archer were the sponsors of Ibsen. But I fought in the critical trenches for the new art from the Land of the Midnight Whiskers. And it was a hard battle as the entire press was dead against him. We took our theatrical fashions from England and great was the name of Clement Scott. An honourable exception to the prejudiced critics was Charles Henry Meltzer, who had translated Hauptmann's "Hannele," and for the Sotherns "The Sunken Bell." To-day I find Ibsen rather trying. "A Doll's House," "An Enemy of the People," for instance. Problem plays soon stale. Consider the twaddle foisted on an unsuspicious public by Shaw—"Mrs. Warren's Profession" sounds as if written for the kindergarten. And "A Doll's House"—the best Nora I saw was Agnes Sorma, with Réjane a good second. Mrs. Fiske and the Russian, Nazimova, are well remembered. The play is dating. Nowadays no woman would leave her children in that dreary door-slamming coda. I wrote of it thirty

years ago that the slamming of that front door by Nora
was heard the world over. It was the tocsin of female
revolt. What nonsense! As young men are getting
scarcer owing to the war, it would be Helmer who might
go away, not his wife. There are always plenty of
women waiting outside. Duse asked Ibsen's permission
to change the original ending, and after considerable
grumbling the Norwegian dramatist consented. The
new ending was thus: Helmer stunned by his loss is wondering if the "miracle" will ever take place. Time
elapses. Suddenly Nora enters, radiant, a bundle in
her hand. "Torvald! Torvald!" she cries. "The miracle! Didies for baby are marked down half-price.
The miracle!" Quick curtain. The late E. A. Dithmar,
critic of *The Times*, wittily named "A Doll's House"
and "Margaret Fleming"—by Herne—"The Didy
Drama."

It was unfortunate for Henrik Ibsen that the Ibsenites
discovered him. In this misfortune he keeps company
with Browning and Meredith. There are dark places in
the heart of every poet, yet these obscurities should not
be hailed as illuminations. Long ago Daddy Ibsen's
plays were seized by the propagandists; at first by the
socialists, then the individualists, then by the women in
search of a message. Now the women have cooled off a
little in their devotion. Ibsen at a banquet in Christiania
told the ladies present that their place was in the home.
Shades of Nora Helmer! He said that he was primarily
interested in them as human beings, not in their sex or
their "wrongs." But the mystery-mongers found him
too tempting a subject for their busy exegetical pens,
hence the huge and absolutely useless literature that
has accumulated dealing with the "meanings" of his

works, when his chief significance is as a creator of characters and in his dramatic construction. Technically he stems from France; the influences of Scribe and Dumas fils are not to be denied. But the unhappy man fell into the clutches of the college professor and exegesis slew him. To-day he is played with the vivacity of an undertaker at a preacher's funeral. Every phrase is packed with esoteric meaning, and the itching to discover strange symbols in his dialogue causes an atmosphere of gloom and apathy; instead of a brisk tempo, the players utter their lines as if the earth was on the edge of dissolution. Ibsen's dialogue is natural or nothing. He is a reader of the human heart. And when he is in the roster of all stock companies, as he is on the continent, then he may be appreciated. But I doubt it. He makes you think as well as feel. Not with impunity can genius benefit mankind, has slyly remarked Rodin.

XIX

PICTURES

After writing about art on *The Sun* for a year I made pilgrimages to the principal art shrines of Europe. I had a brief passion for the gorgeous canvases of Monticelli, and while it would be impossible to see them all—he painted one a day for his absinthe—I saw the best. I went to the south of France as far as Marseilles, and discovered some notable pictures. Then—a reaction, I fancy—I fell in love for the hundredth time with Vermeer. I actually saw thirty of his thirty-three or four masterpieces, missing only one "important" example, somewhere in Scotland, a Christ composition. The Rembrandts are not easily traced, but when I got as far as the Hermitage self-portrait at Petrograd I called a halt. In New York I wrote much of the so-called Washington Square School—Lawson, Glackens, Sloan, George Luks, and the group that followed them. They had a hard battle but they "arrived." The group named "The Ten," which gave annual exhibitions at the Montross Gallery, had some strong painters: the late William M. Chase, Childe Hassam, Willard Metcalf, and Alden Weir. Arthur B. Davies is to my way of thinking the most individual artist we have to-day in this country. He has vision, and is a master of his material. When Alfred Stieglitz opened his little Photo-Secession Gallery at 291 Fifth Avenue he practically inaugurated a new movement in art. The exhibitions of Independents that I had been visiting at

Paris for ten years were suddenly transplanted to New York. We were shown Matisse, Picasso, Picabia, Brancusi, Cézanne, Gauguin, Van Gogh. Their artistic impact on the younger generation was marked. We had John Marin, Rockwell Kent, Samuel Halpert, Marsden Hartley, Weber, Jo Davidson, and Walkowitz. Robert Henri held aloof from the movement; he was self-contained and influenced more by Goya. The mystic, Albert P. Ryder, has passed away but his spirit lives.

Not to go back to the deluge, there was a time when Bouguereau occupied a pedestal in New York, and his worshippers went to the Hoffman House bar to stare at his meretricious "Nymphs Pursued by Satyrs." All manners of schools have had their little hour of triumph. Fortuny and Meissonier, Corot and Millet, Troyon and Turner, Whistler, too; and after the Barbizons, Manet, Renoir; also Bastien-Lepage. Even in New York as late as 1906 I found, to my amazement, that Manet was considered terribly audacious; that he was neither an expert draughtsman nor a colourist. Stupendous! And then the deluge: Cubists, crazy clowns, Futurists, Neo-Impressionists, and a swelling host of other charlatans and mediocrities. Paul Cézanne had intervened. He became the rage. Spry collectors pursued him (in the haunt of every collector there is a bargain counter). Dealers yearned for him. Elderly painters execrated his name. Guileless folk pronounced him "Suzanne" and secretly wondered why he is so ugly. And though not "the greatest painter of all," nevertheless his was a philosophic temperament. The chiefest misconception of Cézanne is that of the theoretical fanatics who not only proclaim him chef d'école—which he is—but also declare him to be the greatest painter that wielded a brush since the Byzantines. The nervous, shrinking man I saw years ago at Aix-la-Provence would have been astounded if he had known that he would be saluted by such uncritical rhapsodies. If ever an axiom is contradicted in practice it is that there is no disputing tastes. As if we don't spend part of our existence battling with other people's prejudices. Note, also, that the other fellow is always "prejudiced" in favour of his own opinions, usually considered by us as stupid or narrow. Our judgments are wellnigh infallible, and our special mission is to set our neighbour right. This conflict is perpetual. It makes life bearable. In matters of art I find the same intolerance. Because I like Henri Matisse, I am told that I suffer from optical degeneration. The same was said of me when I admired Manet, Monet, Degas. Matisse has confessed: "I condense the signification of the body by looking for the essential lines," which is slightly different from the cockney Cubists and their chatter about "significant form." Mr. Berenson has pronounced Matisse to be "a magnificent draughtsman and a great designer." The Chinese are his masters, also the masters of the world in art, though we are only beginning to find it out. Japan, which originates nothing, borrowed its art from the older kingdom. I don't care whether Matisse is a Poster-Impressionist, a sensitivist, expressivist, or a snark, but I do know that he is a master of line that, as Frank Mather, Jr., asserts, has had no superior since the time of Pollajuolo and the Florentines. What if the concubinage of his colours screams in rhythms that make the flesh creep? There is power, profound sophistication, subtle rhythm, all couched in novel terms. He can be suavely harmonious. He is sometimes as sunny and simple as Mozart or Monet. Since the death of Cé-

zanne, Gauguin, and Van Gogh, Matisse is the master
of the field. But Cézanne is the enthroned pontiff of
the modern pantheon.

It was at Saratoga I met a man who called himself "a
common gambler." In reality he was uncommon. Seldom was one in his "profession" as cultivated. A
pagan, he was refreshing in his freedom from hypocrisy. Clerical in appearance, so clerical that James
Whistler, who painted his portrait, and the artist he
most admired and cherished among the moderns, had
nicknamed him "His Reverence." The portrait bore
that title when exhibited. He had no illusion as to his
social position, nor was he a snob among sports. When
he alluded to his calling he was neither shrinking nor
vainglorious. He maintained that his was the next oldest of professions. Place aux dames! He asserted that
a man had a run for his money when he gambled; at
least he could see his cash planked down on the green,
see it swallowed by the turn of the wheel, or rapt away
by an unlucky card; whereas on the "Street" you seldom see the colour of your bank-notes after they leave
your hands. "And," continued my friend, "the game
on Wall Street is not always as fair as at Saratoga, Newport, or Forty-fourth Street." Yet this hardheaded
money-getting man was soft-hearted at the proper time.
In 1906, during the palmy days of his Casino, I saw him
send away a young fool who had whimperingly confessed
that the money he had staked at roulette was not his; in
a word, stolen. The gambler said: "Here is your money,
young man, return it to the bank," adding with an
ironical smile, "Go, and sin no more!" But when a
sporting millionaire wished to play, then the wheel

whizzed its merriest. A Robin Hood of the Green was our gambler. His love of pictures and old furniture became a veritable passion. His taste was impeccable, his judgment seldom at fault. His chief god in art was Velasquez. We always called him The Spaniard. He bought Whistlers at a time when it was a courageous act. I often crossed with him to Europe and his good graces introduced me to Whistler, who was exceedingly uncertain in likes and dislikes. He liked the gambler and was not rude to his friends. When the Whistler collection was shown at the Metropolitan Museum, we were amazed at its quality, yet he had no illusions concerning Butterfly James. "He will live by his etchings, not his pictures," an opinion I had heard from the mouth of William M. Laffan, an expert who predicted that owing to his poisonous paint the canvases were doomed to blackening and desiccation. This prophecy is, I am sorry to say, being fulfilled. Charitable and, according to his lights honourable, my gambling friend was a complex of confusing and contradictory traits. A psychologist would have enjoyed as I did unwinding the tangled skein of his character. When his wonderful Whistlers were sold, and with them his prized Sheraton furniture— I studied them at his Madison Avenue home, and also at his house across the street from the St. Regis—the art world was aflame with curiosity. He died of a fall in the subway, and left more friends than he knew. His name was—need I tell you?—Richard Canfield.

While writing of old-time theatrical topics, I forgot to relate a story about Adelaide Neilson and her manager, Frederick Schwab. There had been some gossip when the "star" went to San Francisco. A report of their matrimonial engagement was circulated. As Miss Neilson was not on the best of terms with Schwab, she threatened to discharge him if he didn't contradict the rumour. He answered: "I don't know who ought to get most angry about the gossip. If you feel yourself disgraced by it, what should I feel?" Which was the retort courteous. Miss Neilson was fond of Schwab because he was the first man to greet her on her arrival in New York. Years afterwards when he was manager for Vladimir de Pachmann, the slightly eccentric pianist— I think in 1890—he had a trying time to keep the little artist in order. One morning at Schuberth's music store on Union Square, Fred Schwab entered. De Pachmann (his right name is Waldemar Bachmann without the "De"), who had been playing, rushed to his manager crying, "I love you so much I must kiss you!" He kissed Schwab on the neck, not a kiss of peace, but a bite, so nasty, indeed, that the manager had to wear a silk scarf to hide the teethmarks. He did not have de Pachmann arrested for mayhem—surely a Chopinzee then—but, so it was whispered, made an iron-clad contract for the next season, by the terms of which the manager would not be altogether the loser. At the time I remarked of de Pachmann that his "Bach was worse than his bite." At a piano recital in old Chickering Hall, given by his wife and pupil, Margaret Okey —now the widow of the French advocate, Ferdinand Labori, counsel for Dreyfus—de Pachmann after uproariously applauding her, became censorious when she finished a Henselt étude (Thanksgiving after the Storm). A sharp hiss was heard in the auditorium. It was from the lips of her husband.   Oscar Hammerstein, I remember, had hissed a performer in his Manhattan Opera House, but for a husband to hiss his wife in public we must go to the pages of "Wives of Artists," by Alphonse Daudet.

XX

NEW YORK IN FICTION

Anyone with good red blood in his veins has made in London and Paris fascinating pilgrimages to the fictitious abodes of Dickens and Thackeray, Balzac, Zola, and De Maupassant. Even the less popular Flaubert has become an object of veneration, and the places mentioned in his Sentimental Education—a vast reconstruction of Paris in '48, or the tomb of the real Emma Bovary, are visited by pious people. New York, noisy, dirty, politics-ridden, her mighty flanks gashed by greed is daily reborn in the imagination of her admirers. Walt Whitman sang her praises, Charles Dickens registered her defects. But there she stands. Take her or leave her, it is all the same to our Lady of Towers. Love her as did O. Henry, and from that love something is bound to result. Magic, mud, moonlight, money, misery, and multitudes may be discovered as befits the temperament of each wooer of her favours. Such men as Poe and Sydney Porter (O. Henry) found her a "stony-hearted stepmother," yet contrived to weave from their defeats magical carpets that transport their readers on the wings of fancy. When the town was young, Washington Irving, Cooper, Poe, and their contemporaries recall to us Battery Park, Bowling Green, and old Wall Street. There is the later Wall Street of Edwin Lefèvre, Frank Norris, and Edith Wharton—in Custom of the Country. Wall Street was also visited by Robert W. Chambers, David Graham Phillips, George Barr McCutcheon, Rex

169

Beach, Owen Johnson, Samuel Merwin, and Thomas
Dixon. It is the most alluring lane in the world. Many
writers who enter it emerge without spoils literary or
otherwise, yet not shorn of their desire for it. More
than one painter has succumbed to its golden glamour;
witness the canvases of Childe Hassam and Colin Campbell Cooper.

How much fiction there exists in which the young
protagonist views the frowning battlements of the city
from the decks of an incoming ferry-boat. He may not
shake his fist at the Woolworth tower as did Rastignac,
Balzac's sorry hero, when watching Paris from the heights
and melodramatically muttering: "The fight's between
us two now!" But some spirit of antagonism blended
with ambition must fill the bosom of adventuring youth
as he beholds what may be the home of realised hopes,
that is, unless he comes by way of the Hudson Tubes,
and then the old ferry-boat is no longer a stage set for his
noble gesture. In Arthur Bartlett Maurice's The New
York of the Novelists, may be found invaluable material
for the curious student. The author slowly works his
way up-town, not overlooking "The Big Canyons of the
Money-Grubbers." That journalistic Bohemia, Park
Row, of which wrote Jesse Lynch Williams, Richard
Harding Davis, Graham Phillips, and Stephen Whitman
—like Davis, a Philadelphian—is not slighted. And
when we reach the name of Edward W. Townsend,
we exclaim: "Wot t'ell! Chimmie Fadden." Chimmie
still lives in the memories of his readers, though the dis-
reputable Five Points has vanished. Mr. Townsend,
an old *Sun* man, added to the civic picture-gallery a
strongly individualised and amusing type. Potash and
Perlmutter are definitely localised, and "Wasserbauer's

Café" is still in existence. Police headquarters, which ever intrigues the fancy of newspaper writers, and Pontons, wherein knotty legal problems are discussed across tables, are not missed. The mysterious East Side always has been a drab cloud by day, but a pillar of fire by night. Julian Ralph, Davis, Rupert Hughes—in his exciting Empty Pockets—and a host of other novelists have explored this region, and like pearl-divers, the deeper they dove the more precious the treasure they brought to the surface. In the Ghetto, "Sidney Luska," the pen-name of Henry Harland, was the pioneer. As It Was Written, The Yoke of the Torah, and Mrs. Peixada are yet to be bettered. Sidney Rosenfeld, Abraham Cahan, James Oppenheim, Bruno Lessing, Rupert Hughes are names that occur to one as the pearl-fishers in those dusky waters. Such artists as George Luks, Jerome Myers, Glackens, John Sloan, Eugene Higgins have portrayed the East Side with sympathetic pencils. The East Side of O. Henry is set before us: The Café Maginnis, The Blue Light Drug Store, Dutch Mike's Saloon, and No. 12 Avenue C. He whimsically calls New York "Little Old Bagdad on the Subway."

Among the forerunners of the present generation were Henry James, William Dean Howells, Marion Crawford, Brander Matthews, H. C. Bunner, Thomas A. Janvier, Edgar Fawcett, Frank Stockton, and Edgar Saltus. Pfaff's, where Mr. Howells met Walt Whitman and Fitz-James O'Brien, was then the Bohemia; Washington Square the Belgravia. What a playground for dazzling antithesis! Henry James visited the Square in his earlier novels and Saltus and Edith Wharton. That brilliant and compelling fiction, The Truth About Tristrem Varick is laid in Gramercy Park, in the old house

of Stanford White. During the eighties Edgar Saltus
played the rôle of social secretary to the fiction of the
Four Hundred; and not always to the satisfaction of the
people he painted. He told the truth. Mrs. Wharton
told the truth. Never tell the truth in fiction if you wish
to repose sweetly upon the breast of your readers. It
may be confessed without contradiction that the majority
of our fiction writers are sadly given to sickly senti-
mentalising. O. Henry was a prime sinner. Our drama
and novels must be lined with pink cotton because of the
sensitive epidermis of the man and woman in the subway,
who, nevertheless, digest without shock the "tough"
facts of life in the newspapers. That apocalyptic genius,
Benjamin De Casseres, once divided our native fic-
tion-mongers into four groups: Punk, Junk, Bunk, and
Bull. Punk includes the ladies with triple-barrelled names
—there are plenty with two; Junk, all the writings on
so-called social-science, pollyannas, new-thoughters, and
pseudo-psychologists; Bunk is the fashionable novel;
and Bull applies to the Jack London School; ramping,
roaring, robust rough-riders and heroes from the wild
and woolly West; bastards of the Bret Harte fiction. It
is a just classification. We needs must have our "art"
dosed with saccharine. War fiction for a period will
destroy this syrup, but it will be in evidence again.
Several of Theodore Dreiser's novels deal with New York,
The Genius in particular; a book moral to the sermon-
ising point, it is full of the sights and sounds of the city.
Mr. Chambers fashioned the scene of A King in Yellow
from the neighbourhood of Washington Square. He
sails through Society in most of his work. Sister Carrie
fled to New York. Predestined, by Stephen Whitman,
one of the few well-written stories on this day of vulgar

diction and typewritten rubbish, depicts with a vivid brush certain sections not far from Second Avenue, and pugilist Sharkey's (Sailor Tom) old place on Fourteenth Street.

Irving Place and Lüchow's have often figured in tales of the town. Van Bibber and his pranks showed Richard Harding Davis at his most entertaining. The heart of O. Henry was in Irving Place, not far from Gramercy Park, the Hotel America, Old Munich, and Little Rheinschlossen. His readers will recall these places. Scheffel Hall is still open. It has been a resort for Bohemians nearly fifty years. But O. Henry did not see it in its glory. Thanks to his friend, Gilman Hall, I met Sydney Porter at the Hotel Seville. The pace was beginning to tell on him. He was a hard worker and a furious candle-burner. Humorous and emotional, he was like a hero in one of his own stories. He never had the leisure to polish his anecdotes. New York was his magnetic rock. He became a cockney of the cockneys. But when he is called the American De Maupassant and Davis our Balzac, then criticism should go hide its head. After Madison Square another marking spot is Gramercy Park: In What Will People Say? which is Rupert Hughes at his best, we catch glimpses of "tea, tango, and toperland." About the Metropolitan Opera House the mists of memory have not yet mounted; it is not old enough to have its legend, as has the Academy of Music. But William J. Henderson has not passed it by in his The Soul of a Tenor. Mrs. Wharton's The House of Mirth plays near it. F. Hopkinson Smith knew the city and its outlying districts. How we followed his trail to "Laguerre's," its cheap wine and innocent diversions. A city passed out of existence while "Hop" Smith wrote and painted. Fickle, shifting, protean New York! You cross the bridge to Brooklyn in the morning and on your return at night you may find a big hole blasted through the house you had left intact. Anything is apt to happen in Manhattan except monotony. The department stores have not been overlooked by the younger tribe of purveyors— the "new" short-story, as far as structure is concerned, is amorphous, invertebrate. Montagu Glass, Edna Ferber, Samuel Merwin are diverting. There are mushroom Bohemias springing up overnight, canned mushrooms; compared with them the Sixth Avenues, Bohemias, Mouquins and Jacks seem eternal. Like the queer little resorts off South Washington Square and its vicinage, these serve as a file upon which budding genius sharpens its teeth. The wine, too, sets your teeth on edge.

Old Delmonico's has gone forever, and a few months ago Sherry's followed suit. No longer may we lounge with Van Bibber in the Fifth Avenue windows and ogle passing petticoats. With a sigh we admit that dear old intimate New York, the city that once contained Americans, has been submerged by an anonymous mob from across seas. The prophecy has come to pass: The East has conquered the West Side. Manners, like good cookery, have gone the way of all flesh. Soon the last American will disappear. I wager that his name then will be either Smithowski, Brownstein, or Robinsonio. Yet the cry will always be New York Redivivus! In a moment of discouragement I said that American fiction was largely written by imbeciles for the delectation of idiots. This was not only uncritical, it was unfair. I should have reversed the order and included the playwright and public.

Just now the right of free speech is not so important as free speechlessness. Old Joe Howard used to tell the newspaper boys of my time that the man wasn't yet born who could write a column of wit and wisdom every day of the year. If he had lived to read Don Marquis in the New York *Evening Sun* (a charming poet) and Franklin P. Adams (F. P. A.) in *The Tribune* he might have revised his opinion; furthermore, he would have been forced to add to his category the art of poetry. Despairingly, I wonder how those two clever chaps manage to keep the machine running. Day after day they throw off verse and prose suffused with humour, fancy, and common sense—the last is not the least negligible. And such verbal virtuosity! Thinking over the problem—the inexhaustible conjuror's bottle comes as an analogy, but filled with ideas, not water—I blew up the other morning immediately after breakfast, making a noise like a "blurb," and Gelett Burgess has defined a "blurb" as a noise like a publisher. Now, my meal had been light, tea and cereal. The ancient maxim runs thus: Grapefruit for brilliancy, for profundity sip chocolate. I don't believe it. Yet it wasn't the tea, it must have been the "pent-up aching rivers," as Walt Whitman says, of accumulated reading and a mild mania of imitation. I sat down at my writing-table, as wide as a well. Jamming on full speed I manufactured phrases. Aphorism or epigram? Or just plain hot-air, a windy reflex from other men? Note the lack of continuity, a dangerous symptom of senility.

Some people lose their ideals when their teeth begin to go. (What retrogression is here, my friends?) According to Havelock Ellis the basis of love is tumescence and detumescence. Tolerance is often a virtue of scep-

tics—but is it a virtue?   Good art is never obscene; the
only obscene art is bad art.   After the war is over, it
would seem that the Almanach de Gotha will have to be
changed to Almanach de Ghetto—especially in the land
of the Muscovite.   Envy is only a form of inverted admiration.   Joseph Conrad speaks of pity as a special
form of contempt.   Stupidity is the great humourist, says
George Moore.   We live too much on the surface of our
being.   A philosopher has said that we live forward and
think backward.   Sorrow is the antiseptic of sick souls.
Woman, declared the Fathers of the Church (shrewd
psychologists), is the most potent engine of dolour that
God has given Man.   The French Revolution only de-
stroyed ruins; the social edifice had been tottering for a
century.   Who was it that so proudly boasted: My
knowledge of thy knowledge is the knowledge thou cov-
etest?   Peace on earth to men of good-will—and fixtures
(above all, the latter).   Intimate friends are, as a rule,
disasters.   Mythomania is a malady that spares few.
Its real name is religion.   Walt Whitman may have been
a yellow dog, but he had a golden bark.   Truth is always
original.   But what is Truth?   Happiness is an eternal
hoax.   Only children believe in happiness; as well say
that the wise are children.   A delightful masculine convention is the virtue of woman.   (George Meredith said
this better.)   Be virtuous and you will be bilious.   (Venerable Hindu proverb.)   She was old enough to gossip
frankly about her new upper-set, but had not reached
the age when she would admit that she was out of the
marriage market.   The average author is not unlike the
average father: his first, his second book, he is interested
in as is the father of a newly-born baby; but after that
he regards his growing family with indifference, often

with dismay. There is always a silent corner in the most sincere confession of a woman. If you closely study a man you will discover that his marriage resembles him (what many-sided men must be polygamists). In the château of chimeras nothing is insignificant. Suspicion of the beloved one is like apoplexy; you may be cured after the first attack, but the second is always fatal. (This sounds like Paul Bourget.) After forty a man survives himself; which is a companion to the impolite epigram of Labouchère that all women over forty should be slain—except the suffragettes. What is all modern literature but a reek of regret that we are all but bubbles on a stream? (George Moore.) I pause for breath.

Most politicians are patriotic vegetables. Man is more significant than his creed. The heart has only one season. Books never kill. In music the cadenza is a parenthesis, except with Franz Liszt, who composed cadenzas with orchestral accompaniment and called them concertos. Charles Dickens said: "We are all going to the play, or coming home from it." "Since they can only judge, who can confer?" wrote Ben Jonson. The meaning of life is just the living of it. German fresco-painting is the white of an egg dipped in frigid ennui. One of the finest things in Hazlitt is his lusty yeoman in The Fight, who impatiently cries: "Confound it, man, don't be insipid." A philosophy in a sentence. Insipidity is the cancer of modern art. Men change, mankind never. The woman who goes about with a chastity chip on her shoulders—*i. e.*, aggressively boasting of her virtue —should be suspiciously viewed; she is painted fire. A Polish proverb tells us that you must kiss the hand that you wish not to sever. It's the severed head that makes the seraphim, wrote poet Francis Thompson. Do you remember the old story, so old that it is new, about Mrs. Bloomfield H. Moore and her titled visitor? She was entertaining him, probably talking about the Keely motor, when another visitor was announced. The Baron politely arose. "Don't disturb yourself, my dear Baron," sweetly remarked the hostess, "it's only my architect." This architect happened to be a member of the Furness family. Apochryphal or not, this anecdote tickled Philadelphia's rib in the early eighties or late seventies. The essence of music is silence. Hamlet said the rest is silence, thereby proving that he was a musician. The rest is always silent. Alice Meynell, essayist unique, wrote that it is not the eye but the eyelid that is important, beautiful, eloquent, full of secrets. The eye has nothing but its colour, and all colours are fine within fine eyelids . . . expression is outward, and the eye has it not. There are no windows of the soul; there are only curtains . . . the eyelids confess, and refuse, and refuse to reject. They have expressed all things since man was man. She also said that Hamlet, being a little mad, feigned madness. Truly a subtle distinction. She also said that Man is Greek without and Japanese within. Our face and figure; our insides. Symmetrical and asymmetrical. And in her Hearts of Controversy, she says, "the note—commonly called Celtic, albeit it is the most English thing in the world." . . . This is enough to startle the staid ghost of Mat Arnold. The Celtic note English! Alice, where art thou? Matthew Arnold averred that in America the funny man was a national calamity. British humourists have ever since made careful note of this warning.

XXI

A VOCAL ABELARD

I had always liked the old man. I met him first at a dingy little table d'hôte just off Fourteenth Street, a quiet, retired place where the spaghetti smoked, the wine was cheap, and not too nasty, and the tariff very low. Understand me, I didn't spend much money on food, preferring to invest it in books, books easy to procure —if one only has the price. I care little for black-letter editions; I would even allow an Aldus or an Elzevir to pass me if a copy of Flaubert's Temptation were nigh, or the music of Mallarmé's poetry available. I actually did give my watch to one of those gentlemen who lend money at high per cent., on account of a first edition. Ah! but what a copy. With illustrations by Manet. But I'm forgetting about Agnani. Ettore Agnani, to give him his full name, was one of those operatic waifs cast up by the ocean of music and stranded in the city with only the shreds and shards of a bass voice. He was a musty-skinned, high-nosed Italian, with some evidences of gentility still hovering about his person, a lover of Italian sauces and an inveterate raconteur.

In those days the table d'hôte was a hobby of mine. I have discovered many good places and remained with them till their inevitable decadence, and would then begin my search anew. I have eaten at an Irish table d'hôte where "Saucissons Patrique" were served, and at Rumanian restaurants where pepper reigned and beef was a side issue. Finally, I discovered Varsi's and was satisfied. Soup that savoured of cockroaches was hardly to be commended, but the spaghetti! For forty cents I dined royally, drank Chianti from Hoboken Heights, and waxed fat and lusty. Chance one evening brought Agnani to my table and the aristocratic deliberation with which he placed his eye-glasses on the bridge of his skinny nose as he scanned the menu pleased me. His hands were lean, brown, withered, and he sported one ring, a blood-stone, as antique as its owner. Agnani was a character. We became friends, for, while I am not much of a lover of music, I like its literary side. I am enamoured of gossip, memoirs, recollections which concern distinguished people and otherwise—and Agnani as he ate his fritto would ramble through the mists of his past and occasionally dig up something of interest. How the old rascal laughed as he slashed a woman's reputation, and with what zest he recounted his early operatic triumphs. He had a little dog to which he was devoted. I simply loathed it. It was one of those shrewish rat-terriers not big enough to make a meal for an honest Newfoundland, and it always bared its tiny gums at me in the most malignant manner. Agnani was crazy over the beast, and I'll never forget the night when in a stifled voice he said: "Nina is dead." Nina was the name of the little animal, and I hadn't the heartlessness to let him know how glad I felt at the news.

Agnani seemed the most frank of men till his private life was touched upon, and then his soul flew behind bars and bolts, and he would become unapproachable. I am not too curious but I have an aching nerve called by the psychiatrists "a craving for psychical insight." To believe that this brain-barren Lombard had "soul-states" would be rather ridiculous, for his greatest concern in life had seemed the tomato sauce on his spaghetti and Nina. After the little dog died he would work himself up into a green rage with Pietro, the one-eyed garçon, when the sauce was scorched. Otherwise, an acid smile lurked under his dyed and gummed mustachios, and his laugh was crackling. He wore a red necktie and I have heard that he had achieved his greatest artistic success as a buffo-basso. He baffled me, did this broken-down singer, to whom I frequently extended dinner invitations with the hope of getting a story—a rich, live story which would repay me for my trouble. (This may sound cruel, but I am a newspaper man, and ink, not blood, circulates in my veins.)

I took Agnani to a Chinese table d'hôte and fed him on bird's-nest soup and chop-suey. I took him to old Martin's where they breakfast like epicures. I dined him at the Maison Félix, but even the artistic dinner in that rare spot failed to warm the cockles on his soul. At last one warm June night, I met him tottering up Third Avenue, looking ill and dogless; his scarlet tie had less of its flamboyancy and the man was meek and dusty. The hour must have been ten and his eyes plainly implored: "Give me to drink." I brought the old chap to Scheffel Hall and bade him drink beer, and to my surprise he drank it greedily. Italians are not fanatical beer drinkers. They are more given to cordials, which they sip after a river of oily eloquence. Not so Agnani. He developed a colossal thirst, and about the twelfth or thirteenth glass light broke at last. He was drunk, serenely so, after the manner of the family Agnani. Then it all came out. He was the second son of a Lombard family whose name made me blink when he told it. You will never know as I'll go to the crematory with his secret. Besides, what does a name amount to except it be at the bottom of a certified cheque? He must have been a wild spendthrift and had "bonnes fortunes"; but of the inchoate mass of reminiscences he hurled at me I recall only one story—a story so improbable that it set me to dreaming of the loves of Abelard and Héloise, and for the moment transformed the faded features of Agnani into the stern lineaments of the implacable Canon Fulbert. Here is the anecdote:

The Milan Opera Company which had left that capital to go on tour in the provinces, comprised as its personnel Rosati, prima donna, soprano; Lahn, a Swiss, contralto; Dimali, tenor; and Agnani, basso. There were others, of course, but these were the principals, and with the impresario, Negri, and the Conductor Pinuti, dined at the first table and travelled second-class. The rest of the company went "au troisième." The real artist in the troupe, Dimali, was a tenor of the robust type, with a voice like steel, and a determined lover of women. The soprano and contralto were mediocre, but handsome and close friends.

"I liked them both," said Agnani in a quavering voice, "because they were good-looking women, and I always had a weakness for female beauty." This was so ingeniously accented, and he looked such a crumbling ruin even as he boasted that I ordered two more beers. He drank both—by mistake, I fancied. Then he continued:

"I was never on very good terms with Dimali. He was so conceited; he was a fine-looking man; no one could gainsay that, but he made eyes at every petticoat, and no chambermaid was ugly enough to keep him at bay—that is, if there were no prettier women around. And how that fellow could drink! He fairly swilled,

always took a treat and never stood one. Ah! he was a
mean rascal, but before the footlights he was superb."
Agnani rolled his eyes and lighted another cigarette.
Its thin, cool smoke curled above his shining pate and
straightway I forgot the clangour of Third Avenue, and
my fancy lit up the stage of some shabby opera-house
in a second or third rate Italian city, as on its boards
moved to tones the passionate puppets of transpontine
opera.

"Dimali never knew when to stop," pursued the basso,
his ancient jealousy of the man favoured by women
breaking forth when his feet were treading, one might
say, the very edge of his grave. "He was aware of his
artistic superiority and always impressed you with it.
He disdained the two women principals, and while en
route usually devoted himself to some pretty chorus
girls, riding third-class, and only turning up at meal-
times. We sang with varying success in many of the
smaller cities and in a few of the larger ones, and our life
was one of the customary cheap triumphs, cheaper lodgings, and general depression. Rosati and Lahn kept
together; the manager, conductor and I played our dom-
inos after the performance. The conductor, Signor
Pinuti, was the most cold-blooded wretch I ever met.
He had formerly been a surgeon in Ravenna, but want
of practice drove him into the musical profession—for
which he had a marked talent. He would, in his drawling
tone, recite damnable stories of surgical operations till
I shivered—my nerves were a woman's, and I feared the
sight of blood. I hadn't been much with Pinuti before
I discovered that, despite his harsh, frigid nature, he
was passionately in love with Rosati, the big blonde

soprano, who, apparently, cared for no one. It was in
Ravenna, Pinuti's native city, that I first noticed Dimali's queer behaviour with the contralto, Lahn. Out of
bravado he began to make love to her, desperately,
without shame, and when a man like this tenor becomes
earnest he may prove dangerous. He fairly haunted
Lahn, and the pretty, silly brunette showed she was
conscious of the handsome singer's wooing. Rosati sul-
lenly watched the game, but was she indifferent? Our
conductor had apparently ingratiated himself into her
graces, and they became inseparable. Thus we split
into three camps, for I associated with the manager,
Negri. We watched the conductor and soprano, and
they in their turn spied upon the contralto and tenor.
Pinuti by this time was crazy in love, and the once cold
Rosati seemed to favour him. Ah! my boy, how little
do we know of women and their tricky ways. One
morning after rehearsal, I overheard Pinuti speaking
with Dimali, rather arguing. I was in my dressing-room,
and every word came to me clear cut. Of course, I
listened.

"'Let her alone, I beg, I command you!' cried the
conductor.

"'Ah! Ah! Am I poaching on your property?'
asked Dimali in his most irritating style. There was a
significant silence, then Pinuti said in a hollow, strained
voice:

"'You insult Lahn. As for me I am betrothed to
Signorina Rosati.'

"'Perhaps the shoe pinches there,' responded Dimali,
laughing villainously. Then I heard no more. Later I
could see that the Rosati had become Dimali's enemy.

Evidently Pinuti had told her of the tenor's nasty speech, for she never noticed Dimali except when singing with him. Lahn seemed conscious of a change in the moral temperature and avoided her former chum; beyond doubt she was succumbing to the fervour of the tenor. Things couldn't go on this way much longer. I told Negri so. He only laughed and said I had too much imagination, at the same time bidding me not to mix up in the affair. Each day Pinuti grew gloomier, and when not conducting was scheming. He was constantly with Rosati, and they watched the other pair of lovers like detectives. These were aware of the espionage, yet never acted as if they wished to be alone. Like true Italians they made love in public and parted every night after a public embrace that made Rosati wince and Pinuti turn pale. What extraordinary reasons had these people for objecting to the love of the tenor and contralto? Was Pinuti also in love with the brunette? Or, perhaps the soprano was really in love with the tenor and jealous of the coquettish Lahn. I couldn't make it out. Suddenly to my amazement, happiness reigned in our little circle. The conductor threw off his dark mood and sparkled with jests and cheerfulness. Rosati, too, forgot the two lovers, and peace once more unfolded her wings above us.

"'What did I tell you, old Grandmother Goose?' jocosely remarked the manager to me; but I held my tongue. I am a Lombard and the Lombardians are naturally suspicious. Soon Pinuti and Dimali became thick as sheep at pasture and continually drinking and pledging each other in strong wine. Dimali was a roisterer who always drank too much while Pinuti, the man from Ravenna, was too cool-headed to be affected by his potations. The two women were once more on good terms, and I was simply a bewildered looker-on in—how do you say it?—Sì! in Vienna. I knew it couldn't last, but I was not, I swear to you, prepared for what followed. One night, after the lovers had literally torn themselves apart, Dimali went with Pinuti to the wine-house. I was soon off to bed, for we had been singing 'Rigoletto,' and I was tired. It must have been long after midnight when the sound of footsteps awoke me, followed by a noise as if some one were lurching from wall to wall. A moment later, I heard Dimali's voice, thick with wine, lustily trolling. A muttered exclamation from Pinuti and the song ceased. Doubtless a hand had been clapped over the tenor's mouth to prevent him from arousing the sleeping household. I arose and opening my door ever so little saw by the dim lamplight the two men careening along. Only Pinuti did not seem to be very drunk, for he easily supported his companion. He led him, much to my surprise, to his own room, and after a few minutes came out into the corridor and, passing me unsuspectingly, went directly to Rosati's door and knocked three times. I counted those knocks, they were like the knocks at the gate in your Shakespeare's 'Macbeth.' In a moment he was admitted, and I smiled at myself for my silly suspicions, sillier fears.

"I was turning to my bed when my attention was once more caught by the sound of a door softly closed. I instantly tiptoed to my old post and saw with a surprise that merged into horror the conductor and the soprano moving towards Pinuti's room wherein lay the drunken Dimali. As he passed under the lamp Pinuti paused, put his hand in his pocket and brought out a black oblong box.

"This sinister drama so upset my nerves that I fell on my bed incapable of motion, above all incapable of raising my voice in alarm. But my brain was excruciatingly alive. I suffered ten thousand hells as I laid there, and years seemed to pass, though I dare say it couldn't have been more than ten minutes before the guilty couple emerged from the blood-stained chamber of crime. Pinuti silently conducted to her room the wretched soprano, Rosati. As they passed me in the semi-darkness they looked like the Scotch family—yes, like the Macbeths." The old man trembled at the ghosts his memory had dug up.

"And did they murder the tenor?" I interrupted in agitated accents. Agnani hiccoughed, the strong beer was beginning to tell on his venerable brain. He responded in mumbling tones.

"No, they didn't kill poor Dimali. Worse. He went away in a few weeks. Pinuti was heart-broken when he at last realised that he had been used as a handy tool by the soprano—she, too, disappeared soon after. The manager failed, the company broke up, and I"—I became impatient with his drolling evasiveness.

"But what became of Dimali?" The now thoroughly intoxicated old ruffian regarded me with his cynical, disconcerting gaze. He asked with a leer:

"Have you ever heard Popelli's opera, 'Abelardo e Eloisa?'"

"Never."

"You have missed much. It is a beautiful score. Dimali made the hit of his career in it." I was puzzled.

"As Abelardo?"

"No, in the rôle of Eloisa."

I commanded two more bocks. When he left the café he was giving an excellent imitation of the Leaning Tower of Pisa, only more dignified.

XXII

"M'LLE NEW YORK"

Vance Thompson is a Caveman. Don't be deceived
by his books on Woman, Drink, Eat and Grow Thin, or
by his activities in Europe with the Y. M. C. A.
—where Cavemen were needful. He is a Caveman, despite his poetry and prose. I first met him at the old
Eden Musé on Twenty-third Street, in 1893, where he
put on a pantomime of his own with his wife, Mlle.
Severine, and Pilar Morin in the cast. He was writing
for *The Commercial Advertiser;* later he joined the staff
of *The Musical Courier.* Then he went to France as correspondent. He published his French Portraits while on
The Musical Courier. But it is of his *Mlle. New York*
that I would speak. Modelled after some of the Paris
weeklies, audacious, fearing neither God nor man, nor
the printer, yet this fortnightly was unlike any publication I have ever seen. To-day collectors know it;
a complete set is hard to come by and the price is
high. The first series comprises eleven numbers, the
second four. Vance Thompson, Thomas Fleming, illustrator, Thomas Powers, illustrator, and myself comprised
the staff. There was no office except under our
hats, and the publisher mailed the copies. Frankly, I
wonder how we escaped Anthony Comstock. Perhaps
our "precious" prose saved us. But the illustrations!
Simply gorgeous. The "mighty line" of Fleming, the
tricky humour and skill of Powers—still a force among
New York caricaturists—the wicked attacks of Editor

Thompson on society and government and women, all these made *Mlle. New York* unique. The make-up, too, of the sheet was unusual. Printed in colours, with wide margins, there were tiny pictures across the letter-press, and impertinent marginal comment. In a word, *Mlle. New York* was more Parisian than Paris. It cost us a lot. We had to dive down "into our jeans" to pay the printer and paper-man. But we had lots of fun.

It was a safety-valve for our rank egotism and radicalism. Every institution was attacked save the church. Philip Hale wrote a masterpiece in miniature about Jack the Ripper, entitled "The Baffled Enthusiast." We had a Philip Hale cult then. No wonder. An artist in prose, he literally educated Boston in the gentle art of paganism. Why, even in such a deadly task as inventing analytical notes to the Boston Symphony Orchestra programmes he brings a touch that lightens the inherent dryness of the subject. Papa Krehbiel, as each number of *Mlle. New York* appeared would run his fingers through his blond curls and desperately exclaim: "What are you boys up to?" We didn't know ourselves. Possibly to startle people. We didn't succeed either in startling or in making the enterprise a paying one. *Mlle. New York* faded from the news-stands. Marc Blumenberg generously came to the rescue. At a loss he published the last section of four issues. We gave up, and after the shouting was over, rather the wailing of the mourners, the casualty list was depressing. Eventually all indebtedness was cancelled. We had the experience and fifteen copies of a costly literary and artistic experiment. And *Mlle. New York* was both literary and artistic. When the young chaps nowadays talk about Free Verse, I mind me of the verse we printed twenty-three years ago. (We began in 1895.) When a clever literary hoax is discussed I recall the poetry, personality, above all, the ferocious portrait of Lingwood Evans, an Australian rough-neck, writing decadent verse that alternated between the muffled morbidities of Verlaine and the roaring free-verse of Verhaeren. It was one of the most successful of hoaxes. From editors and librarians came pouring in queries as to the new man. His poetry was copied, praised, and decried. Anarchist, libertine, mystic he was. "The Father of Livor" and "The Avenue of Farthingales," the terrific and sinister parody on "My Country, 'Tis of Thee" made people sit up. If an I. W. W. boasted such a poet to-day, he would get short shrift from the government. Yet it was pure fun-making of a fine quality. Vance Thompson was Lingwood Evans, Tom Fleming made the woodcuts, so vital and original in design.

Vance introduced European writers and painters who since have become celebrated. Knut Hamsun, the Pole, Stanislaw Przybyszewski—not a fiction, this name, but the author of Homo Sapiens, which has been translated—Maeterlinck, Ibsen, Verlaine, Verhaeren, and the entire lyre of the younger French, Italian, Spanish, and Belgian poets. Edvard Munch, a powerful Norwegian artist, and Strindberg, the Swede, probably had their names printed for the first time in America in the pages of *Mlle. New York*. Rupert Hughes wrote his most brilliant short-story for us, When Pan Moves to Harlem, in which he relates a nocturnal adventure of Slab-sided Sal told in purest Americanese. (O. Henry is insipid compared with this tale, a forerunner to many.) I looked after the new names in music. Thompson wrote some musical verse and in all sorts of free-rhythms,

He had been class-poet at Princeton, but that stony fact
did not prevent him from developing. His slender
volume, Verse, I have by me and read. My favourite
is his Ego Book, replete with charm and wisdom.
Drink and Keep Sober—the original title—is amusing,
and like his brochure on Woman is stuffed with fallacies.
Except in Dickens and in Zola (Doctor Pascal, the taking-
off of Uncle Antoine Macquart by spontaneous com-
bustion), there is nothing to equal the explosion of a
young Philadelphian on the terrace at Monte Carlo.
It is simply joyous. Rum did it. And at table surrounded by his family, who were spattered with the remains of the unhappy drunkard. I wonder how this
"awful warning" escaped the eagle eye of Billy Sunday.
As for the woman question, I can only quote a few sentences from *Mlle. New York* (an editorial, first fortnight
in November, 1898). Mind you, a man has a right to
change his mind, but he should not leave behind him an
armoury of arguments to refute himself. He did this.
I was then the "Gynolatrist." How he mocked my old-
fashioned attitude towards Woman! Among other things
this is what he wrote:

"Here in the United States the worship of Woman is
carried to ludicrous lengths. . . . And perhaps in these
days when the hens hold conventions and their fritinacy
disturbs the ears of thoughtful men, it may not be superfluous to iterate the old truth that woman is physically,
mentally and morally inferior to man. She bears a certain resemblance to the masculine type. She is, indeed,
an undeveloped man. Her place in the scale of human
life is midway between the adolescent and the viril.
As a matter of fact, her entire physical constitution—
fine skin, frail, bony structure, beardless face, feeble

voice—is nearer to that of the boy than the man. This is no place for the consideration of the physiological proof of the statement. The proportion of red and white corpuscles, the caudal vertebræ, resembling those of the embryo or the ape; her very method of breathing, which is thoracic and not from the diaphragm; the shape of the head, like that of a child or a Kaffir, the grey substance of the brain, lighter than in man—on all these points and a dozen others the craniologists, biologists and anthropologists have spoken with authority. Woman's physical inferiority to man is a fact beyond question. . . . She is indeed an interesting study, this adolescent animal with the great white (not grey) brain, the phlegmatic senses, and the dulled finger-tips. But what a damnable noise she makes at this century's end! . . . In letters, painting, science, music, sculpture—nothing. When with simian—the feminine is nearer the simian than the masculine—ease they imitate the gestures of an artist one must always look in the background for a man. Behind George Sand loom the pitiful figures of Jules Sandeau, De Musset, Chopin; behind George Eliot one sees the bearded face of Lewes; and so when a female novelist deteriorates or improves, takes up a new subject or dons a new manner, one need but lightly say: 'Eh bien! She has taken a new lover.' . . . Sorotic women argue that man and woman started equal; that it is only man's tyranny which has degraded woman in the scale of life. So be it. Perhaps this is as good a way as any other of satisfying the feminine mind. It begs the question by acknowledging the very inferiority at issue. And when will woman overtake man in his ascent? A and B start from a given point. A travels at a speed of ten miles a day; B travels at a rate of six miles a day; when will B overtake A? . . . The hen has a right to cackle only on one occasion—when she lays an egg; she never has a right to crow, and by reason of imperfect thoracic development she never can crow. . . . Dear God! the crowned and laurelled eunuchs of American literature—professors with dandruff on the coat-collar, and bearded ladies, and the chaste, pantelleted spinsters, and the little, hairy poets, all hungry and timid and all bought and sold——"

A man may alter his views twenty times, as a snake sloughs its skin, but when he writes such words, words like the virile ring of crossed blades, then he is primarily a Caveman. Who knows whether as a sexagenarian he may not doff the garb of civilisation and emerge hairy, rugged, in a bearskin, and over his virile shoulders a mighty club! Beware Woman! Even in his Woman, the old masculine condescension peeps forth. He alludes to her as "little woman." In Vishnuland what Vance?

I wrote many, so-called prose-poems, seduced by the examples of Baudelaire, Mallarmé, and Huysmans. They are to be found scattered through *Mlle. New York* and *Melomaniacs.* Here is one, never before reprinted, from *Mlle. New York:*

"She lay in the Hall of the Mirrors where, repeated in evanescent gestures, her person moved with processional precision. She had disrobed to the accompaniment of soft, hidden music, and to the unconscious miming of the mirrors; something of fear and something of shame were in her heart as she pulled to her pretty chin the royal counterpane. It was the first time she had ever lain in a palace, and the night seemed to hum with a thousand harps. It was the music and the beating of her heart that she heard, and she wondered most at the heavily scented atmosphere, and smiled at the face that smiled down at her from the shining ceiling. Her plump body sank in relaxing curves; the very couch seemed to embrace her. Then she heard footsteps and dared no longer gaze into the ironic mirror overhead. As the prince approached love loomed nigh. There was no tenderness in his eyes, and his young forehead was slightly wrinkled. It was his nuptial night; for him was waiting a fair girl, whose pulses leapt to the sound of his voice. But he had no words for her when he reached the royal bed that stood in the Hall of the Mirrors. His troubled gaze drove the blood to her heart, when he sat beside her and the music ceased and the mirrors grew grey and misty. She had waited for this moment since her birth; their souls had been woven together by imperial decree, yet now they circled about each other like two tall stars in interstellar depths, bound for eternity to tread in the stately dance of the spheres, æons apart, and destined never to embrace. With outstretched, despairing arms she welcomed her image in the air above her, and her impassioned, sorrowful glance married her to her own soul. The prince told her in falsetto tones of his desire for rest, and she welcomed him as one would a pet poodle; beside his sleepy escaping soul she lay in the Hall of the Mirrors, where, repeated in evanescent gestures, her person moved in processional sadness."

What does it mean? Do you remember the story I told you of that farewell stag dinner given at the Maison Félix to a certain tenor by his friends—principally

brothers-in-law—before he married an operetta soprano?
My cryptic prose is the sequel of that marriage, which
was speedily dissolved, because it was not consummated.
But no one would know this from my tortured style. I
was very "precious" then, and suffered, though briefly,
from the green-sickness of too ambitious writers.

I tried my hand at all sorts of imitations. I was
practising my scales in public. I imitated Maupassant
in a tale, Fog, my first and last essay in that genre of
demi-monde; imitated Zangwill in The Shofar Blew at
Sunset, which brought from him a very pleasant letter;
imitated myself in Music, the Conqueror, and in Frus-
trate, both of which appeared in Melomaniacs. How we
rioted in extravagant comparisons! I was mad over
Maggie Cline and in pompous prose I saluted her as A
Brunhilda of the Bowery, I wrote of her, and Apollo,
forgive me! "As Whitman was a great natural source,
an impulsive in our native literature, so Maggie Cline,
the exponent of muscularity in song, is in the musical
world. . . . At the magic of her voice the sights and
sounds of the present fade and you are straightway
transported to Eldridge or Hester Street and witness
with beating heart and brain on fire the downfall of that
good man and true, the doughty Donovan, or the epical
fracas at McCloskey's ("Throw him down, McCloskey!")
I treated her as if she were a Lilli Lehmann or a Sarah
Bernhardt. It was saluted as a "new note" in criticism.
Yvette Guilbert didn't escape. I plastered her with epi-
thets until her own mother wouldn't have recognised her.
"She is a singing Zola, this Yvette Guilbert. She sings
of the rogues, beggars, outcasts, drunkards, the shards
and estrays of life, the human offal, the gutter's refuse.
She is a singing Zola, this Yvette Guilbert; a porno-

graphic Zola, a realist Zola, a Zola of bestiality supreme, a Zola of the love that lies in wait and supplicates with a grimace." It must be remembered that Yvette then was not the sweet singer of old French lyrics. She was the "modern" Yvette, a wonderful "diseuse," and thrice as fascinating as in her latest incarnation.

XXIII

MY DREAM-BARN

About this time I began to suspect myself. My spiritual axis had shifted. There was somewhere a leakage of moral gas on my premises—as Henry James remarked of D'Annunzio. I had become dissatisfied with my life. Why all this interest in the work of other men! Couldn't I play off my own bat? Vance Thompson encouraged me to write a book. So did Philip Hale. (I must blame my subsequent crimes on some one.) Why waste hours every day hearing music, seeing pictures, and worse, writing of them? What's Hecuba to me? I was becoming neurotic. I could sympathise with Berlioz when he sneered at the Sonata. Why just a sonata or a symphony? Why music-drama or Shakespeare? Why not rum and rebellion, or gals and gallivanting? I knew by that time I couldn't have all these things. What shall it profit a man if he gains his soul but loseth love? I was seizing the shadow for the substance, like the dog in the fable. I couldn't marry more than one woman at a time because of certain social prejudices. And sometimes a man's wife won't let him marry the girl he likes (women are so unreasonable). What was I to do? Which way to turn? Sensibly, for the first time in my life, I concluded that my only hope was a philistine life. Poor old bourgeois, always getting pounded by poetical Bolsheviki; in reality the bourgeois possessing horse-sense. Flaubert warned his pupil, Guy de Maupassant, that to achieve masterpieces he must

be peaceful in his life that he might be violent in his art.
Zola swears that Flaubert led the life of a bourgeois,
writing instead of selling groceries; Flaubert, who his
life long pursued the bourgeois with gibes! Vance
Thompson used to say that an artist, whether poet or
painter, musician or sculptor, should marry the feather-
bed type of woman. She protects and consoles; also
cooks a good dinner. When artist mates with artist
then comes the tug of tongues. No family can harbour
two prima donnas—that is, not without fur flying. The
artistic temperament is "catty," whether male or female.
Hence these tears. Therefore, I steered a middle course.
It was in 1895 I began to study hard. Again I drew
up a formidable manifesto for my private use. I assailed
my laziness (of course, I've never been lazy. I've never
had the time. It is my spiritual sloth I mean.) Goaded
by my self-admitted mediocrity, I determined to be a
contemporary, if nothing more. There was leaking gas,
and my moral meter had failed to register it. If I had
gone down on my shin bones, and echoed Durtal's despairing prayer in A Rebours, by Huysmans, it would
have been better for the health of my soul. Do you
recall it? "Take pity, O Lord, on the Christian who
doubts, on the sceptic who desires to believe, on the
convict of life who embarks alone, in the night, beneath
a sky no longer lit by the consoling beacons of ancient
faith." It has a liturgical ring, this invocation.

But, as I wrote of Baudelaire, I had patiently built
up my soul as a perverse bird builds its nest:—bits of
straw, the sobbing of women, clay, cascades of black
stars, rags, leaves, rotten wood, corroding dreams, a
spray of roses, a pebble's sparkle, a gleam of blue sky,
arabesques of incense and verdigris, and for a ground-

tone, the abomination of desolation. My soul was a cemetery of the seven sorrows. I had rented an Ivory Tower, but I had lost the latch-key. When She beckoned to me from the topmost cell, my Princess of Mirrors and melancholy, I could only shrug despairing shoulders. I was a steeplejack—but there were no step-ladders wherewith to climb to her. A man can't be both a steeplejack and a carpenter. I could only whistle down to the wind and the Ideal never comes in answer to whistling. I even mixed moral values by quoting what Coleridge attributed to Sir Joshua Reynolds: "The greatest man is he who forms the taste of a nation; the next greatest is he who corrupts it." As I hadn't the power to form the taste of my neighbour, much less that of a nation, I proceeded to corrupt my own. I muddled the Seven Arts in a grand old stew. I saw music, heard colour, tasted architecture, smelt sculpture, and fingered perfume. A mad carnival of the senses. I sympathised with Des Esseintes in Là-Bas, though I didn't care for his "mouth-organ" of various liqueurs. But I believed that an art could be interpreted in the terms of another. I read a book by Suarez de Mendoza, L'Audition Colorée, to relieve my anxiety. It is a searching study in false secondary sensations, and deals with "colour-hearing," or "pseudo-photoesthesie." This results from association of ideas early established. We have, most of us, been reminded of some far-away happening, usually sentimental by the odour of faded flowers. The sense of smell plays a commanding rôle in all sex manifestations. The Fathers of the Church knew this: hence their stern admonitions to women using heady sensual perfumes. Certain musical tones evoke certain colours. And if you investigate you will discover that the æsthetic terminology of painting resembles that of music. I believed in employing the whole keyboard of analogies, so my criticism often proved trying to my readers, but not to me. I needs must educate them. The arts are separate, yet, as Walter Pater says, all aspire to a condition of music, as our sun and planets travel towards a central sun in some remote constellation. But I abused the scheme, and I am not sorry. "You write of music as if it were a living thing," said Arthur Symons to me in a memorable letter. Music is a living thing for me, as living as any vital organism. It lives when it enters the porches of my ears, and it is a living memory. To write about it is quite hopeless. You can describe a picture, a statue, a cathedral, and quote a poem; but you may not describe a symphony. The best way out of the dilemma is to follow in the footsteps of the music-reporter. Tell me a news story. If you attempt a subjective explanation, you run the risk of not being intelligible. The technical method has its perils; it is understood only by musicians. None the less did I persevere in my endeavour to achieve a synthesis of the arts. The result may be foreseen. Yet, I have heard music that gave me the illusion of light, of air, music that was as diaphanous as the spider's web in the gold of the setting sun; music as keen as a Damascene blade that halves a lace veil, as melancholy as the thoughts of a woman in travail—but it demands high courage to make one's self ridiculous, and to write in such a style would be grazing the fatuous. Chopin and Shelley are alike to me, as are Wagner and Browning, Raphael and Mozart, Beethoven and Shakespeare.

I lived at the corner of Madison Avenue and Seventy-sixth Street for fifteen years in the Carrollton, one of the first tall apartment houses in that section of the city.

Big old-fashioned rooms, high windows, stone balconies
on the tenth floor, gave me plenty of light, air, and a
view that was inspiring. There were few obstructions
in 1899 between my Dream-Barn and Staten Island. I
could sweep all the East River and the Hudson, too. I
could see the harbour maculated with craft, see the bay,
the Statue of Liberty, steamships going and coming.
From my wide windows facing Central Park, I caught the
copper gleam of the erect synagogue at Seventy-sixth
Street and the Avenue; beyond was the placid toy lake
with its rim of moving children; the trees smoothly swept
in a huge semi-circle, at their verge was the driveway.
The glow of summer afternoons, the purity of the air,
and the glancing metal on the rolling cars and carriages
made a gay picture for me. My studio was rather bare.
I hate cluttered-up rooms. The severe line of the low
bookcases was relieved by the curves of my beloved
Steinway grand. A few pictures, Ernest Lawson landscapes, a head by George Luks, a study by Thomas Sully
completed the ensemble. Add a desk, once the property
of Thaddeus Stevens, and the inevitable cast-iron lamp
depending from an oak beam, and you may realise that
it was not a difficult task to write a dozen books amid
such surroundings. Only—those skylights! The roof
was almost composed of glass. There was an excellent
northern light for artists old-fashioned enough to believe
in any particular lighting; and during a rain-storm the
patter and swish kept me awake. I've heard sentimental
persons say: "Oh! to be here as the rain gently drips.
What an inspiration!" But it seldom dripped, it usually
cannonaded, and during a thunder-storm the lightning
flashes were too intimate for nervous people. I recall
one night when Rafael Joseffy was there. He looked

JAMES GIBBONS HUNEKER
(1900)

ANTON SEIDL

under the pianoforte, saying it was the one spot where he could escape the blaze of the electric tempest. Francis Hackett, the critic, came in, and Edward Marsh, of Macmillan's, and Frederick James Gregg, of *The Evening Sun*, but we could not persuade Joseffy to stay. He said that we might as well be on the deck of a ship, which was true, and when the building rocked in a hurricane, the illusion of being afloat was strengthened. I loved my old Dream-Barn, and, as one chap remarked, a newspaper man lives on views, and I had from my windows not one, but a dozen.

Life and letters, pictures and music! They were woven into a close strand. I read, I wrote, I played. An excellent epitaph. I was forced to create my own atmosphere, else grow stale and perish in the vacuum. The artistic roots of our life are not deeply bedded in the national soul. I was, and still am, a lover of the new Irish literature. I wrote much of Yeats, George Russell, and Synge, later of James Stephens and James Joyce. I believe that George Moore on his native soil is better than he is in England, or even France, which is saying a lot. Ireland not only has produced her greatest novelist in Moore, but her most alluring lyric poet in Yeats. I met Yeats at the home of John Quinn. Synge, with his Maeterlinckian atmosphere, which modulates into the melancholy mists of the Ould Sod, created a new thrill. James Stephens and his rich fantasy, squeezing golden wine from leanest grapes, a genuine Irish genius in whose heart bubbles fantasy and tears; and Joyce, a gloriously bitter Banshee, wailing Ireland and the Irish in a voice all his own—these and many of the minor lyrists quite overflowed our horizons. Contemporary English literature has nothing to equal these men in originality, raci-

ness, spiritual depth, or magic. Edgar Saltus always
has been one of my pet authors. He is elect among lovers
of style. Setting aside his fiction, what writer, with the
exception of William James, can make such charming
and conclusive expositions of philosophy as Mr. Saltus?
And without pretensions as a professional metaphysician.
We must go to France for his counterpart. I possess,
thanks to him, one of the rare impressions of his Oscar
Wilde: An Idler's Impression, which fairly sums up the
personality and gifts of that unhappy Irishman. Mr.
Saltus writes as a coda: "Apart from that, it"—he is
speaking of morality—"has nothing whatever to do
with the arts, except the art of never displeasing, which
in itself is the whole secret of mediocrity. Oscar Wilde
lacked that art, and I can think of no better epitaph for
him." This is Wilde in an epigram. But Saltus is our
most brilliant writer, and epigrams may be expected from
him.

I have no grievances. I am what I made myself,
therefore, I blame myself for my shortcomings. As I
loathe the brand of any particular school or movement in
art, so I detest the fellow who lays the blame of his
troubles on some one else—usually his wife. Friends
have praised me, but I don't deserve that praise. I
never aimed at anything and if I anticipated others in
"discovering"—presumptuous word—certain of the new
men in Europe and America, it was because of my critical
curiosity; also because a newspaper man has a scent for
news. I mention "America" as some critics believe me
to be on my knees before European culture. The late
Percival Pollard, a capital critic, devoted a chapter to
me in his book, Their Day in Court. He said that I
neglected Americans, when, as I told him, I gained my

living by writing about the painting, composing, literature, and modelling of my fellow-countrymen, in *The Etude*,
*Musical Courier, Recorder, Commercial Advertiser, Sun,
Times*, and the Philadelphia *Press.* For nearly four
decades I have done little else but praise or blame our
native talents. Many a swan has turned goose, but I've
had white swans also. American painters and sculptors
in particular have I studied, from Arthur B. Davies and
George Grey Barnard to the fledgling illustrator or clay
modeller of yesterday. I leave the American composers
to tell my tale. Nor do I fear that I shall be accused
of tepidity concerning the merits of our literature. Humbug I hate. And one venerable humbug was punctured
when our new school of landscape—in this form America
is eminent—proved triumphant. I quite agree with
Willard Metcalf when he declared that the further back
we go in the history of American art, the worse we find
the painting. This is not only true of the Hudson and
kindred schools, but it holds good in the case of our por-
trait-painters of the past century. Such leathery effi-
gies! I never could understand the superstitious veneration entertained for second-rate painters like Gilbert
Stuart, Copley, Peale, and the rest of the imitators of
Joshua Reynolds and Thomas Lawrence. One brush-
stroke of Raeburn is worth the lot of them. A Sargent
or Chase portrait can't be mentioned in the same
breath with them. They manufactured historical portraits, like the wooden heads of Washington by Stuart,
and it is as historical painters only that they possess artistic justification. Mediocrities all. And mediocrities
were the mid-century Landscapists. Imitators of Con-
stable and Gainsborough and Claude. George Inness
is an example of over-rated merit. He was an amiable

mediocrity who saw our native scene through English spectacles. Yet he fetches big prices. The mystic vision of Albert Ryder, the grim power of Winslow Homer, or the sumptuous paint quality of Lawson are absent from his work. Our new landscape-painters have used their own eyes, and paint from a personal palette. Their predecessors are bogies for the art dump in auction-rooms.

It must be nearly twenty years ago, anyhow eighteen, that I entertained Vladimir de Pachmann in my Dream-Barn on Madison Avenue at Seventy-sixth Street. The tenth floor, a room as big and as lofty as a cathedral. Alas! where are such old-fashioned apartments to-day? After eating a duck, a kotchka, cooked Polish fashion, and borsch, beet soup, with numerous Slavic side dishes, preceded by the inevitable zakuska—those appetite-slaying bonnes bouches—de Pachmann fiercely demanded cognac. I was embarrassed. Not drinking spirits, I had inconsiderately forgotten the taste of others. De Pachmann, who is a child at heart, too often a naughty child, cried to heaven that I was a hell of a host! He said this in Russian, then in French, Italian, German, Polish, Spanish, English, and wound up with a hearty Hebrew "Raca!" which may mean hatred, or revenge, certainly something not endearing. But the worst was to come. There stood my big Steinway concert grand piano, and he circled about the instrument as if it were a dangerous monster. Finally he sniffed and snapped: "My contract does not permit me to play a Steinway." I hadn't thought of asking him, fearing Chopin's classic retort after a dinner-party at Paris: "Madame, j'ai mangé si peu!" Finally I saw the hole in the mill-stone, and excused myself. When I returned with a bottle of abominable cognac, the little man's malicious smile changed to a look of ecstasy, and he was not a drinking man ever, but he was accustomed to his "petit verre" after dining, and was ill-tempered when deprived of it. Such is human nature, something that puritans, prohibitionists, and other pernicious busybodies will never understand. And then this wizard lifted the fall-board of my piano, and, quite forgetful of that "contract," began playing. And how he did play! Ye gods! Bacchus, Apollo, and Venus, and all other pleasant celestial persons, how you must have revelled when de Pachmann played! In the more intimate atmosphere of my apartment his music was of a gossamer web, iridescent, aerial, an æolian harp doubled by a diabolic subtlety. Albert Ross Parsons, one of the few living pupils of Tausig, in reply to my query: How did Joseffy compare with Tausig? answered: "Joseffy was like the multi-coloured mist that encircles a mighty mountain; but beautiful." So Pachmann's weaving enchantments seemed in comparison to Godowsky's profounder playing.

And what did Vladimir, hero of double-notes, play? Nothing but Godowsky, then new to me. Liszt had been his god, but Godowsky was become his living deity. He had studied, mastered, and memorised all those transcendental variations on Chopin studies, the most significant variations since the Brahms-Paganini scaling of the heights of Parnassus; and I heard for the first time the paraphrase of Weber's "Invitation to the Valse," a much more viable arrangement than Tausig's; also thrice as difficult. However, technique, as sheer technique, does not enter into the musical zone of Godowsky. He has restored polyphony to its central position, thus bettering in that respect Chopin, Schumann, and Liszt. I have called attention elsewhere to Godowsky's solo sonata, which evokes images of Chopin and Brahms and Liszt —Liszt only in the scherzo. Instead of exhuming such an "ungrateful," unpianistic composition as Tschaikovsky's Sonata in G, pianists of calibre might more profitably introduce the Godowsky work. He is too modest or else too indifferent to put it on his programme. It "lies" so well for the keyboard, yet there is no denying its difficulties, chiefly polyphonic; the patterns are intricate, though free from the clogging effects of the Brahms sonatas. De Pachmann delighted his two auditors that night from 10 P. M. to 3 A. M. It is safe to wager that the old Carrollton never heard such music-making before or since. When he left, happy over his triumph—I was actually flabbergasted by the new music—he whispered: "Hein! What you think! You think I can play this wonderful music? You are mistaken. Wait till you hear Leopold Godowsky play. We are all woodchoppers, compared with him!" Curiously enough, the last is the identical phrase uttered by Anton Rubinstein in regard to Franz Liszt. Perhaps it was a quotation, but de Pachmann meant it. It was the sincerest sentiment I had heard from his often insincere lips. We were all three surprised to find a score of people camping out on the curved stairway and passages, the idealist, a coloured lad who ran the elevator, having succumbed to sleep. This impromptu Godowsky recital by a marvellous pianist, for de Pachmann was a marvel in his time, must have made a hit with my neighbours. It did with me, and when Godowsky returned to New York—I had last heard him in the middle nineties of the previous century—I lost no time in hearing him play in his inimitable manner those same works. A pianist who can win

the heartiest admiration of such contemporaries as de
Pachmann and Joseffy and Josef Hofmann—I could
adduce many other names—must be a unique artist.
And that Godowsky is.

Among the younger American poets I find one of
genuine importance, not alone because of his potentiali-
ties, but because of his actual performance. George
Cabot Lodge, son of Senator Henry Cabot Lodge, died
in the very harvest time of his undoubted genius. In his
Introduction to the two volumes of the Poems and
Dramas, Theodore Roosevelt has never written with such
a mingling of perspicacity and tempered enthusiasm.
Young Lodge was a poet and his versatility may be noted
in these books. In his sonnets and lyrics he paid the accustomed tribute of youth to influences such as Milton,
Wordsworth, Meredith, Browning, Tennyson, and Swinburne. He could mimic Walt Whitman, and he early
succumbed to Schopenhauer and Baudelaire. In at
least one of his dramas, I find the cosmic ecstasy of
Nietzsche, the doctrine of the Eternal Return. But
Lodge had assimilated a half-dozen cultures, and had
passed far out to sea the perilous rocks of imitation upon
which so many lesser talents have come to grief. When
we consider as an achievement his "Herakles," we are
amazed. The poet, the Maker is before us, and in re-
clothing the antique and tragic myth in his own lovely
garment of speech, he is, nevertheless, a modern of his
own times. I know few poets with this sense of the vital
present, added to a divination and an evocation of "old
unhappy far-off things, and battle long ago." His figures
are not fashioned with scholastic black magic, but are
living beings, loving, hating, suffering, and in conflict

with ineluctable destiny. He had the lyric art and also
the architectural. He was a singer and a builder of the
lofty rhyme. George Cabot Lodge had voice and vision.
His Life, by Henry Adams, proves him to have been a
young man beloved by his friends, among whom were
Langton Mitchell and the late Sir Cecil Spring-Rice.
I can only add here my humble mite of admiration and
affection to the names of the vanished genius.

"Men need not be common because there are many;
but the infection of commonness once begun in the
many, what dulness in their future! . . . more piece-
meal pictures, more colonial poetry, more young nations
with withered traditions. Yet it is before this prospect
that the provincial overseas lifts up its voice in a boast,
or promise common enough among the incapable young,
but pardonable only in senility. He promised the world
a literature, an art, that shall be new because his forest
is untracked and his town just built. But what the new-
ness is he cannot tell." Ponder these words. They
occur in an essay by Alice Meynell, entitled "Decivilised,"
and contained in a slender volume called The Rhythm of
Life. Most of us dislike, as did James Russell Lowell, a
"certain condescension in foreigners," yet the mellow
wisdom of this Englishwoman should not be missed. The
deadly hand of vulgarity is upon the Seven Arts. Never
have the lowlands so overflowed their ooze and muddied
waters above the level of our once aristocratic highlands
of taste. Music alone has thus far resisted the invasion
of low ideals, but in opera the edifice is already tottering.
Poetry, fiction, the theatres— Alas! But I am optimistic withal. No nation boasting such high heroisms,
no nation after such a baptism of blood and fire can long
dally in the swamp of the banal or the vulgar. And I

know that I am not alone in my hope of an approaching renascence of the arts in our beloved America.

New York, like London, is a city where you can disappear from the view of your own little world by simply crossing to the other side of the street. When I left the theatres for art, I also left Broadway and patrolled Fifth Avenue, which is picture-land. I was reported "missing" by my friends the actors, dramatic critics, and managers. When I ceased writing about music and musicians and devoted my time to literary criticism, I was supposed to be in Europe. Curious vast city, where you are dead if you stay away from your usual haunts a day! (I fancy the wish is father to the thought.) Yet I never was idle, not even in Europe. I was breasting in another current; that's all. There were rumours that I had retired to a monastery. I read this in a musical journal. "What a recluse our erstwhile ubiquitous friend, James Huneker, has become." I was not a recluse, I merely stayed away from Carnegie Hall and the Opera House, where musical folk mostly do congregate, hence the hasty inference. It is true, the story that one family can live next door to another for years and not know names. That is a little trait of Gotham. We are not neighbourly, and while I remember Yorkville and Harlem when people sat on their "stoops" of summer nights, that time has gone. New Cosmopolis is no place for provincial customs.

I mention this "recluse" story because I have been often teased by my friends on the subject. When I turned up at the opera, I would be greeted with "Hello, Farmer!" I begin my morning with Bach, end with Bach. Bach the Alpha and Omega of music. But enjoyable as it is to read the charming fiction of an unknown listener, an inscription in one of his books by

Arthur Symons is still more gratifying. It runs: "To
James Huneker in memory of the night when he played
Chopin at Lauderdale Mansions. May 31, 1905." I
had played there in May, 1903, when I first met the distinguished Englishman, one of the few critics since Walter
Pater who writes criticism as if it were a fine art and not
a "dismal science."

I love the high places of our world. I am never giddy
when standing on balconies, or looking over precipices,
or swooping aloft, in an airplane. Possibly fifteen years
on a tenth floor accustomed my eyes to vast perspectives.
But, contrariwise, when I am in a small room, or under-
ground, or in a cave, even though it be the Mammoth
Cave in Kentucky, I feel that death is not afar. Once
in the catacombs at Rome I nearly suffocated, more from
the idea than the reality, of being buried alive. I believe
the name of this aversion to enclosed space is Claustra-
phobia, and I am convinced that in my case it is a pro-
drome of apoplexy. Important, if true. Yet the trait
may have influenced my mental attitude towards the
arts. I shan't say that I have no prejudices, for then I
should be a colourless monster. It is his prejudices that
makes vital a critic's work. George Moore has rather
horridly suggested that a critic is always remembered
by his mistakes—which are his prejudices expressed.
Catholicity in taste and judgment has been my aim,
sometimes my undoing. The half is better than the
whole, but for me the too much is too little. Again a
case of personal temperament.

XXIV

MY ZOO

In my artistic and literary Zoo there are many queer creatures, but it is a mistake to suppose them all freaks. Brahms and Stendhal are not freaks, though, with the innate perversity that lurks in the heart of critics, I was asked why I didn't write of Beethoven when I had made an elaborate study of Brahms, or about Balzac, when I revived the name of Henry Beyle. My answer is simplicity itself: because at the time I preferred Brahms and Stendhal. Not that I placed them near the thrones of Beethoven and Balzac, but as worthy of the sincere attention of a critic; besides, Beethoven and Balzac, like Shakespeare, have been the themes of the master minds of criticism: Goethe, Sainte-Beuve, Taine, Georg Brandes. It was the same when I defended Ibsen, and "discovered" Strindberg. I suppose that my titles aroused the notion that the talented men and women of whom I wrote were semi-lunatics. Nietzsche died a melancholy invalid, but he was never mad; neurasthenic, I should say. Maeterlinck is the sanest of men. So was Liszt, so Chopin. However, I am not setting up an alibi for the sanity of my favourite artists and writers. It is not necessary. There is, take it by and large, more madness among mediocre persons. A little madness is a necessary ingredient in the composition of genius. Nor do I claim that my apes, peacocks, unicorns, egoists, visionaries, melomaniacs and steeplejacks are all geniuses. Again, mediocrity is to the fore, a mediocrity tempered by eccentricities. There is no bigger humbug than the fellow who sports the insignia of "genius," the long hair and doubtful linen, the alcoholism and the boresome boasting. As Charlie McLellan said of one man—who thought he looked like Shakespeare because he had a high, bald forehead, and hair worn as in the Chandos portrait—"I dare him to keep his hat on!" The shining dome exposed the man, and made an impression on the unthinking; his hat on and he became Mr. Everyman. Shave some of the Shavians and naught remains. But I never bothered with the externals of such "geniuses."

My most successful book was Iconoclasts (1905). It is my "best seller," though Chopin is a close second. My favourite book is Egoists, consequently, it has been the most assailed. I have never attempted the didactic, not even in my various educational editions of Chopin, Brahms, Tschaikovsky, or Richard Strauss. I collaborated with Rafael Joseffy in the new Schirmer edition of Chopin, but confined my analysis to non-technicalities, though in my Chopin, two-thirds of the volume is purely technical. In the case of Egoists, I let the grouping signify its individualistic tendency. William James in one of his letters complains that the book lacked "consequenz," to which I cheerfully agreed. I prefer to suggest rather than explain; it is an oblique method, but so am I constituted. That is why I am, in a minor degree, a symbolist. The majority of critical writings, here and in England, are as insipid as a bald hoarding. In France criticism is an art, and I have long worshipped at the shrines of Sainte-Beuve, Taine, and Anatole France. But my favourite books, because they were despised and rejected, are my Melomaniacs and Visionaries. Mr. H. L. Mencken, brilliant and individual critic, to whom I owe

more than a lakh of metaphorical rupees for his interest
in my work, wrote that I hadn't much talent for fiction. And it was the one thing of which I had hoped he
would say the reverse; not that I think I have, but when
you possess a weakness it is always nice to be coddled.
But Mr. Mencken is no coddler. Furthermore, he best
likes a little volume of parodies, entitled Old Fogy, which
first appeared in *The Etude*. None the less, I shall not
lose courage. One of my stories, The Lord's Prayer in B,
is in three foreign languages. It was written while musical tones drove me frantic. Hence the leading-motive;
torture by tonal reiteration. Octave Mirbeau used the
same theme in his Le Jardin des Supplices; a bell is tolled
over the head of a criminal in China, who dies from the
noise. My Lord's Prayer in B first appeared in *The
Musical Courier*, March, 1896; later it headed the tales
comprised in Melomaniacs. Therein I tried to bottle
my chimeras. After the book came out, I met Jeannette
Gilder, and she reproached me: "You of all men, from
you I expected the real fiction about music." I replied:
"It is not only about music, but it is music itself," and
then wondered what I meant. I had avoided the sentimental raptures of the Charles Auchester and The First
Violin type of musical novels, endeavouring to make music
the hero. That is why Arthur Symons said that I wrote
as if music was a living thing. I know of no other book
of musical fiction, that is, music dealt with imaginatively,
like Melomaniacs. It derives a little from E. T. W.
Hoffmann and his grotesques, and it leans a lot on Poe,
who with Chopin was my earliest passion. But the
treatment is my own. The trouble is that these stories
demand both a trained musical reader and a lover of
fiction—not a combination to be found growing on

grapevines. Visionaries is less novel. In it The Third Kingdom is the best invention, and that may have unconsciously stemmed from that golden casuist, Anatole France. But enough of this gossip about my stepchildren, my paper hostages to fortune. I have referred to my writings for one reason: I believe such references will help my publishers up the steep and stony path of their profession. One's publishers should be encouraged. By giving your precious ideas between covers to a world eager for them they also, after infinite pains, may earn an humble competency. You have done a good deed.

XXV

MY BEST FRIEND

Enemies are sometimes friends in disguise. Listen! When I heard the news I was writing a letter to John Quinn, my legal counsel, in which I exposed with merciless logic and rhetorical emphasis the deceit and villainy of Fulbert. The thing was as plain as daylight. Not a link in my chain of wrathful accusations seemed weak or misplaced. The man was a liar; perhaps worse; in any case, a cold-hearted wretch. Had he not said in public print and under a flaring, a vulgar head-line that an aunt had been the muse of Ibsen, hence my admiration for the Norwegian and his work. It was pure falsehood. My aunt probably read Tupper and Felicia Hemans, and while she had been in Norway—she was the wife of a sea-captain, a Norwegian, Thrane by name—she may have seen the poet, but that she played the flattering rôle of his muse is doubtful. His own wife's sister, Camilla Collett, was one for a brief period. It was the way Fulbert put the thing that had infuriated me. And as I paused in my writing, Tarver rushed in with the evening paper. Fulbert was dead. Yes, Fulbert, my chief foe, the foe that had watched and blocked every move in my career, had dropped dead after leaving his office, where, no doubt, he had written another of his vile attacks upon my new book. But Fulbert dead! I turned towards the window so as to keep from my friend the emotion that wrinkled my lips. Fulbert

217

dead. At last. Had I even longed for this consumma-
tion? How often had I not prayed to the gods, prayed
in the night that the malicious devil who boldly signed
himself Fulbert, would, when besotted by drink, drug
himself into imbecility. And now he was dead, the
venomous dog.

"Fulbert dead?" I said in almost a jocular tone.
"What in the world will I do for an enemy? You
know, Tarver, he was mine ancient enemy, and I hold as
a theory that a man's enemies do him less ill than his
friends, and—" "For heaven's sake, stop your cold-
blooded chatter and let the poor devil rest." When we
reached the street Tarver proposed a drink, but I refused.
I did not feel in the humour. He lifted cynical eyebrows.
"Oh, very well, if you expect the same fate as your friend
Fulbert. I'll leave you to your meditations. I suppose
you will send a wreath to the funeral." And this from
the man who a moment before had called me cold-
blooded. I was glad to be alone. What beastly wit.
No, I wouldn't send flowers, nor would I write to the
widow. I had known her long before her marriage to
Fulbert. Poor Fulbert. Well, why not? The fellow
was dead, and as Helen had married him, it was her
affair—pshaw! He had never wanted her—really. Only
—Fulbert. Why that particular man? Why Fulbert?
I walked rapidly, unconsciously frowning. Several ac-
quaintances passed, but I pretended not to see them.
They smiled. Decidedly they took me for a queer bird.
All writers are queer. One man familiarly hooked my
arm with his stick: "Hello there, old chappie. I see your
friend has passed in his chips. Going to wear crêpe?"
"Oh! for God's sake!" my humour was black; "don't
mock at death." "Phew!" was all I heard as I turned

into a side street, ruminating on that already old yet ever new text: Fulbert dead.

At the end of a fortnight I began to suffer from a certain inquietude. Some poison was fermenting in my veins. My nerves played me tricks. I could not work. Instead, I stared at the city, streaked like a map, beneath my tenth-floor apartment. I could see the two cities meet at the Battery, and I watched the white, fleecy cloud-boulders, vanguard of a thunder-storm, move in processional splendour across the lower bay. I could not read, I could not write. My new book had appeared and a glance at the press-clippings told me that it was being praised. Not a club stroke from hostile critic, not an acid stab from an enemy. Had I enemies no longer? Had they been concentrated in the person of Fulbert, that Fulbert who was dead and cremated? I pondered the idea. My own careless words like curses were coming home to roost in my skull. Without an enemy, I had often said, a man of talent is like unploughed soil. What an infernal paradox. An enemy—why, I had them by the score. Yet not such a master-hand as Fulbert. Fulbert it was who had eagerly awaited my first book and, with a devilishness almost feminine, had praised it, pouring into every phrase a double-distilled corrosive flattery that withered all it touched. The poor little volume soon shrivelled up and died. In the face of such diabolic appreciation all other criticism must perforce pale or seem fatuous. This had been a favourite method of the dead man. He alone possessed the subtle syllabic tact for such critical assassinations. And my first fiction! That had succumbed to the trumpet-blasts of laughter; consummately Rabelaisian; ventral laughter permeated by false bonhomie. Focussing the strong light of ridicule upon my ideas, perverting my intention, and caricaturing my heroics, Fulbert slaughtered my book so merrily withal that no suspicion attached to the butcher; the butchery itself had been irresistibly comical.

So it had gone on for years; book after book had been attacked in the same surprisingly cruel and original fashion. The ingenuity of Fulbert was Satanic. He always bowed pleasantly to his victim. Once, at a friendly board we met. Mrs. Fulbert was in the company, and her husband, as if to show off his critical paces, cried across the table to me: "Ah! my old friend the writer. Are you going to give us your accustomed 'improvisation' on the piano this evening?" Mrs. Fulbert turned her head so as not to smile in my face. The others laughed. So did I. But I almost strangled in the effort. I felt sorry for the widow. Of course, the critic had died without leaving her a penny—after a manner of most critics—and the poor woman in an uninteresting condition, was forced to move from the city. Did it concern me? I couldn't gloat over her trouble. I couldn't revenge myself by asking her hand in marriage. I am not of a melodramatic turn. Fulbert was dead. And I would follow him in a few years; perhaps sooner than I expected. I gazed across the East River. The bridges with their gaunt framework evoked the image of some archaic heaven-storming machine, some impious Babel built by God-hating men seeking to emulate the secret of the skies. Without knowing why I sighed. Life seemed empty. My old ambitions relaxed and fell away. Wasn't my hatred only a surface irritation, an author's lacerated vanity? Hadn't Fulbert's attacks stung my sensitive epidermis forcing me to fight, urging me to finer work, to wider conquests? Would indiscriminate praise have accomplished a like result? In a grim mood, I again turned to the window and launched my gaze towards Long Island. Over there, over at Fresh-pond, what was once Fulbert now lay enclosed in an urn. I could not keep my thoughts from that urn. In it were the burned bones of my adversary. Mechanically I picked up my hat and went down into the street. Presently I was riding across Williamsburg bridge.

The approach was like the road to any cemetery. Little one-story edifices with black gaping entrances, displayed mortuary ornaments, metallic wreaths, hideous emblems, banners of supreme ugliness, marble shafts pointing dirty white digits to the sky, botched carved angels perched on shapeless lumps of granite—all inviting the sorrowing, sentimental poor to purchase, and at bargain prices. Opposite the cemetery was a huge hostelry for man, beast, and mourners, which funeral parties frequented, there to enjoy the baked meats and copious fluid refreshment. Oh! the desperate jollity of those gatherings at which the bereaved were inwardly strengthened and helped by their friends to bear their burden of woe in an unfeeling world. No matter the doleful faces coming, on departing they were flushed and bore an expression of specious comfort. Every day there was a sepulchral comminglement of black-robed women, children, men, hurrying to and fro, gabbling, excitedly swallowing the food hastily set before them; while the waiters, accustomed to this bedlam of gluttony and grief, rushed in and around the groups, seated or standing, frantic because of conflicting orders, glad to pitch anything on the table, hardly waiting for their fees, and never thanking guests for tips. From the adjacent crematory, a veritable mausoleum, came the sound of solemn music. And from a tall chimney could be seen a clear flame, the essence of some burned body winging its way to the infinite inane.

I hastily passed this melancholy banquet hall and found myself in the Columbarium. It was an impressive chamber. No hint of furnace. The architecture with its calm classic touch was thrown into relief by the severe tones of an organ, hidden from view. A service had concluded. Some lingered to watch their precious dead consigned to the purifying fire. With reverential feelings I saw the speedy end of a fellow human, contrasting this antique mode with a ghastly open grave, clods of earth harshly falling upon the coffin. The music ceased. Questioning an attendant I was directed to an upper gallery. There, after a short search, I found a compartment in which was lodged a new urn. It bore the name of my enemy. A great loneliness invaded my soul. There was Fulbert dead, and forever dead. No one had so hated me. No one had taken such an interest in me. When I had felt this critical surgeon's knife in my innermost fibres, I realised that the surgeon had performed his task with a loving hatred. He knew every line I had written. He had read me, studied me, gloried in me as a field on which to display his wit and cruelty. What if he did wound the victim? Does the life-saver hate you when he scientifically carves your leg from your body? Are you not merely a subject for his technical skill? Did Fulbert ever hate me? Did I not serve him as an excuse to exhibit his pen prowess? Who had so faithfully kept my name before the public? Who would ever take the same interest? He was my spiritual running-mate. I was made to go in double-harness with him; created by the ironical gods on high who mock at the

teased destinies of suffering humanity. With blurred
eyes, I spied upon the urn. I read the inscription:
"Henry Fulbert. Aged 45 years." Nothing more. And
then leaning heavily against the enclosure, my cheeks
feverish, I spoke aloud: "He was my best friend. I am
lonely without Fulbert."

XXVI

AUTOGRAPH LETTERS

Yes, and autographed pictures, how many? My correspondence with famous men and women, well-known writers, musicians, painters, sculptors, actors, clergymen, and men in political life would make a fat volume, especially if I included their signed photographs. Many of my correspondents I never met, never even saw. Yet truly I could borrow Browning's title: "How It Strikes a Contemporary," as a caption for copious comment on interesting people. In 1884 or 1885, I received a letter, undated, from Friederich Nietzsche, written in French. I believe that, setting aside the late Karl Knortz, of Tarrytown, a poet, I was one of the first American correspondents of this poet and philosopher, who has written the most savage attacks against his fellow countrymen since Heine and Schopenhauer. His hatred of the Prussian régime is openly expressed. He said at a time when Richard Wagner was giving lip-service to the conquerors of France, that war had brutalised Germany, with a consequent deterioration of its culture; and remember that despite his delicate health, Nietzsche had served in the ambulance section during 1870. Yet he is quoted by uncritical persons as a fomenter of war, though he has defined Prussia as "long-legs and obedience." His doctrine of the superman should be taken in a spiritual sense only. I saw his sister at the Nietzsche Archive, Weimar, where I went after data for my Liszt book ten years ago. Elizabeth

Foerster-Nietzsche is a good-looking intellectual lady, devoted to the memory of her brother and writing much about him. She told me that his Polish blood was a delusion. There is no Polish blood in the family. The father was a God-fearing, old-fashioned pastor, and I recognise in the son much of the evangelical spirit. I saw the piazza on which he looked from upper Weimar over the Thuringian landscape. There he would sit and read—the book usually upside down—and when his sister wept he would say: "Don't cry, little sister. We are happy now." Nietzsche's nervous breakdown was caused in part by the contumely of German critics. He was forced to earn his living in Switzerland, at Basle. Madame Foerster-Nietzsche didn't mince words when telling me of the neglect and insults he had been subjected to. A Dane discovered him to the world, Georg Brandes. In his autobiography, Ecce Homo, Nietzsche says that the Germans are the Chinese of Europe. His own culture was Greek and French. And in France he first was welcomed with open arms by the Intellectuals. The French translation by M. Albert was the first and is the best. Poor, persecuted, unhappy, misunderstood poet and philosopher, what a shock it would have been for him to have heard his name coupled with such mediocre pedants as Bernhardi or Treitschke, he the foe of militarism, of tyranny. He had never been persona-grata at Potsdam. Like Goethe's the genius of Nietszche is universal.

Nearly twenty-five years ago I received from Tolstoy a postcard on which he wrote in English: "Sir, I do not like the story of the Devil you sent me. I cannot see a fair future for your sinister and ennobled talents. Lief Nicoleivitch." Mobled Queen is good! cried Polonius. But why "sinister"? The story was in *M'lle New York*.

The letters I have from Georg Brandes are personal, and there is many a gleam of humour and philosophy in them. He writes with equal fluency in four languages, and in each tongue not only the precise idiom, but the essential character are present. "Alas! the two-thirds of my writing—all that regards Scandinavian literature, and some other books—are not translated. I have even a volume of verse to my account. And I always try to give my Danish style a certain melody . . . which is impossible to render in translation. You do not know how happy you are to be read in your own language, and to have a language spread over the earth. My old book on Russia was not the cause that barred me from Russia in 1913. I have lectured in Russia many times since I wrote it in 1888. But the Minister of the Interior feared the enthusiasm of the young students in Helsingfors. . . . I have made many attempts to help the poor oppressed Jews in Russia, Poland, Finland, but I have always found rich Jews in my way; they own the newspapers, are in business relations with the oppressing government, and print nothing that would prove disagreeable to it." This was written in English from Copenhagen, dated July 14, 1914. Since the war Brandes has had one thought after his own land—France. His hatred of Russia, like Zangwill's, is easily comprehended. In despair, he wrote me, he took up his big book on Goethe, begun twenty-six years ago, and as we know, had the courage to finish it. In 1909, after the publication of my Egoists, he wrote from Copenhagen congratulating me, though he objected to the inclusion of the name of Anatole France. Yet the gentle Anatole is an individualist notwithstanding his socialistic tendencies; the general tone of his writings gave me that impression.

For Barrès, Georg Brandes holds no brief of admiration. He disliked his Dreyfus activities, naturally, but how long ago that seems. He speaks with extreme cordiality of our former Minister at Copenhagen, Maurice Egan, an old friend of mine and a Philadelphian born.

I never saw George Moore till 1901, and then at Bai-reuth. Mr. Moore, I need hardly tell you, belongs to the old Wagnerian guard. His Evelyn Innes is the best novel about operatic singers that I know. The August afternoon I spoke with this remarkable Irishman he wasn't aware that I wrote about music. My name, usually mispronounced (Ah! the delightful little Amy Hoppin, who in 1875 translated my long booming name into French as "M. Mielcœur"—literally Honey-Heart) had not been clear, and when he later wrote from Dublin he spoke of my Chopin, and regretted that he hadn't known it at the time. In a letter also from Dublin, dated April 2, 1904, Mr. Moore wrote: "In The Confessions of a Young Man I give a description of a servant-girl in a lodging-house, but I did not think of her at the time as a heroine of a novel. It was some years after that I conceived the idea. I was walking down the Strand reading a newspaper. It contained an article on servants, and in the article the following sentence occurred: 'We often speak of the trouble servants give us, but do we ever think of the trouble we give servants?' The sentence was illuminating. 'Of course,' I said, 'we give servants a great deal of trouble. I wonder if a novel could be written about a servant. A lady in love with her footman?' 'No,' I said, 'that is very common, very obvious. A cook has a trade to learn; some one who learns a trade —a cook-maid. Now what could happen to her? Sooner or later she would be seduced; she would have a child; she would be sent away. If she did not kill the child, she would have to bring it up on her wages. Her wages would vary from fourteen to sixteen pounds a year; on fourteen she could not rear her child, on sixteen she could. A human being's life dependent on two pounds a year. These thoughts passed through my mind in the space of fifty or sixty yards, while walking from Surrey Street to the Temple. And the writing of the book is as unlike Goncourt as anything could be.'" I had written in Overtones that, no doubt, in a general way, Germinie Lacerteux suggested Esther Waters; but Mr. Moore gave the genesis of that very human story in his letter. He continued:

"I admit I was influenced by Zola in the writings of my three first books, A Modern Lover, A Mummer's Wife, and A Drama in Muslin. But Evelyn Innes was not suggested by Huysmans's book; it was conceived and planned before Huysmans's book was printed. Mary Robertson, the poetess" (Mr. Moore means A. Mary F. Robinson, the widow of Professor James Darmesteter, and later the wife of Professor Duclaux), "told me of some little French actress who had scruples of conscience about her lovers and went into a convent, but she could not remain there because the nuns were so childish; she was three and twenty and most of the nuns were sixty, but they seemed to her like children. 'What a wonderful subject for a novel,' I said. 'I must write that.' I made the actress a singer, she couldn't act in a convent —and as I was under the spell of Wagner (I heard the story in Paris on my return from Bayreuth) I made her a Wagner singer. Huysmans writes of the convent from the outside, I write of the nuns from the inside. There is no faintest resemblance between me and Huysmans.

GEORGE MOORE
As seen by Jack Yeats

I have a word to say about the paragraph at the bottom
of the page in which you say, 'From this the reader will
be able to judge of Mr. Moore's knowledge of music.'
My knowledge of music is the very slightest, but it was
sufficient to save me from the mistake which you thought
I fell into. When I wrote, 'The last composer who had
distinguished between A sharp and B flat,' perhaps I
should have written, 'The first composer who ceased to
distinguish between the two notes, and tuned his instrument by semi-tones and wrote forty-eight Preludes and
Fugues.' My meaning would have been clearer, and I
remember when I saw the words on the proof I thought
of altering them, and I'm sorry I did not, as you misread
them. . . . I have just returned from London; I went
over to hear the Elgar Festival, but was so much bored
by 'Gerontius' that I did not go to hear 'The Apostles.'
He seems to me quite a commonplace writer. Some
excitable ladies leaned over to ask me what I thought of
the music, during the interval, and I said: 'Holy water in
a German beer barrel.'"

That's a capital criticism. In the first edition of
Evelyn Innes he made another witty epigram when he
called Parsifal a "stuffed Christ." Who dare say that
Mr. Moore is not a humourist? Not "the funny man in a
boarding-house," which he said was Bernard Shaw, but a
humourist whose humour permeates his writings throughout. As to the convent scenes in Sister Teresa, Pearl
Richards Craigie, "John Oliver Hobbes," told me in
New York that she had supplied Mr. Moore with "local
colour." She wrote a convent novel. I've forgotten its
title, but I remember "Sister Teresa," which is a case of
fiction being stranger than truth. A human ass, whose

tribe grows no less, said to me many years ago that the reason he didn't like Dickens was because of the novelist's predilection for low company.   And someone, it must have been a college professor—that Eternal Sophomore— wrote long ago that George Moore preferred low company; witness Esther Waters, A Mummer's Wife, Mike Fletcher—by the way, his most virile, original performance.   I much prefer Mike to De Maupassant's Bel Ami.   Now what sort of a mummy mind has such a critic!   I can quite understand people not liking George Moore.   With Baudelaire, his books are a touchstone for imbeciles.   No man of his time in or out of England has written with such imaginative sympathy in his fiction, or with such critical insight.   His versatility is remarkable, his culture sound.   And what an artistic writer.   Vance Thompson has spoken of college professors with dandruff on their coat collars.   The one I allude to—and I've forgotten his name and habitat— may sport an immaculate coat, but the dandruff is inside his skull.   John Quinn wittily calls them professors of Comparatively Literature.

In 1906 (October 26) Mr. Moore wrote from Dublin: "You say that Ibsen's technique is entirely French. Will you allow me to disagree with you on this point? No writer since the beginning of the world invented a technique so original as Ibsen's.   It seems to me to have fallen from the moon.   First quality: the omission of any statement regarding his subject-matter; every other dramatist states his subject in the first act, Ibsen never, in any of the important plays.   Second quality: his manner of telling a story backwards.   Rosmersholm is all told backwards, and the difficulty of this form is enormous.   I experienced it in the first fifty pages of The Lake;

to write fifty pages in the past participle is no easy task, and Ibsen did that in dialogue without anybody perceiving that the characters were asking and answering questions."

I suppose I had said something about Ibsen's debt to Scribe in Iconoclasts; and he did owe a lot on the purely technical side. As stage-manager at Christiania or Bergen he adapted many plays from the French repertoire, Scribe's in particular. Scribe is a wonderful technician, despite the emptiness of his "ideas." From him you may learn the playwright's trade. But Ibsen benefited from many sources, Scribe and Dumas fils among the rest. The Greek dramatists have written plays backwards. There is no new thing behind the footlights. Ibsen is like a clear still pool of icy water in the ultimate Scandinavian pine forests; a pool mirroring the sky and stars, and the stately shapes of tree; also the shapes of the men who go to his waters as on a secret errand to dip their little pails therein, and later assert that they had drawn from their own private artesian wells. Oh! St. Bernard of Cork, not Clairvaux!

Like Brandes, Mr. Moore is not an admirer of Maurice Barrès. He writes: "Barrès is not a great favourite of mine. I have always found him very antipathetic, and his literature always seemed to me ineffectual; a well out of which a dry bucket is always coming up, a clock that never strikes the hour." That I do not agree with this damning dictum is known to readers of Egoists. Another time he writes: "It is extraordinary how interesting you Americans make your writing; you never produce the stodgy mess that Englishmen do; they write reviews that interest nobody." Mr. Moore doesn't know that over here we smoke the opium of optimism. He is an avowed admirer of Edgar Saltus, telling an interviewer that Poe, Walt Whitman, and Edgar Saltus were our best writers. Walt's superiority, he maintains, is because he writes with his whole body, not alone with the head. (I am quoting from memory.) There are some of us who believe that W. W. never used his head at all; only his body from the waist down. In 1909, I told Mr. Moore that I was contemplating a monograph on Franz Liszt. The news filled him with enthusiasm: "You know that I am such an egoist, such a dog in the manger, that I envy you that subject, though, of course, I could not write it myself. To write a life of Liszt must be a charming thing to do; much better than writing a life of Wagner. Oh, much! He was so many-sided, so quaint a personality—his mistresses, and his music and his friendship with Wagner, and a hundred other little turns in his character. It is a book I hope you will spend a good deal of time upon; not rewriting it as I write my books, for that is madness. Never do that!" No, I never rewrite my books. The "dog returns to his vomit" when an author reads his proof. That is bad enough. But I didn't enjoy writing my Liszt. The subject required too much research, and research requires time, and time is money; ergo: I had to hurry the book through in a year. Moore is a rich man, and he has always had leisure, which, I am happy to say, he never wasted. Poor Dostoievsky, the profoundest of the Russian novelists, and that means the profoundest of all, Balzac excepted, was harassed by poverty and could not write his powerful fiction in the artistic way he wished. It was a tragedy in the life of a tragic soul. Tolstoy and Turgenev were rich. Flaubert till he was fifty had ample means, and he had not wife or children. I repeat it needs a competency to write books. My Liszt was not what I had wished for. I dislike it—but then I dislike all my books; "detritus of me," as Whitman yawps. None the less it is a handy volume of reference. Before I finished it the subject had ceased to interest me. Liszt and the ladies! There Mr. Moore was clairvoyant. It is the major motive in the Abbé's life, crowded with incident and the tragedy of being a transitional composer. Moore would have handled the woman side of Liszt better than I.

Mr. Moore was excited when I told him of a rumour that The Lake was to be dramatised. Why not? he asked, and he wrote me a long letter from London— dateless, only "105 Marylebone Road"—which is practically a scenario of the novel. It is too lengthy to transcribe now. He once wrote a full-fledged comedy, and a very readable one, which I fetched to Daniel Frohman. Nothing came of it. When I last saw this Irishman of genius he didn't look his age by ten years. He was born in 1857. The Marquise di Lanza—who was born Clara Hammond, and daughter of Surgeon-General Hammond—wrote me that George Moore was born in 1852. He told her in 1889 that he was then thirty-seven. Madame Lanza still has the letter. Oscar Wilde told her on his visit to America that he was twenty-six. He was really twenty-nine. Not that it matters. A man is as old as he writes—I mean a writing man. And I've noticed that men are as vain and "tetchy" as women on the subject of their age. Why not? Cock-a-doodle-doo! crows the chanticleer at dawn.

I have related my impressions of Joseph Conrad the man: His letters resemble him; our letters usually do re-

semble us.   As is the case with the majority of great
writers, Mr. Conrad is the most human of humans.   His
unfailing kindness, and politeness in recognising other
men's work is very comforting to writers who are swarm-
ing around the base of his mountain.   I had compared
him with Flaubert, and he wrote me (1909) that "when
you overwhelm me with the mantle of Flaubert, it is an
ominous garment to put on a man's shoulders.   Yet
there is one point in which I resemble that great man;
it is in the desperate heart-breaking toil and effort of the
writing; the days of wrestling as with a dumb devil for
every line of my creation. . . .   Mais laissons cela! . . .
I must go back to my MS. on a page (just like this one)
bearing the No. 890 of the novel I have been at for the
last sixteen months.   And the end is not yet!   And
that end also does not bear thinking about."   I believe
that the novel he mentions is Chance.   In another letter
he speaks of Flaubert.   It was written from Kent the
same year, 1909: "I, too, began my communion with
Flaubert by Salammbô.   I might have seen him—but
in 1879 I was somewhere at sea, au diable boulli, Kerguelen
Land, I think, or thereabouts.   It was another life I remember with much tenderness, as a transmigrated soul
might be supposed by a miracle to remember its previous
envelope."   What is more fascinating than a peep into
the laboratory of a great artist's mind!   Involuntarily
you exclaim: "O rare Joseph Conrad, who has wisely
written that 'Imagination, not invention, is the supreme
master of art as of life!'"

While I was speaking of Nietzsche, I should have quoted
a striking remark made by Edith Wharton in a letter
from Paris some years ago (1909).   She had read his autobiography Ecce Homo, and she found that it held more

of the philosopher than any of his other works, and she added: "The farther I go the more I feel that Goethe contained most of him (Nietzsche) and most of everything else! He was the most Super-est of them all." Mrs. Wharton could have joined to Goethe's name that of Dostoievsky. I have been rereading The Brothers Karamazov and The Possessed (Englished by Constance Garnett; Besi is the Russian title of The Possessed. It means, aptly enough, Devils) and my opinion is strengthened that from the great Russian novelist, Nietzsche absorbed much of his mysticism; the Eternal Return, the Superman. In these books, also The Idiot, may be found some of the most significant utterances of the German philosopher—the most un-German thinker of his epoch. In all modern literature, dating from Dante—and I called Dostoievsky the Dante of the North in an essay to be found in Ivory Apes and Peacocks—there is no such grandiose vision as the story of the Grand Inquisitor in The Brothers Karamazov.

When I spoke of my Zoo and its queer inmates, I was probably thinking of what Paul Elmer More wrote in 1915: "How in the name of heaven do you have the will-power to read all those eccentrics and maniacs whom you seem to know by heart? A week of them would kill me with ennui. After all, there is nothing that really lasts and maintains its interest but the sane and the reticent." Words of wisdom. But sane genius also has its crazy wards, its padded cells: Dante, Shakespeare, Milton, Goethe; besides, my "maniacs" are a pretty sane lot. Some drank. Some murdered sleep, yet Chopin, Stendhal, Anatole France, Richard Strauss, Pater, Wagner, Baudelaire, Manet, Brahms—the list is long and far from insane, for I take it neither Poe nor Chopin were quite

mad. Drugs and alcohol did for Poe. Mad, naked
William Blake was rather peculiar, to say the least.
Yet a god-intoxicated man. No, I don't hold with the
eminent critic that is Mr. Moore, and I yield to no one
in my admiration of Wordsworth, of the Lake School, of
the placid and delightful eighteenth-century essayists.
A chacun son poison!

Richard Mansfield I never personally met, but I wrote
about him critically from his "Prince Karl" days on.
I have several letters from him, undated, but written during the stress of the "Peer Gynt" production. He invited
me to dine at his home, No. 316 Riverside Drive, and
when I gave my reason for refusing his hospitality—also
my regret—he fairly exploded. A European born and
European in culture, he couldn't understand my attitude.
In London and Paris there are clubs where actors, artists,
writers, and critics meet and mingle, and no harm comes
of it, indeed, good results. But in New York the dramatic critic is taboo. If he dines with an actor, or an
actor takes luncheon with him, then the alarm-bells are
rung all over town. "Mansfield has bought up Mr. X."
I didn't say this in my letter, but the sensitive Mansfield
understood. He had wanted to talk over "Peer Gynt"
with me, because he had read what I wrote of Ibsen's
tragi-comedy. They were then rehearsing at the New
York Theatre and Will McConnell had instructions to
admit me. I didn't go. I now regret it. The production quâ production was picturesque, but the spirit of
Ibsen missing. Mansfield was nearing the close of a brilliant career. He was exhausted by work. He had few
intimate friends, I mean genuine friends, who could advise
him. Edward A. Dithmar was one, but to him Ibsen
was repugnant. He was sincere in this his dislike and I

respected his sincerity. Yet, what an Ibsen interpreter Richard Mansfield might have been. What an Oswald, what a Rosmersholm. When Orlenev, an extraordinary Russian actor, played here with Alla Nazimova, we saw for the first time the possibilities of the Master-Builder. Mansfield was made for the part, and for many other modern rôles. But fate willed otherwise, and he went on year after year, wasting his dramatic powers in such tawdry stuff as "Parisian Romance," "Dr. Jekyll and Mr. Hyde"—crude melodrama—and the silly "Prince Karl." For Shakespeare, neither by temperament nor training, was he suited. In "Rodion the Student," Charles Henry Meltzer's admirable adaptation of Dostoievsky's The Crime and the Punishment, Mansfield was in his element. But to his letter:

"Here is another grudge I have to record against the unfortunate choice of a profession that debars me from the more intimate acquaintance with brilliant men. . . . In this city, in this country, one is forced to eat one's own heart—Garrick and the rest of them had better luck —they had the stimulus of fine minds, their opinions, their encouragement. . . . Still, I feel that we could have discussed "Peer Gynt," and I could have got from you a lot of points that I may miss—even at a sacrifice to yourself and of yourself. . . . I can't begin to enumerate the essentials. I should have to talk it act by act, scene by scene, the necessary cuts, my appearance (my looks), et cetera. Scribners should have published our (acting) cut edition. . . . Chicago will probably d—n it, the Associated Press will do the rest. . . . As to Anitra" (a character in the play), "being the Eternal-Womanly, I have my doubts. We have Solveig—the one is no more eternal than the other, or the other than

the one on earth; if it had not been for Solveig, I should
not have undertaken to do Peer, but, of course, the
much esteemed author I know only meant that the
Eternal-Womanly, all of them, write these days. I
shall not allow the 'dread passenger' to refer to 'midmost
of Act V'—because that is one of Ibsen's mistakes in
good taste. It is hard enough to drag the people off
the earth without knocking them back to it of a sudden
and reminding them that after all we are in a theatre
and only actor-folk. But Lord, I could write on forever.
Throw it in your waste-basket and let it go at that.
Don't write about it and me, but come and talk to me;
the public would be the loser, but I shall be the gainer
and perhaps in the end the public too." This letter
shows what Mansfield's friends knew—that the actor
was not only a charming man but amenable to reason.
He was often caricatured by irresponsible writers. The
biography by Paul Wilstach demonstrates that. It was
my loss, not meeting the gifted and musical man. And
what a lot he did for Shaw, for he literally gave "Arms
and the Man" and "The Devil's Disciple" their first
artistic production in America. Mr. Shaw was charac-
teristically "grateful," judging from the letters that
passed between actor and author. But could "Peer
Gynt" have been possible here? I saw it in its entirety
somewhere in Europe, and it took two nights to play it.

A crumbling letter written in London (July 8, 1895)
is signed Kyrle Bellew, and what memories that name
evokes. Mr. Meltzer had made an adaptation of the
Dumas Collier de la Reine, in which Mrs. Potter wore
the largest hat I ever saw on a woman's head. Incident-
ally, Bellew speaks of Mrs. Pat Campbell. "She is the

vogue, the real thing is not there. She must be written around. It is the skittishness of her personality that has set London crazy" (he is referring to Mrs. Campbell's memorable impersonation of Paula Tanqueray in the Pinero play; all said and done, her best dramatic assumption). "As an artist she is impossible—as a producer of a certain kind of suggestion she is immense. She will never be a great actress. She is Pat Campbell, and she will never be anyone else. Nethersole has killed herself playing 'The Notorious Mrs. Ebbsmith' in London. She has challenged reigning favourites and got hopelessly sat upon, or ignored." Kyrle Bellew then goes on to speak of Barney Barnato and Albert Beit, who were splurging in London with their millions. A single letter from the beautiful Mary F. Scott-Siddons is dated from Berlin, February, 1896, and chiefly deals with the troubles she was undergoing in producing an opera composed by her protégé, the English pianist and pupil of Liszt, Henry Waller. "Fra Francesco" was its title, and Arthur Sullivan had approved of the music. I dimly remember that it was given in Germany. But by far the most interesting part of the letter is the account of her Shakespearean reading before the Kaiser and Court at Potsdam. Oddly enough some selections from American humourists best pleased the Hohenzollerns. Other days, other ways.

My correspondence with Remy de Gourmont covered several decades. It is chiefly literary, and there is so much in it about my books that my well-known modesty estops me from reproducing these letters. Senator Lodge made a happy quotation at the close of a certain letter: "I look with amazement at the flood of books that I see pouring over the news-stands and counters. It is not that they are meretricious or immoral, but they seem to me so feeble and so full of weak sentiment. I think constantly when I look upon them of Carlyle's phrase that 'they are intended for immediate use and immediate oblivion.' Your George Sand" (in Unicorns) "brought back distant memories. She was still a conspicuous figure, still writing when I was a boy and a young man. She had a great reputation then. I remember that I tried to read her books and they bored me . . . it seems to me as if the years in their movement had justified my original attitude. On the other hand she has, as you say, immense interest as a personality." Of the so-called, and still-unborn "Great American Novel," William Dean Howells wrote: "We all have to have our shy at that monstrous misconception, that grotesque impossibility, and I like to see you bang it about. But we shall never bang it out of the heads that have so little in them." One of my treasured letters is dated May 8, 1902, and signed Frank Norris. Well I remember his earnestness when he asserted that poor or mediocre books were for the mass of the people better than none at all. "Only get them to read—anything," was his plea. Of my Melomaniacs he wrote some words that pleased me, for Norris was a craftsman: "You certainly have attained what has always seemed to me the most difficult of all achievements. I mean originality without grotesqueness." I was tickled to death over that. You see, even professional critics have feelings.

It was as long ago as 1893 that I began corresponding with Israel Zangwill, for whose work I have genuine esteem. When he visited the United States in 1898, I met him in New York. I had imitated him in such stories as The Shofar Blew at Sunset, and in The Cardinal's Fiddle, and he was duly amused. Like most Englishmen, he can't understand that I am tired of Whitmania, probably, as Lawrence Gilman suggested, because I had suffered from a bad attack in my youth and had recovered. What I chiefly resent is the implication that Whitman voices our national feeling, or even pictures us as we are. He does neither. We are not Camerados, closely knit, as the war has made us. Mr. Zangwill finds in him the "real insight of a seer." Granted. And still one swallow doesn't make a summer. "These States," as John Jay Chapman pointed out years ago, are not peopled by Walt Whitman characters. The Lord forbid! Max Nordau, for example, doesn't agree with Mr. Zangwill in his estimate of Walt, calling him a rotten sensualist, as may be noted in the Calamus section of Leaves of Grass, and of patriotic yawps he has this to say: "In his patriotic poems, Whitman is a sycophant of the corrupt American vote-buying, official-bribing, power-abusing, dollar-democracy, and a cringer to the most arrogant Yankee conceit." (Degeneration, English translation, page 231.) How Max admires us!

John LaFarge, the critic, interested me more than John LaFarge, the painter. He is called an eclectic, which simply means an artist who lacks originality. His pictures never attracted me, not even the South Sea examples. Paul Gauguin, not LaFarge, is my man for exotic art. But an extraordinary raconteur was the American according to Royal Cortissoz. I never met him, although I went to his Tenth Street studio to see his stained glass, which I liked. I have a stack of letters from him. They are of equal interest. I quote a few sentences showing the curiosity of the thinker concerning art and life. In 1907 he writes: "I want to tell you what always interests me, because I cannot tell myself how it is done—though it is very well known, that is, how a painter can carry out the enormous mass of detail of a painting from Nature, in the few minutes that make an hour, or two or three hours. Several of the pictures you mention—the water colours in the South Seas, are only a couple of hours' work, and the big one, which you may remember, is an afternoon's work. . . . You yourself, if you ever have the chance, ought to go down and live in those wonders of light and air. But what I wished to write to you about was your paper on the etchings of Rembrandt and Whistler" (it appeared in *The Sun*). "What you have said is, to my mind, very much needed. Some excellent people confuse the limit of things, and in their enthusiastic admiration for Whistler, put him where it is unjust to be. . . . I have never been exactly a Stendhalist" (I had quoted Stendhal), "but I remember Henry James, who, himself, of course, admired him more or less, was interesting in his expression of dislike when we were in Italy together. In Paris some fifty odd years ago, I met people who had known Stendhal (Beyle). You may remember that my grand-uncle, Paul de Saint-Victor, was a successful rival in some one of the love affairs of your man. . . ." John LaFarge was one of the first American artists who "went in for" the Japanese, for Blake, for Goya. His mural compositions are pasticcios.

W. B. Yeats wrote me in 1903 that John Quinn had told him I wrote the article in *The Sun* on the Irish movement in two hours; which was true. Yeats adds: "That seems to me a wonderful feat, for it is precisely what journalism is not—detailed and philosophical and accurate. . . . Of course, my critic in *The Evening Post* was right in one sense in calling me decadent. We are all decadent, our sins are the sins of our forefathers. But I am struggling against it, always trying to get the fire to the centre, not to the circumference. I don't think this critic knew that Lionel Johnson, who is his type of classic health, never got up till dark or went to bed till daylight, wrote poems to absinthe, and died, poor man, of a fall he got when intoxicated. Of course, this isn't the same thing as literary decadence, but I imagine it would have seemed so to him. I have a notion that everybody has been decadent since Shakespeare, and the reason for it is partly a question of language— but that is too big a question for a letter." Mr. Yeats might have recommended his critic, all critics, to read the masterly exposition on the theme of decadence in Affirmations, by Havelock Ellis. After the Nordau humbuggery the word "decadence" was used as a club to smash an author's reputation. Nowadays, it's a joke for Washington Square Bohemia.

Paul Hervieu is another writer with whom I came in contact at Paris. His dramas are still in the repertory of the Théâtre Français; "Les Tenailles" ("Nippers"), "Le Reveil"—with Julia Bartet, Bargy, and Paul Mounet-Sully—the brother of the tragedian, and "The Enigma." These pieces were poorly interpreted in New York—"The Awakening," with Olga Nethersole, hardly a substitute for Julia Bartet, whose exquisite art is for me an exquisite memory. I spent a pleasant hour with M. Hervieu at his apartment on the Avenue du Bois de Boulogne No. 23. He was a reserved man with an English bearing, which I set down to his fondness for things

English; he informed me that he spent his summers on the Isle of Wight. He impressed me as a man suffering from secret chagrin; perhaps an unhappy love-affair. His artistic successes were numerous. I was all the more surprised when he advised me not to give way to cynicism; irony he detested, he, the skinner of souls, whose surgeon's scalpel was deeply dipped in irony; he, the novelist, whose use of the so-called "cruel terms" was as disconcerting as Henri Becque's. Doubtless because of his abuse of verbal corrosive-sublimate he sought to restrain younger men from his mistake. His letters, a dozen, are full of technical gossip about his plays. The tall, slanting handwriting of Alla Nazimova recalls the time when she made her debut here in company with Orlenev at a little theatre off the Bowery, East Third or Fourth Streets. Emma Goldman was the press-agent, and called herself Emma Smith, on account of her numerous tiffs with the police. I can go back still further to the days when Emma was a disciple of Johann Most, the anarchist. It was not the law that ended Johann's days but John Barleycorn. He was a thirsty dreamer. Nazimova afterwards played Grushenka wonderfully in a dramatisation of "The Brothers Karamazov," at the Lexington Avenue Theatre, near Forty-second Street. Orlenev was the Dmitri, a half-crazy drunkard falsely accused of parricide. The company generally was excellent; the intellectual aristocracy of the town present. Miss Nazimova's career since then has been confined to the English-speaking stage. But she was at her artistic best when playing in Russian.

A note that I received from William M. Laffan, then proprietor of *The Sun* (1907), exhibits his native decision and Celtic humour. "Yes, sir, I am, or more rightly,

I was, an etcher; and none of your damned amateurs, either, I want you to understand. Twenty-five years ago I converted sheets of otherwise blameless copper into bread and butter. I don't know how many I did, but I don't mind telling you that the art of them was on a high plane, a very high plane, indeed; a fact which is not necessarily impugned by my having been able to sell them. There is nowhere, thank God, a proof extant (I think I possess only one), so that I may say what I like about their quality and run no measurable danger. The bad proofs that a man pulls will always come home to roost; but I am the exception that proves the rule. I will read your article about Rops with pleasure. Why not have a go at Meryon? There's provocation for you." I did. The study appeared on the editorial page of *The Sun*, and later was included in Promenades of an Impressionist. William Laffan was too modest. I have seen a woodcut of his representing a covey of birds, which betrayed observation and knowledge of technical process. His handwriting is etched. With the exception of W. C. Brownell's pen-and-ink miniatures, I never saw such tiny lettering allied with such diamond clearness. Pearl Mary-Teresa Craigie, as she signed herself, was not in private life like her masculine pen-name, "John Oliver Hobbes." She was shy, feminine, sympathetic. I only saw her once and at the Hotel Netherlands. She spoke of her favourite writers, of George Moore and Bernard Shaw—evidently not her favourites —and she confessed to being an anti-Wagnerian. Her handwriting, too, in the half-dozen letters I have saved, is small and clear. Another human being who made me unhappy in her presence because of her inquietude. Her last communication is dated April 24, 1906, and was written at her home, Steephill Castle, Ventnor, Isle of Wight.

In reading some of the letters Havelock Ellis sent me during the past fifteen years, I note the same quality of charm and wisdom that informs his published writings. Now, to write a book that is both wise and charming seems a task beyond the powers of most of our young authors. They are in such a hurry, tumbling head over heels to court the favours of the Great God Success, that they give us hardly the bare ribs of literature. Charm—isn't it a lost art? And haste and charm are mutually exclusive. You can't be charming on a type-writing machine. Worst of all, few miss the quality. The reading public takes its literature dished up with advertisements, and only asks that the story be told with cinematographic velocity. To concentrate one's intelligence on a phrase is inconceivable; to linger over an idea or a prose cadence—that way folly flies. Hurrah for the Movies in print! Yet there are some serene souls left, with brains and art to interpret them; a few who refuse to mingle with the vast mob of tripe-sellers in the market-place. One of these elect is Havelock Ellis, known as a psychologist, nevertheless a literary critic of singular charm and acuteness. His New Spirit made a sensation twenty-five years ago; Affirmations was another revealing book, with its studies of such disparate personalities as Zola, St. Francis, Casanova, Nietzsche. The note of catholicity sounds throughout the fluid prose of this master's pages. Recall The Soul of Spain, the most sympathetic book on modern Spanish art and literature that I have read; Velasquez and Goya are not overlooked. His Impressions and Comments is charged with kindly wisdom, garnered from a life rich in experience and thought, not more than a page or two in length, on a thousand-and-one themes, saturated with the tolerant Ellis philosophy, which he once defined as the difficult art of holding on and letting go.

But I must brisk up my tempo, else I'll be rambling on till next summer. A Homeric catalogue of names would be the quickest way to dispose of my letters. There is a hastily written scrawl from the English painter, Augustus John, whose canvases are among the jewels of the John Quinn collection. There are letters galore from that witty and erudite New York barrister —who the older he grows looks more like Cardinal Manning—Quinn, the avowed friend of the Irish literary movement, of Synge, and Moore, Yeats, Stephens, James Joyce, Lady Gregory, and also a friend of Arthur Symons and Joseph Conrad. He is not so ascetic as he looks; but a letter-writer born. The name of Jules Gaultier is at the bottom of a finely written page. Of this brilliant philosopher I wrote years ago; I even introduced his books to William James, but the American thinker was just then absorbed in Henri Bergson, and Pragmatism, and he never expressed an opinion of Gaultier, for me the superior thinker of the pair; above all, one without a trace of sentimental charlatanism. You can't say the same of Bergson, that weaver of glittering specious phrases. In his letter Gaultier deplores the death of Remy de Gourmont. That writer did much to spread the ideas of Jules Gaultier. As I have told you, my friendship with Maurice Maeterlinck dates back to 1903. His letters are personal. I have only one letter from James Joyce, a man of genius. His play, "Exiles," has the same poignant quality we find in "The Master

Builder," or in some of Strindberg's one-act dramas.
The same intensity, oppressiveness, and lurking tragic
terror. I couldn't help thinking of Strindberg's "Credi-
tors"; but Joyce is individual and Celtic to the back-
bone. A bitter brew, but stimulating is his play.
From the master, Paul Bourget, I had a letter in 1909
saying pleasant things about my study of Stendhal, in
Egoists. M. Bourget it was who revived the cult of
Stendhal in the early eighties of the past century, and so
timed that he fulfilled the great writer's prediction that he
would be understood about 1880. Bourget is not much
read by the present generation in America, though he was
popular when The Disciple and Cruel Enigma were translated. Why hasn't someone translated his Duchesse
Bleu, one of his most charming fictions?

Bernard Berenson, art critic, Jean de Reszke, Jules
Lefebvre, Isidor Phillipp, Paul Adam—who was called
by De Gourmont "a magnificent spectacle," and a magnificent writer he is—Auguste Rodin, glorious sculptor;
Ignacio Zuloaga, Spanish painter, the biggest since the
death of Goya; a post-card signed Strindberg—but not
addressed to me—Yves Guyot, French economist; Florian
Parmentier, critic; a cordial greeting from W. W. Mesdag,
the Dutch marine artist, whose collection of French art
at The Hague is one of the many attractions in that
lovely, tranquil city; of his wife, also a painter, I have a
small water-colour; Fourcaud, Viardot, Widor, the organist of St. Sulpice, Paris; J. H. Rosny, Sr., the novelist;
Charles Gounod, Jules Massenet—these autograph letters
were given me by Brander Matthews out of sheer kindness, Jules Claretie, Catulle Mendès—need I tell you,
the incomparable writer and once son-in-law of Theophile

Gautier, himself surnamed the impeccable—Camille Saint-Saëns, Conductor Felix Weingartner; the composer of "The Attack on the Mill," Alfred Bruneau, and last, not least, a card from Madame Franklin Grout, dated 1909, Villa Tanit, Antibes. She thanks me for the Flaubert study in Egoists. Madame Grout was formerly Carolina Commainville, the favourite niece of Gustave Flaubert, who, supposedly egotist, gave up his personal fortune when the husband of his niece became embarrassed in business. As you already know, I am an enraged Flaubertian, and have been spreading his gospel for thirty years. The very name of her villa, Tanit, has a touch of Salammbô. Her second husband, Dr. Grout, was one of the physicians at the private sanatorium of Dr. Blanche, where unfortunate Guy de Maupassant was confined and died. Henry Labouchère wrote in London *Truth* at the time of De Maupassant's death that Guy was a natural son of Flaubert's, and that he told his own story in his best novel, Pierre et Jean—best after Une vie. There is not a scintilla of evidence to support this romantic yarn. Flaubert formed the talents of his pupil, Guy— a mere child in comparison with his mighty master, and one who was grateful enough to testify to that fact, a fact sometimes overlooked by young writers, who prefer his elaborately carved cherry-stones to the Massive figures chiselled from the solid marble. My autographic treasure of treasures are three pages of a manuscript in the handwriting of Flaubert, corrected for the printer, exceptions and errors noted. Madame Bovary —one of the glories of French literature, as Henry James has said in a moment of unusual expansion (he alternately admired and disliked Flaubert)—in the making. I reproduced one of these pages in Egoists. I also possess a letter of the Master, probably addressed to his lady-love, Louise Colet, the woman whose epitaph was written by Maxime Ducamp thus: "Here lies the woman who compromised Victor Cousin, made Alfred de Musset ridiculous, calumniated Gustave Flaubert, and tried to assassinate Alphonse Karr. Requiescat in pace." A reader of the heart of woman, poor Flaubert, nevertheless, stumbled in his judgment of the spitefully shrewish creature who had tried to rob George Sand of her literary laurels. Robert Browning said: "God be thanked, the meanest of his creatures boasts two soul-sides, one to face the world with, one to show a woman when he loves her." Flaubert, one of nature's noblest, showed his love for a worthless woman by facing the shrugs and sneers of the Parisian literary world.

XXVII

MID-VICTORIAN MAX

I never believed in criticising a criticism, *i. e.*, a criticism concerning myself. That way lies confusion of spirit; besides, it's a waste of time. Because a critic doesn't like your work and says so, he is not necessarily in the wrong. He is often right. I mention this as a mild preparation to the pleasing story of a verbal warfare indulged in once upon a time by Mr. Shaw and Mr. Huneker. No blood was spilt, no bones were broken. Our native bad tempers only peeped out at intervals; as the Colonel would say, we had a bully time. But first I must begin with Max Beerbohm, whose too few books have been a source of joy to me as they are to lovers of prose as palatable as dry sherry. In Unicorns I ranked Mr. Beerbohm with the stylists who produce slowly and with infinite pains an astringent liqueur for connoisseurs. "Precious?" Yes, at times, but as irony is his happiest medium, his form and utterance are conditioned by it. Max is a born classic, as readers of the delightful Works and Zuleika Dobson need not be told. Well, in 1903, on the appearance of my Iconoclasts, which had a fair measure of critical and public success in London—Mr. G. K. Chesterton wrote appreciatively of the book—a copy fell into the hands of Mr. Beerbohm, then writing for *The Saturday Review.* Result: one of the old-fashioned critical scarifications. My unfortunate group of Iconoclasts were bowled over by a pen, so often languid and affected, but become vigorous, ferocious,

possibly because I was a Yankee.   It was a page of brilliant, destructive criticism.   It did the book much good
as far as sales were concerned—adverse criticism is better
than none—and Bernard Shaw wrote me a letter congratulating me on the honour of being slashed in *The
Saturday*.   I didn't precisely see the honour, though I
understood the kindly interest displayed by Max.   Over
here the review attracted the attention and the late
Harry Thurston Peck tried to "sic" me on the English
critic.   He said that the Beerbohm style was constipated,
mine copious; therefore, we must be antipathetic to one
another.   This reasoning did not appeal to me, and I
refused to be drawn into controversy.   Two exceptions
I did take to the article, mentally, of course, and without
impugning the general conclusions of the writer.   One
was being called a "yellow journalist" when everyone
knew that my colour was "purple."   I wrote "purple
panels" then, or tried to; the other exception was being
described as writing like a "drunken helot."   That
struck me as a contradiction, for helots, drunk or sober,
did not write at all, not even on the tablets of their
memory.   However, that is a mere scratch, and I did
not explain it to Mr. Beerbohm, knowing how busy he
was at the moment demonstrating to his cockney readers what a great dramatist Mr. Shaw was; infinitely
greater than Arthur Pinero.

As for the demerits of Iconoclasts, I have naught to
say, except that it has sold better than any of my books,
possibly an ominous sign in the eyes of Mr. Beerbohm,
who has, no doubt, forgotten all about his clever review.
That other critics did not agree with his verdict has
nothing to do with the case; notably Remy de Gourmont
—who also gave me the opening review in the *Mercure*

de France, a long article on "Chopin," now included in
a volume of his Epilogues.   That absence of "tendenz"
which William James complained about in my Egoists,
a refusal on my part to indulge in so-called "general
views," in any neat little theory or "problem," met the
approval of Remy de Gourmont, who detested phrases
and empty formulas.   I am speaking now of Iconoclasts.   But in *La Plume* (July 15 to August 1, 1905)
Paul Hyacinthe Loyson—the son of the one time famous
priest and orator, Père Hyacinthe Loyson—seemingly
agreed with William James.   He wrote, inter alia:
"l'auteur est un fin gourmet des belles-lettres . . . je
ne sache pas de plus beau sujet pour un thèse de doctorat
es-lettres.   M. Huneker auquel il ne manque plus que
la Sorbonne, le trouvera en latence dans chaque page
de son livre vivant.   Ce qu'il manque, c'est une préface
d'ensemble que l'éditeur dramatique est fort capable de
nous brosser à traits larges et drus. . . .   Précieux vade-
mecum, le livre de M. Huneker leur offre je le répète,
un répertoire analytique et critique . . . son essai sur
Ibsen, qu'il faut mettre hors pair, est inestimable à cet
égard."   We are here far from the "yellow and drunken
helot" of Mr. Beerbohm.   Nevertheless, I did not write
a "préface d'ensemble" as suggested by the French
critic.   I preferred letting the title, Iconoclasts, serve as
the "tendenz" of the book; in it all are image-breakers
save, perhaps, the cynical Paul Hervieu, who strayed in
by mistake.   (To-day I loathe the book.)

Now for a little elliptical escape:
Here is a post-card dated 9th May, 1905, 10 Adelphi
Terrace, London, W. C., and signed by Himself—"G.
Bernard Shaw."   (He is fond of using post-cards and has

written some memorable things on them.) He wrote: "*John Bull* is not yet published" (he means *John Bull's Other Island*), "I am too busy rehearsing and producing to attend to my publishing business for the moment. I proposed to Brentanos that they should get you to edit a selection from my musical feuilletons in *The World*, etc. They said it was an excellent idea to get you to edit my dramatic feuilletons and that they had bought up the old numbers of *The Saturday Review* accordingly. Knock the difference into their heads if you can. My sister in Germany is furious because you have compromised her social position by describing me in Success (which has reached Germany) as a 'peasant lad.' The Shaw peasants! Good God! You know not what you say. Why did you give me the slip last fall? G. Bernard Shaw."

The "peasant lad" I shall presently deal with; of the Dramatic Opinions I would speak first. The late Volney Streamer, literary adviser of the Brentanos, had collected all the critical articles of Mr. Shaw from *The Saturday*. I was asked to write a Prelude to the book, which contains some of the author's always engaging and often fallacious criticisms. In my preface or introduction, rather, impertinence, I happened to speak of Mr. Beerbohm as "Mid-Victorian Max." If I had tried to be funny and had written "Mud-Victorian"—for London was clogged with literary mud during the Yellow Book period of the nineties—or even "Max-Victorian," I might have understood what followed in the pages of *The Saturday*. Max went up into the air. Another page of loving invectives followed, worse than the first review, and I began to feel famous. He informed his readers that he was proud of the ascription, Mid-Vic-

torian. If he were, why so hot, little man? as Emerson
asked. If I wrote the precise phrase that pleased him,
why should he foam at the mouth, metaphorically speaking? In classic parlance I "got his goat," and also a lot
of free advertising. That was better than my publicly
objecting to his "purple helot," wasn't it? I suspect
that Mr. Shaw was not overjoyed with my preface, as
later he wrote one for the English edition. The projected collection of his musical criticisms did not appear—
a good thing, as Shaw, whether writing of pictures or the
tone-art, is distinctly amateurish. Glittering generali-
ties are his, but not backed up by technical training, wide
experience, or genuine musical temperament. John Runciman told me that he had a poor opinion of Shaw as a
music-critic.

The "peasant boy" caused all the trouble, and although I tried to explain to Mr. Shaw that the head-line
in *Success Magazine* was none of my making, he would
not listen to me. Robert Mackey, then associate editor
of *Success*, wrote that head-line, and he has since deplored
doing so. However, his sorrow is about as deep as mine.
Why should Mr. Shaw heartily dislike the "peasant"?
Scratch a socialist and you come on a snob. Max Beerbohm has said in effect that socialism will never succeed
till snobbishness ceases. He is right. Mr. Shaw is not
of peasant origin though he has written that most Irish-
men originally came over from Liverpool on cattle-boats;
he is middle-class Cork (with a Cork soul), and his
family was not rich. He was a poor youth when he went
to London, and he is none the worse for his struggle.
The newspapers created the Shaw legend; that he was
a vegetarian, a teetotaler, anti-vaccine, anti-vivisection,
anti-evening clothes, wearing Jaeger flannels, anti-every-

thing except notoriety. Yet for repeating in my article
what was common talk, thanks to his own self-propa-
ganda, St. George—who has slain so many dragons—
fell foul of me in a certain letter, calling me the short,
ugly word on every count.

XXVIII

G. B. S.

My main offence, however, was the "peasant lad";
that rankled. I met his cousin, Robert Shaw, a newspaper correspondent for the New York *Sun* and some
London journals in Berlin. He had not seen *Success*,
and I suspect Mr. Shaw's sister did not see it then.
The foolish part of the affair was that Mr. Shaw didn't
believe my story of the mistake; he fancied a lurking
insult when none was intended; indeed, I could only
plead ignorance of another's error. So when he wrote
me, August, 1905: "My dear Huneker: You really must
come over here and have your mind properly trained;
you will never be anything but a clever slummocker in
America," I knew that further argument was useless.
And who was I to succeed where the only Shaw had so
signally failed? I wrote a weekly column for years in
the London *Musical Courier;* I had lived in London
and I loved the city, not evidently to no purpose, for if
thirty years' residence couldn't change Shaw from being
a clever Irish slummocker, what chance had I for spiritual
redemption? I remained in America—the America that
first recognised him, thanks to Richard Mansfield.

I was the first to write of him as early as 1888. In
1890 I persuaded Marc Blumenberg to buy an article
of Shaw's for *The Musical Courier*, which he did. It
was printed in June or July of that year, though I shan't
swear as to the year, as I have not kept my files of that
journal; it may have been 1891. But it was the first

musical "story" by Bernard Shaw to appear in an American publication. What was it about? If I remember, it preached the superiority of the forerunners of the pianoforte over the modern instrument. I have often noticed with amusement that literary persons usually like tinkling music. They speak of dulcimers, harpsichords, clavichords, they prate of cymbaloms, harps, and lutes, but for full-blooded, highly-coloured compositions for the keyboard, whether by Bach or Beethoven or Chopin, they have an abhorrence. The subdued light of Chinese lanterns, the Bohemian studio atmosphere, the tinkle-tinkle of music made by young men wearing bangles—Ah! that is lofty art. George Moore in Evelyn Innes goes into the matter heart and soul. So did Shaw; and recently I read in Ezra Pound's Pavannes and Divisions a fresh eulogy of Arnold Dolmetsch and his old instruments. We had Dolmetsch over here many years ago. He is all right, so is the antique and charming music he plays, but when Shaw begins abusing the modern concert grand pianoforte, I can't help recalling his other article, amusing enough, in an English monthly or fortnightly, in which he tells how he studied the piano.

He unblushingly gives his reason for mildly abusing me, which reason corroborates my claim as being his "discoverer" over here. Under date 16th September, 1905, he writes: "The reason I call you a slummocker and heap insults on you, is that you are very useful to me in America, and quite friendly; consequently, you must be educated or you will compromise me." The blind leading the blind! I don't think his allusion to my usefulness cynical. What else is a critic good for but to make himself useful? What is still more amusing

was his communication on music in a letter dated 13th
August, 1905, from Cork.   It is, like the others, in his
small, distinct handwriting.   "Some day I shall talk to
you about music.   I haven't the time to write now.
Last winter I heard Liszt's 'Faust' symphony played for
the first time in London—old-fashioned before it was
born—an obsession, with the new chords of the fifties!"
We had been listening in New York to the "Faust" symphony for how many years?   How shallow is Shaw's
judgment may be noted in his neglect to study Liszt in
a proper historical perspective.   "The chords of the
fifties" were Liszt's original harmonic inventions, not to
speak of his themes, some of which were utilised by
Wagner in "The Ring," "Tristan," and "Parsifal."
I'll go further: Without Liszt "Parsifal" would not be
as it is.   Liszt contributed much to the mystic "atmosphere."   So much for George, the clever musical slummocker!   He continues: "I know a lot more than you
do, especially about music.   What I said about Liszt's
music is exactly accurate.   Go and study the operas of
Cornelius (delightful music) if you want to understand
that particular moment."

But George, dear old son!   It was not necessary for
me to study the music of Peter Cornelius as I had listened
to his masterpiece, season after season in the Metropolitan
Opera House as conducted by Anton Seidl, sung by
Emil Fischer.   And don't you know that Cornelius was
a pet pupil in composition of Franz Lizst during your
famous "fifties"?   That "The Barber of Bagdad" was
produced in 1858 at Liszt's suggestion in Weimar?   You
probably do know more than I; you know more than
anyone, living or dead; like the little girl in the play,

for you the King is always naked; but you didn't know
about the "Faust" symphony and the important part it
played in Wagner's music-drama because you never read
with understanding the Wagner-Liszt correspondence;
and you didn't know about Cornelius and his acknowledged indebtedness to Liszt—though his is individual
and truly "delightful music"; yet you know more about
music than I?   Very well, then take the trouble to read
my "Liszt" study (1911), and in the future you will
make no such absurd "breaks."   George was annoyed
because I had challenged him to play the first movement
of Chopin's E minor concerto, but as he was a one-
fingered virtuoso—he now works a mechanical piano,
bless his musical soul!—and he answered me as above.
I had studied the Chopin concerto with Rafael Joseffy—
my copy is full of his pencilled fingering and phrasing—
and with that incomparable master at the second pianoforte, I had played the allegro.   At least I can play it
better than the Aged Mariner of Adelphi Terrace (isn't
all this lovely and childish, our "daring" and boasting?).
I had answered a letter from Shaw, August, 1905 (13th
inst.), in an equally abusive key.   It was at Sorrento,
Italy, and I had been drinking the hot, heady, generous
Capri wine, which primed me for retort; I must have
made such a judicious person as G. B. S. grieve.   I
dared him to take off his shoes and show the world the
web-foot of a bog-trotter.   This charming remark I had
remembered in some Lever novel.   Uncle George must
have smiled, but he never turned a hair.   His reply was
characteristic Shaw: "Your chest being now relieved,
we can resume cordial relations."   What is there to be
said to such a saintly man who can thus turn the other
cheek in so diplomatic a manner?

I forgot to tell you that after the "peasant lad" episode he wrote an article for the New York *Metropolitan Magazine*, in which he briefly alluded to my supposed slip. (Ah! the honour of the Shaw family was at stake; Shaw the socialist!) He ended with a denial of the "fiction" that I was trying to pass off as truth, and after rallying me came to an abrupt close with: "Now, James!" —It was very funny to me and to my friends, who sent me numerous clippings of the sly little coda. Mr. Shaw is as dangerous as an army with brass bands to argue with, especially in public, and the only reason I am telling all these highly unimportant things is because someone else may do so and get the facts muddled. I am now convinced that Shaw was grooming me as his future biographer; hence the hint about being "useful to me." But I was not a bird of his feather and could not be persuaded to alight on his twig, there to be snared. Professor Archibald Henderson fell into the trap, and what he endured while spinning his yarn—fancy writing the life of a man not dead!—really the "autobiography," for he worked with Shaw—he alone can tell. The meanest part of the thing is that recently Mr. Shaw said that Mr. Chesterton was the only man who understood him. O gratitude, where is thy Shaw? O Shaw, where is thy Archibald?

I have been told that another of my offences was what I had printed in the chapter devoted to "The Quintessence of Shaw." I asked there if Mr. Shaw is brilliant on bran, what would he not be on beef and beer? This question angered Mr. Beerbohm; possibly I might have asked that Mid-Victorian if his imitation of the essay style of Charles Lamb did sometimes turn out cold mutton.

Perhaps Bernard Shaw does furtively eat roast-beef sandwiches, and at midnight; perhaps he does secretly sip Shandygaff—not Kit Morley's hippocrene draught, but the garden variety of half ale, half porter. Perish the proposition! Shaw eating meat would cause more of a row than did the revelations of Anna Seuron, the governess in the Tolstoy household, who had caught old man Tolstoy in his bare feet and at the pantry gobbling raw beef. And the hour was midnight. That beef leading-motive resounded the world over. In a roundabout fashion, I heard that one morning while at Lady Gregory's, Mr. Shaw came down to breakfast in a truly masculine mood. He must have glanced cannibalistically at the cutlets, for Mrs. Shaw warningly exclaimed: "Now, George." He is said to have uttered Banshee curses and to have pitched in and eaten a pound of meat—or was it hog and hominy? Ochone! And he may have smoked a pipe in the hidden gardens of Coole Park! But I shan't vouch for the respectability of the anecdote, nor am I violating confidence, as it was told me without restrictions, though not by Lady Gregory.

I met Mr. Shaw at Baireuth, in 1896, on the esplanade of the Wagner Theatre, where he informed me of the whereabouts of John Runciman, music-critic of *The Saturday Review*. I liked the looks of Shaw—tall, weedy, a bearded man, with a gangling gait. I liked him better in 1903 when I saw him coming from a performance of his travesty in blank verse, "The Admirable Bashville, or Constancy Rewarded," at the Imperial Theatre. Reformers are usually dyspeptic. When I speak to them I always turn my head the other way, especially if I am close to a man who doesn't drink or smoke. That sort is pestiferous. But Bernard, the

Shaw, is eupeptic. He may have a weak stomach, irritable nerves, like most thinkers, but personally he is as sweet and wholesome as John Burroughs or Edwin Markham. He has magnetism when he chooses to turn on the current. He looks like Everyman. He is far from handsome, and his brogue is Corkonian. Careless as to dress, he is extremely courteous. He is said to be a physical coward, but boasts the rarer quality of moral heroism. He wrote at the time of McKinley's assassination that Czolgoz was the bravest man in America because he stood alone. Shaw proved that he didn't lack moral bravery when he bearded ex-Premier Asquith and his ministry amid the execrations of the press in England and America. Lloyd George owes his fellow-Celt a candle. Yet this dauntless ink-slinger once ran away as fast as his long legs could carry him from a socialistic gathering in Hyde Park. He didn't propose to dodge brickbats and dead cats, realising the truth that he who fights and runs away will live to fight another day. He did. William Morris, magnificent man and poet, would always roar when he related this anecdote. Daddy Long-legs, he called Shaw. In the deep and earnest eyes of Mr. Shaw are humour and kindliness. He begged me not to write anything more about his charitable disposition, "else," he added, "I'll be having all the beggars in London at my backdoor." And a mighty good thing it would have been for the beggars, though they might have got more advice than ha'pence. ("Keep it up, Shamus, keep it up!" I can hear George muttering as he reads this. "You are again advertising me, again being 'useful.'")

XXIX

HIS LETTERS

An extract from letter dated August 13, 1905: "You are quite right in saying that I lead the life of a saint; that is my trade. But a saint is not what you allege me to be. There is a convention that saints are disinterested and ascetic, just as there is a convention that sailors are frank and generous and unsuspicious. . . . When you try to make out that I pose as Diogenes (I don't), that I am at the heart just the same sloppy, maudlin, coward—making a metre of it as the feeblest of my readers, I fly at you promptly for debasing the moral currency." (The spectacle of Preacher George accusing anyone of debasing the moral currency after his successful efforts at the game is enough to make poor old George Eliot sit up on her eternal gridiron.) "I am really a coward speaking with authority of the dangers of cowardice, a sort of conceited prig who has found out the weakness of the current morality by practising it, a voluptuary who finds himself not on the infinite illusions of a monastic imagination, but on a sufficiency of actual adventures, and a dozen other things that I have not time to enumerate."

Far be it from me to insinuate that the spirit in my "Quintessence of Shaw" was an ironical spirit, and that both Beerbohm and Shaw missed it, whether wilfully or not, I can't say; but the fact remains that the entire chapter was written in the key of irony, extravagant irony, and that a professional ironist like "Max" and a

Brummagen-Englishman like Shaw did not see this is another confirmation of the suspicious hatred entertained by Europeans generally towards our playful American manner. I did call Shaw a saint—jestingly. I did address him as St. George or St. Bernard. I did say that, secretly, he was a sloppy sentimentalist. And he, of all men, became enraged at my very palpable fooling. Really, I am beginning to believe in Paul Hervieu's remark to me:—that indulgence in the mode ironical sterilises the sense of humour. Nevertheless, I cling to my superstition that Shaw is a wingless angel with an old maid's temperament, but one who can't take a joke. John Quinn is right:—the Irish are witty but lack the saving sense of humour.

Shaw never had an original idea, but decorated himself with tall feathers pulled from Ibsen, Strindberg, Hauptmann, Sudermann, even Maeterlinck, in his stage directions; above all with the feathers of Marx, Nietzsche and Samuel Butler. He made a fortune out of the Nietzsche philosophy, and his native Irish wit and impudence imposed on a public innocent of the sources of his knowledge. But oh! the box-offices of this "peasant lad" from Cork, who sold his Celtic birthright for a golden mess of British pottage. Neither with Synge and Yeats, nor with George Moore, Joyce, or Stephens, will he be ranged, though he had talent for fiction, witness his clever novels. And now after lecturing on the evil of being Bernard, let me say that the more I write about him the more I love him; as Oscar Wilde said—according to Vincent O'Sullivan—in reply to the question: "Do you know George Moore?" "Yes, I know George Moore, know him so very well that I haven't spoken to him for ten years." I revere Mr. Shaw the

man, though I dissemble my love, and I admire the
writer who succeeded in England where Ibsen and
Nietzsche did not, while exploiting their genius to his
own uses.

But the letters of George Bernard Shaw! Masterpieces, some of them. Superman Billingsgate, also.
We had another tiff over a letter he had sent me relative
to "Candida," in which he confided to my "discreation"
to use what I wished, and from which I extracted just
one paragraph, to be found on page 254 of Iconoclasts.
He had, this St. Bernard, the cheek to accuse me of printing his letters without his permission, he, all the while
hoping and praying I would print them in their entirety;
for notoriety is the breath of his nostrils. He even persuaded several critical friends in London that I had been
indiscreet and I was duly reproved for my "blithe" behaviour in the newspapers. You shall see that he not only
gave me permission but that I only reproduced one paragraph. Possibly he feared that again I might write of
his sporting genealogy that he was "W. S. Gilbert out
of Ibsen"—and an extravagant compliment at that.

Nor have I been the only victim in this respect of his
caprice. There were several of his "disciples" who
could tell the same tale. He assured me that I had picked
up my philosophy from the gutter, meaning that he hated
individualism; but his socialism has always been either
a joke or a puzzle to his friends and socialists alike. In
reality Shaw is the perfect flowering of the individualist,
the moral anarch in action. Just as Henry James expressed his dislike of Stendhal, without whom he and the
entire modern school of psychologists in fiction would
not have been as they are—this includes Bourget, Mere-

dith, even Tolstoy, who has handsomely acknowledged
his obligations to the author of La Chartreuse de Parme
—so Shaw practically admits that he is as much of an
anarch as Max Stirner. Karl Marx he long ago repudi-
ated. He would set up a pontifical throne of his own.
But he is only a condiment in the stodgy stew of British
socialism, a flavour, nothing more. He mocks at my in-
corrigible romanticism, but if the wages of sin is death, the
wages of goodness may be insipidity. Dostoievsky has
profoundly said that "One must be really a great man to
be able to make a stand even against common sense."
Shaw is too sensible. He thinks more of a drain-pipe
than a cathedral; socialism is only another name for
drain-pipes, and while modern man cannot live without
them, by them alone he cannot live. And he has paid
the penalty. It is vision, not open plumbing, that
counts. Vision Bernard Shaw has not; in his heart is a
box-office. He, the champion of liberty, is a philistine.
Little wonder I sent him a post-card from Sorrento in
answer to his rakehelly letters, and with this inscription:
a tomb, and on it the words: "Ci-gît, the first of the Shavians." But I was not exact. There is only one and
last Shavian, G. B. Shaw. And if the whole is better
than the half, then a half-Shaw is better than no bread.

Let us begin with his post-card dated 12 August, 1904,
somewhere in Rosshire: "This is well. I shall be back
in London in October, where we can foregather at our
ease. Meanwhile, give my compliments to the genial
sweet-mouthed Ibsen" (I was then en route to Norway).
"Of Strindberg I have a high opinion, possibly because
I have read very little of him—chiefly a story called
Memoirs of a Madman, or something like that, but ought

to have been called The Truth About My Confounded
Wife." (Probably this meant Strindberg's autobiography, Inferno.) "The truth about Candida is useless; nobody will believe it; and my letter will be scouted as an
obvious invention of your own. I am writing a play about
Ireland and England—study of national characteristics.
Are you going to Vienna by any chance? My German
translator, Trebitsch, can put you on to all the advanced
spirits there. G. B. S." His kind offer I didn't take
advantage of, as I had lived in Vienna and knew all the
modern crowd, Schnitzler, von Hofmansthal, and the rest.
My translator, Madame Lola Lorme, lived there. I was
even accorded a Huneker-Chopin Evening in the Beethoven Saal, so George was fetching coals to Newcastle.

From London under date of 4 January, 1904, he sent
me a very interesting communication, from which I
give an excerpt: "Dear Huneker: I was sorry not to see
more of you on your visit here, as you struck me as being
a likable old ruffian. My wife, since your review of 'Man
and Superman,' will not allow that you have a spark
of intelligence, but you must come and mollify her in
person when you are over next. It always amuses me
to see Candida stirring up oceans of sentiment. I think
I see you wallowing in it. Your writing always interests
me; but you will never really master the English drama
until you study English life and character. I speak as
an Irish foreigner who has had to learn it as one learns
Chinese. My first play, though performed in a crude
version in 1892, was not completed as it stands at present
until I had been more than twenty years in London;
and a great deal of the complaints made of it and other
works of mine by Scotch literary men in London (you
know that the literary life is lived in a vacuum) and by

Yankees, by yourself, is explained by the fact that English life, as I present it with a vestryman's and politician's knowledge of it (to say nothing of my private adventures), is irritatingly unnatural and repugnant. When I am on the general human nature plane, they are delighted with me. When I am on the English plane, they become soreheaded at once. They love Candida; she might be an American, an Irishwoman, a Scotchwoman, any woman you please. But take my specifically Englishwomen—Blanche in 'Widower's House' (only one remove from her grandmother's washtub), Vivie Warren, Lady Cicely Waynflete in that excellent Christian tract, 'Captain Brassbound's Conversion,' and, above all, Ann Whitefield and Violet Robinson in the Superman drama (Ann being my most gorgeous female creation; you can no more appreciate these from the other side of the Atlantic, clever as you are, than you could write Anthony Trollope's novels). The men annoy you in the same way; you can see the fun of Brittannus in 'Cæsar and Cleopatra' and perhaps of the American captain in 'Brassbound' and young Malone in the 'Superman,' where national types are openly made fun of; but the Hooligan in 'Brassbound,' the chauffeur Straker in the 'Superman,' the whole gang in 'Widower's House' arouse your instinctive anti-English prejudice almost as if they had been done by Thackeray, who was so stupidly English that, being a man of genius, he wasted his life for gentility's sake, on silly tittle-tattle relieved by occasional maudlin drivel."

Note: Mr. Shaw forgot that London is not far from New York, forgot that the characters he believed to be incomprehensible and irritating to Americans are old friends from a half-hundred fictions previous to his; and as for his notion of our "national types," yes, we did laugh over them because they were such caricatures, from the Shavian shadow-land. Abandon all reality, ye who enter here! might be a motto for his fantastic plays. There is no "instinctive anti-English prejudice" among Americans, unless they happen to be professional Irish-Americans. Curious, though, the "instinctive" Irish prejudice against Thackeray that endures. They have never forgiven him his stupid strictures on the people and customs of Erin. Shaw continues in the same vein:

"I tell you, you don't appreciate the vitality of the English; you see nothing but their stupidity, their moral cowardice, their utter lack of common sense, their naïve acquisitiveness, their brainless cruelty to children and criminals, their uncritical obtuseness or idolatry (as the case may be), their childish unscrupulousness, their insensibility to, and disbelief in, any means of persuasion except intimidation and coercion, and all the rest of it. And the stupidity, peculiar to the Englishman, which prevents him from knowing what he is doing, is really a stroke of genius on his part and is far more voluntary than the bright American thinks. Cromwell said that no man goes further than the man who doesn't know where he is going; and in that you have the whole secret of English success. What is the use of being bright, witty, subtle, genial, if these qualities lead to the subjection and poverty of India and Ireland, and to the political anarchy and corruption of the United States? What says my beautiful, vital, victorious odious-to-all-good-Americans, Miss Ann Whitefield? 'The only really simple thing is to go straight for what you want and grab it.' How disgusting! How cynical! so say you;

and so also say the Filipino and the Red Indian of you and yours." (Note: To us the chief characteristic of Ann was peculiarly Yankee.)

"Would you like to see what the English think of the Americans? Read Algernon Casterton, by Lady Sykes, a recent English novel. There you will see the English conception of the American woman as a cold-blooded sexless prostitute, who sells herself without scruple and without affection to the men who can give her the best time in London society, and who makes her husband pay for her favours as if he were a stranger. This is a revolting notion to an Englishman, whose chief conception of a wife is a woman who will not only keep house for him in return for her board, but will allow him the use of her person gratuitously.

"Some day I will write a play showing the good side of this American 'sexlessness' of which London complains so much. However, the moral for you is, study the English. There is much to be learnt from them; and I, who have been struggling for more than a quarter of a century with their knavish brainlessness, lose patience often enough; but I get on with them very well personally; find them enormously interesting; have got a good deal of training from them; and, in short, intend to stay here, and be one of the glories of literature. What is this tomfool story about my objecting to Mansfield's Bluntschli? ('Arms and the Man.') I never saw it—never objected to it. All these Mansfield stories are fudge. They are not exaggerations; quite the contrary. Richard's reputation is a feeble, vulgar, blundering attempt to suggest an outrageous but actual truth. But we are on excellent terms. He tells me that the American public will not stand me—that 'The Devil's Disciple' was played by

him to empty houses out of sheer devotion to art. On
the other hand, I call him Pompey and revile him as an
obsolete barnstormer because he funked Cæsar, and would
not even condescend to notice my alternative offer to
let him play the waiter in 'You Never Can Tell.' But
these passages leave no bad blood, because I have in
my desk the returns showing that the American public
spent about $150,000 to gloat over his Richard Dungeon;
and he considers 'Cæsar and Cleopatra' an imbecile bur-
lesque. So we both remain, each perfectly pleased with
himself, and perfectly friendly. Who is Arnold Daly?
Is he anything to the late Augustin? Talking of Augustin, Miss Marbury showed Ada Rehan 'Captain Brassbound's Conversion,' thinking she would jump at such
a part as Lady Cicely. But alas! Ada shared opinion
that Brassbound is rot—could see no point in it at all.
Does not this make you ashamed of yourself? This is
a Christmas-holiday letter, hence its length. I spend the
whole slack holiday time in a mad race to get abreast of
my correspondence. Yours ever, G. Bernard Shaw."
Note: As to the "sexlessness of the American woman,"
some disgruntled males over here believe that female
suffrage is the logical outcome of oversexed women.

How long ago seems 1904! Mansfield gone, charming Ada Rehan gone, Arnold Daly—"nothing" to the late
Augustin—grown up, having made his reputation in
Shaw comedies, Forbes-Robertson, with Mrs. Robertson in "Cæsar and Cleopatra"; Grace George in "Captain Brassbound's Conversion"—Mr. Shaw must sigh
for new actors to conquer. He called me an "inconti-
nent naïve sort of big baby"—this nearly fifteen years
ago—adding apropos of that quotation about Candida:

"I know the risk I ran, and even foresaw as an agreeable possibility that you would blurt the thing out and give me a chance to lecture you." No! George didn't set a trap for me with his smooth phrase "at your discretion," did he? And he didn't wish me to print it, did he, so that he could contradict me? Oh! No! Not to-day, baker, call to-morrow with a crusty cottage!—as we used to say in the dear old days at Dulwich. Follows the fatal paragraph, the one I quoted in Iconoclasts (in 1905):

"Dear Huneker: Don't ask me conundrums about that immoral female Candida. Observe the entry of W. Burgess: 'You're not the lady h'used to typewrite for him.' Prossy is a very highly selected young person indeed, devoted to Morell to the extent of helping him in the kitchen, but to him the merest pet rabbit, unable to get the smallest hold on him. Candida is as unscrupulous as Siegfried: Morell himself at least sees that; that 'no law will bind her.' She seduces Eugene just exactly as far as it is worth her while to seduce him. She is a woman without 'character' in the conventional sense. Without brains and strength of mind she would be a wretched slattern and voluptuary. She is straight for natural means, not for conventional ethical ones. Nothing can be more cold-bloodedly reasonable than her farewell to Eugene: 'All very well, my lad; but I don't quite see myself at 50 with a husband of 35.' It's just this freedom from emotional slop, this unerring wisdom on the domestic plane, that makes her so completely mistress of the situation. Then consider the poet. She makes a man of him finally by showing him his own strength—that David must do without poor Uriah's wife. And then she pitches in her picture of the home, the onions and the tradesmen, and the cosseting of big

baby Morell. The New York hausfrau thinks it a little
paradise; but the poet rises up and says: 'Out, then,
into the night with me'—Tristan's holy night. If this
greasy fool's paradise is happiness, then I give it to you
with both hands; 'life is nobler than that.' That is
'the poet's secret.' The young things in front weep to
see the poor boy going out lonely and bareheaded in the
cold night to save the proprieties of New England Puritanism; but he is really a god going back to his heaven;
proud, unspeakably contemptuous of the 'happiness'
he envied in the days of his blindness, clearly seeing that
he has higher business on hand than Candida. She has
a little quaint intuition of the completeness of his cure;
she says, 'he has learnt to do without happiness.'

"As I should certainly be lynched by the infuriated
Candidamanics if this view of the case were made known,
I confide it to your discretion. I tell it to you because
it is an interesting example of the way a scene which
could be conceived and written only by transcending
the ordinary notion of the relations between the persons,
nevertheless stirs the ordinary emotions to a very high
degree, all the more because the language of the poet,
to those who have not the clue to it, is mysterious and
bewildering, and, therefore, worshipful. I divined it
myself before I found out the whole truth about it.

"Blank is a very decent fellow; but he persists, like
most intellectuals, in dictating conditions to a world
which has to organise itself in obedience to laws of life
which he doesn't understand any more than you or I.
Individualism is all very well as a study product; but that
is not what is happening. Society is integrating, not
individualising; and it is better to lay hold of what is
doing and make the best of it than to sit complaining

that it won't do something else. Trusts are most excellent things—as superior to competitive shopkeeperism as symphonies are to cornet solos; but they need more careful scoring and longer rehearsals and better conducting. The only individualism worth looking at now is breeding the race and getting rid of the promiscuity and profligacy called marriage.

"Is there such a thing in America as a decent publisher—one whom I could trust, in reason, to sell my books on commission if I manufactured them myself? I am tired of wasting time negotiating with fools who are afraid to publish the Superman, and rogues who want to get too soft a bargain over it. It is copyrighted all safely; but it lies there dead whilst *McClure's* and *Harper's* and the like funk it, and others want to grab it forever and each. Yr. G., Bernard Shaw."

Thus Shaw on Shaw. Doubtless he changed his mind many times since 1904. Candida may have become to him charmless. She was transferred from Ibsen's Lady of the Sea with the charm and poetry omitted. Ibsen, too, can be charmless, but his small-town frumps are often vital, intense. Both Ibsen and Nietzsche were butchered to make a Shavian holiday. In Iconoclasts I have paid my tribute to the brilliant gifts of Mr. Shaw, to his invincible courage, love of his fellow beings—for if he chides us it is only to correct our weaknesses—his detestation of cruelty and injustice, his splendid sincerity and superabundance of normal sense—also to his sublime capacity for distorting facts if it suits his mood. With his cosmical intellect he should not be a mere playwright amusing an inconstant public with his profound japes and jests; he should be Premier, Pope, or Kaiser. I proffer no apologies for quoting him so freely; indeed, I think he should feel indebted to me for my generous spirit.   But I'm quite sure he won't.   Yet, as I have said before, I have no grievance against Mr. Shaw.   He is, or was, my most distinguished "enemy."   I must add that he has most graciously given me permission to reprint in part the foregoing letters.

The query about a publisher was soon answered.   I went to my old friend, Arthur Brentano, and within a week Mr. Shaw was provided with the best of publishers. Since then all his books and plays have been handled by this enterprising house, and I think the unsentimental socialist has had no cause to complain over the arrangement.   I need hardly say that as I am not a "literary agent," I was not "interested" in the transaction except as a friend of author and publisher.   It was another case of being "useful" to Mr. Shaw, and he was duly grateful. I should not have resurrected these memories if I had not been delving into the past, as I think it prudent to let sleeping Shavians lie, but when he is naughty he has to be rebuked even if he is a naughty grandfather, on whose banner is inscribed the strange device: Equality, Envy, Indigestion.   Ah! if you had only come over here years ago, Master, we might have civilised, made something out of you, if only a Sachem in Tammany Hall.

XXX

A HALF–HAMLET

I

It is lucky for a man that he doesn't marry his first love; luckier for the woman. Some Russian has said—Dostoievsky, I think—that man is unhappy because he doesn't know he is happy. Most men live in a state of innocence till they marry. Then they awaken and remorse sets in. Women don't believe this because woman is as a rule incapable of remorse. Let me relate the story of my most interesting sentimental hesitations; a story in which the heroine is a half-Hamlet and also plays the rôle of real protagonist. I was in love, yet an onlooker. But what an enchantment of the heart! It happened in Rome, years ago. I was young, green as a green apricot, and overflowing with belief in woman, and a constitutional distrust of myself. That is the beginning of wisdom.

An October sun slanted its yellow glory from the western sky as I entered the narrow gate of the Protestant cemetery, which I had achieved after a dusty walk from my apartment at the top of the Spanish Stairs, by way of the Porta San Paolo. I was warm and craved repose: palms, pines, willows, olives, aloes, and flame-shaped cypresses in shaded alleys promised a pleasing haven. It was my favourite spot. Summer afternoons when Rome was a faded photograph of herself I would read, sitting on the grassy mounds above the bones of the buried. Keats and Shelley touched my imagination

277

here as nowhere. I had become selfish about the place and resented the appearance of strangers, odious tourists carrying red books, who talked loudly, whispered, giggled, or stared condescendingly. So sensitive was I that invariably I questioned Angelo, the smiling guardian of the doorway, as to the number of foreign invaders. On this occasion Angelo held up two fingers. I sighed my relief. A pair of humans I could avoid. Up the gentle slope which leads to the tombs of Shelley and Trelawney I slowly passed. To my annoyance, I saw a man and woman before the altar of the dead. The woman was on her knees. Even that appropriate attitude did not mollify me. They were intruders. I hurried down-hill and went to the grave of Keats. There, at least, was grief made more classic by the appearance of the Cestius pyramid. But again I was disappointed, for the appealing voices of beggar-boys came to me through gratings in the nearest wall. I shook a threatening head at these importuners and strode away. It was one of my gloomy days when all the poetry stored up in me mingled with my spiritual spleen and caused dolorous hours. I was then of a receptive temperament without an outlet for periodical crises of emotion. I would joke about this condition, calling it a congestion of the poetic centres, yet I was bitterly chagrined when I realised my inability to relieve myself in creative verse.

Suddenly my shoulder was brushed and a contralto voice asked a pardon in English. It was the lady I had seen kneeling. She was garbed in green and carried flowers which she placed on the grave of Keats, not forgetting his beloved friend, John Severn, who lies hard by in the ground. She again knelt and, her face in her ungloved hands, she seemed more in meditation than

prayer. Her fingers, pressed against her eyes, were thin
and white, yet suggested nervous force. When she removed them and arose to rejoin her companion, I saw
the features of a young woman which attracted because
of their purity and intense expression. But I could not
conceive how anyone could thus sorrow after a dead
poet. I love Keats, revere his resting-place, but this—
this was something more personal. Perhaps, I mused,
as I looked at the woman's slender figure, she is some
sentimental girl who had especially visited Rome to stand
at the tomb of one whose name is not "writ in water,"
but on imperishable marble. For a moment I was stirred
by the image of the act, and then felt a wave of irritation mount within me. She had reached her former
position and I noticed that the man with her was big of
frame, expansive in his movements, and dressed like an
Englishman abroad. At once I instinctively disliked
him. My nerves told me that I was unstrung, and I
wondered whether I had made a mistake by remaining
in Rome all summer; the notion that I was suffering from
a mild attack of malaria was more grateful than the con-
viction that it was hyperæsthesia. This feeling prompted
me to walk boldly towards the couple as I lifted my hat.
Otherwise, why should I, shy and slightly supercilious,
risk a snub from strangers? They cordially received me,
and the man said in a booming bass voice: "Really, it's
joyous to meet a countryman in this lonely cemetery.
I was telling Mrs. Saint-Hilary—" "But, Lewis, how
do you know the gentleman is English?" interposed the
lady. I made a nervous gesture of dissent. "I am an
American, but I adore your poets." She glanced her
gratitude and would have spoken but for the jarring
laughter of her husband. "After this," he effusively

exclaimed, "I'll never go by clothes.   At all events, you
have an English tailor."

   Annoyed, I bowed, yet without the acrid feeling I had
smothered a few moments before; so sudden was the revolution of my mood.   Bearded, imposing in girth, with the
head of a fighter, of a master of enterprises, Saint-Hilary
had made an immediate impression.   Either one liked
him or got out of his pathway.   He was given to elbowing
his way through the crowds of life—and I realised the
animal force and attractiveness of this new acquaintance.
Presently I was engaged in analysing the charm of Mrs.
Saint-Hilary.   She was one of those rare women whose
air is captivating in its candour.   I set her down as a
poet—and then I remembered in a flash.   Of course!
She was the wife of the robust correspondent of a promi-
nent English newspaper.   I smiled.   "I think we ought
to know each other," I ventured.   "There is at least one
drawing-room in Rome where we may meet some day."
The girl clasped her hands, crying: "I knew it.   The
Bernervilles.   And you are James Huneker who reads
poetry on the tombs of Keats and Shelley and transposes
their poetry to the key of Schumann and Chopin.   What
did I say, Lewis?   What did I say?"   She was all enthusiasm, and my perplexity increased as I recalled her
earlier elegiac expression.   The nonsense about Shelley
and Chopin!   Mrs. Bernerville must have been in one
of her exaggerated gossipy moods.   The husband took
my hand.   "I liked you from the first.   Old Bernerville
told me about you.   You are very solid over there."
He nodded in the direction of Rome.   "Yes, I sometimes read here, oftener dream my afternoons away.   In
fine, I'm a dilettante, and that's why I love Rome—of

all cities it is the one where you can be the laziest with
most dignity."

We talked of our friends, of our preferences in art and
literature, of our beloved poets. Saint-Hilary proposed
departing. "We live up in the Ludovisi Quarter, on the
Via Sallustiana, and darkness soon comes these autumn
days. Let us walk as far as the Porta San Paolo and
take .a carriage there." "And I am at the Trinità de'
Monti." "Our neighbour, practically," said the Englishman. "Come, we must be going, Dottie." I felt
resentful. Dottie! What a name! And how little
suited to her spiritual personality was her good-natured,
tiresome husband. In the carriage facing Mrs. Saint-
Hilary, I studied her face. Her eyes reflected the slaty
grey-green of the sky. For me she was like a harp that
vibrated, yet had never sounded the eternal music within
her.

II

When a young man wishes to resolve the enigma of a
strange woman, to evoke her submerged music, he is
likely to push his curiosity beyond its province, his virtuosity beyond its power. I remembered this as I slowly
walked along the Via Sistina. The weather was chilly,
one of those damp evenings in which sounds a cheerless
autumn, the leading-motive of a rapidly approaching
winter. I did not feel in a resilient humour; if at that
precise minute I could have avoided visiting the Bernervilles, I should have been almost content. I knew that
the Saint-Hilarys were to be there. Mrs. Bernerville
had written me a brief, breathless note full of underlined
adjectives and enthusiastic gasps. O what an impression I had made on her dear friends! Mrs. Saint-Hilary

had not minced her words—I looked like an artist—
while her husband, dear, old, bluff Saint-Hilary—a rough
diamond and a man of importance in the literary world
—he, too, likes you; a good fellow, he calls you, very
different from the average critic! I sniffed. She was
impossibly delightful, cette dame! Why had I given her
my books? I reddened at the ascription "average
critic." What impertinence! What a patronising tone!
I regretted my promise. I loathed strange people. For
me success in life meant avoiding new faces. Even the
memory of Mrs. Saint-Hilary's face, vaguely silhouetted
in the twilight, did not touch me. Her mystery evap-
orated in the flabby phrases of Mrs. Bernerville; besides,
the Bernervilles were too rich; the possession of much
money results in grossness. I had reached the Piazza
Barbarina and its rococo Bernini Tritons. Soon I was
shaking hands with my hostess, wondering why I had
come.

"It's good to see you" were her welcoming words.
"I've asked no one but the Saint-Hilarys. Bernerville
expects his old pirate, as he calls him, the Prince Abbazia"
—that stupid old bore, I thought—"but let us go to the
fire. What disagreeable nights we are getting. I recall
Rome when its Octobers were like the Mays of Florence."
Mrs. Bernerville was in the fading fifties, small, alert,
her face like a wizened pear. She said she was from
Boston, but in moments of mockery her husband would
mention the name of a small Western town as her birthplace. She always endured this sarcasm with placid
humour; under the severest strain her temper always
was admirable. Dressed in black lace, wearing a collar
of black pearls, she appeared to me a richly evolved
beetle, including its celerity—she would circle about a

room, about her husband, or a victim with an accompanying loquacity that compelled rather than charmed. The
Salon was empty, save for our presence. Sitting opposite
the fireplace I forgot my irritability as I listened to her
budget of gossip about people we knew. I longed to put
a few questions concerning the Saint-Hilarys. Who was
the wife? Had they been married many years? But
my companion pursued a zigzag monologue in which she
exposed with touching innocence the troubles of Count
O'Ragan and his pretty spouse. She had her own theory
concerning the course of this unfortunate marital squab-
ble—it was not altogether the fault of the Count and his
passion for gambling. Oh! no. If she dared—why,
yes, certainly the Saint-Hilarys were happy. Whoever
doubted it, Dottie is Irish, her husband, need one ask,
English. He is a trump, his wife a bit of humbug.

Dottie a humbug! For me such familiarity bred frost.
"And," continued Mrs. Bernerville, "she is a poet, like
yourself." I raised deprecating hands. "Dear lady, I
am not a poet—only a dreamer. Pray do not say any
more about my books. My poetry goes into the waste-
basket. After all the praises you have heaped on my
ineffectual head, I fear Mrs. Saint-Hilary will find me a
sad disappointment." "Praise! I! Why I really told
her you were an inarticulate Milton, or was it Browning?
If you would only fall in love and be jilted, you might
possibly overwhelm us with a masterpiece. But don't fall
in love with our Dottie—it would be a waste of time.
Ah! there you are, Bernerville." Glad of the interruption,
I cordially greeted the old man. The Miltonic allusion
had put my politeness to the straining test. Oh! for a
vast wilderness from which the tactless would be forever
barred.

"How are you feeling, young man? Why don't we

see you oftener? If I'm not in, there's the Madame, who can discourse Shakespeare and the musical glasses. And then don't forget, I have some wonderful Burgundy in my cellar. What you miss!" The short, apoplectic Bernerville, with his brilliant, Oriental eyes, his wheedling red lips, and old-fashioned side-whiskers looked more like a Wall Street banker than an American who had lived in Italy thirty years. "Oh! let's talk of music," impatiently broke in his wife. "We were talking of Sgambati and Liszt." I closed my eyes resignedly. I was accustomed to her foreshortenings of the truth. She would talk of Sgambati, with whom she had studied ten or twenty years earlier, and of Liszt and the Princess Sayn-Wittgenstein, before the end of the evening. It was one of my particular tortures to hear from her rapidly moving lips the secret reason why Cardinal Antonelli had interfered with the projected marriage of Liszt. She even insinuated that Liszt had asked the Cardinal to refuse his consent, as the pianist-composer wished somehow to wriggle out of his promise to marry that formidable bluestocking, the Princess. I had been retold that incident at least a hundred times.

"I say, where are our guests? It's nearly ten o'clock. No Saint-Hilary, no Dottie, the passionate pilgrim, no Abbazia! I wonder where that old pirate is?" Bernerville held his wrath in his pudgy white hand and wickedly smiled. His friends often boasted that he could shatter any reputation with a gleam of his shining teeth. The sound of a remote door closing, then approaching footsteps—it must be the Saint-Hilarys. Unannounced they entered, the lady on gliding feet, Saint-Hilary following with his amiable shuffle. Mrs. Saint-Hilary did not seem

too cordial, while her husband with his air of false bonhomie was intolerable. These people, who had been so
desirable the other day, at close range were average folk.
With pessimistic fancy I immediately saw everything
drab. She had not removed her wraps in the anteroom—
she was a privileged person; there was a touch of fur on
her shoulders, and the round Astrakhan hat on her
shapely head gave her an exotic air. A Russian princess
fresh from the Neva, a driver of snow-sledge and rein-
deers! I saw the light from the blazing logs reverberate
from the deep grey eyes. Then she went into the apartment of Mrs. Bernerville, and I wondered why such a
trivial happening as the reflection of fire in a woman's
eyes, sweet-cupped and dark-lashed, should so trouble
my soul.

"Come into the den and have something decent before
you begin to slop tea," growled Bernerville to the two
men. "I will that," was the ready response of Saint-
Hilary. I shook my head. I preferred staring into the
flame, hoping that it might evoke her glance. As the
ladies returned, the expected Prince arrived. He stiffly
bowed and looked in the direction of the smoking-room.
Mrs. Bernerville laughed. "We will excuse you, Abbazia. They are in there." "I'm thirsty," he curtly
replied and disappeared. "Bernerville has odd cronies,
hasn't he?" asked his wife. "You've been coming to
this house for years. Tell me, have you ever met an
intimate of my husband's you could converse with over
a minute?" I replied: "Frankly, no." "Have you
written much?" asked, in her modulated tones, Mrs.
Saint-Hilary. I forgave her the brusqueness of her
salutation. At one swift leap all my early interest revived. It was her voice that held me; it was as tender

as the green of newly put forth leaves. "You are a poet," she gaily asserted; "what image held your tongue in check then? Come, give us the fresh vintage of your fancy." Her husband away, she fairly warmed. O the Celt in her eyes and their melancholy setting! I stammered. My conceit deserted me. An inward necessity bade me keep silent, though I longed to respond in lyric phrase. The first man who compared a woman with a rose was a poet, Voltaire averred, but the second a fool. So I did what infatuated poets have done before me—I kept my peace and drank my tea hot. Not only did I feel like a fool, I know I acted one. The two women chatted over their work. Mrs. Bernerville politely inquired if Mr. Saint-Hilary would soon finish his book on Celtic Antiquities. "He is a desperately lazy man, my husband, notwithstanding his bigness. He thinks he has laboured like a galley-slave when he has finished his daily stint for his newspaper. Aren't men naturally slothful?" She turned to me. "I am, if I may reason from the general to the particular?" "Yes, but you are a poet." "I am not. I love poetry as much as music, but I never write it." "You know what dear Mrs. Bernerville says of you?" "That I'm an inarticulate—" I flushed. "I don't believe it. You will write when the time comes. Some friendly soul should stir you." "Ah, but where is she?" My tone was so mocking that the two women rallied me. The elder vivaciously exclaimed: "If you are going to talk like that, I'll leave you alone and go see what mischief those men are up to. Æsthetics bore me." She scampered away.

The silence endured several minutes. Mrs. Saint-Hilary went to the fire. Her eyes were dark, her face flushed—I thought I detected a certain fatigue in them; the face with its decidedly irregular profile was without distinction at this moment. Perhaps she was not so happy as her friends believed. She spoke: "I think I recognise in you a trait of our time. Every generation produces its share of souls—disillusioned. All sorts of ingenious, also silly, theories are put forth to explain those souls. Some say decadent." "Poor, overworked word," I hazarded. "True, but handy for the phrase-makers." I interrupted: "Candidly, I can't complain of my health. And if I've published no verse, that's no reason why you should suspect me as a pessimist." "You are not a pessimist," she gravely said. "You might be summed up as a half-Hamlet—one who dares not—but may." I was flattered, and wondered with the fatuity of youth why she took so much interest in my case. She read my mood. Then, with a burst of gaiety: "Now don't let us become morbid discussing your hidden ambitions. I know your sort"—"Saint-Hilary?" "Good heavens! He is a steam-engine. And what a gift of expression." She paused, and lightly adjusting with her slim fingers an ornament in her hair, she rapidly moved around the dimly lighted room. I followed her with my eyes, my envy of her husband revived by her warm praise. Yet a few moments before she had called him lazy. Logic from such a temperament! "You are very Celtic," I declared, "very! You ascribe to me a Hamletic quality; half-Hamlet, I think you ironically remarked, but I am an observer enough to ask you whether among your own sex there are not half-Hamlets, quarter-Hamlets. You have known so many among mine?" She smiled. "There speaks the wounded vanity of the man, of the poet. You remember what Heine said about man being the vainest animal, and the poet the vainest among men?" "Yes, but you haven't answered my question. Are you, too, a half-Hamlet?" "Alas, to be a woman with a nomad's heart in me," she quoted. "Do you know who sang that? Dora Sigerson, loveliest of Neo-Irish poets. I, a feminine half-Hamlet? Never! I'm a nomad. I must wander or suffocate. I hate the stuffy life of my sex. The indoor sex, I have named it. Oh! if I had been born a man—a man. The history of heroes is the history of youth. That's Disraeli." "What would you do if you were a man?" I eagerly questioned. "Make love to pretty women, like all of them?" "Pouf! Is that the only ideal of man? No, I should write great poems." Her voice, usually muffled in timbre, rang out: "Where is the nomad you spoke of a moment ago? To be a poet means charming one's spirit to the ink-well." "To live my poems, of course." She was almost pettish.

Then with a gust of laughter Saint-Hilary entered, followed by the others. His face was red and his enormous frame slightly swayed. Evidently Bernerville had something stronger than Burgundy. "Ah! there you are again, my boy." (He sees two of me, I muttered.) "And no doubt entertaining Mrs. Saint-Hilary. I suppose you swapped verses. She is a poet, you know. Now, Dottie, put on your singing-robes and say something nice in your sweet Irish voice. Recite one of your own poems, girlie." Mrs. Saint-Hilary coldly looked at him but did not reply. The giant went to her, sliding across the highly polished floor, and laughingly took her by the wrists. Everyone was amused at his persistence except myself. The party broke up. Saint-Hilary, his high spirits slain by the disdainful countenance of his wife, bade the Bernervilles a glum good-by, and the

Prince was helped down-stairs to his carriage by polite servants. Mrs. Bernerville wasn't shocked, whispering that it was his regular evening performance. Suave and mysterious Bernerville was fresher than all of us. I slipped away. What people! What a misspent night! And Mrs. Bernerville had not failed to drop a last deprecatory word about Dorothea Saint-Hilary. I slowly went home by a familiar route. In my chambers I found a fire, dressing-gown, a supply of tobacco, and a decanter of sherry carefully arranged by the housekeeper. "Now," I ejaculated, "is the time to enjoy myself." I made myself comfortable, and getting pen and paper I proceeded to manufacture an inventory of my platonic soul, a practice I never omitted before retiring. Many ideas crossed my mind. She had said some memorable things. Why did she manifest such interest? And the husband! Happy with such a man? Au grand jamais! I looked behind me in the shadows. Despite my agnosticism, I experience "mystic fear" when alone after midnight. What joy in the reaches of the gloomy hour when the vitality is at its lowest ebb, and the hobgoblins of conscience are stirring, to have the image of a sympathetic companion beside you. Decidedly some men don't deserve their happiness. And lighting a cigar I resolutely began to rewrite the eleventh line of an original sonnet in French.

III

Early the second morning I went out. I had not left my rooms since my return from the Bernervilles. The success of my sonnet—I had finished the remaining lines before I went to bed—gave my muse a boost. In one

evening I had actually written three sonnets, the work-
manship of which was not indifferent; already buzzed in
my head the scheme of a sonnet-sequence.   But the
sharp, glorious blue of the sky that saluted me this second
morning speedily drove rhyming from my thoughts.
Hastily swallowing my coffee, I was soon striding through
a leafy avenue of the Pincio garden, wondering whether
life was not, after all, worth while.   The sweep of the
picture, Rome beneath, the misty dream of a poet, spurred
my nerves from their languor.   I traversed the outer
path of the garden as far as the Piazza del Popolo, and
was hesitating when a hand was placed on my arm.
"Good morning, Sir Poet."   "Mrs. Saint-Hilary!   What
luck!   Only a moment ago I was thinking of you."
"What a fib!   Your eye is too clear for a man that has
been indulging in retrospection.   No!   No!   You thought
what a wonderful morning it is.   You said to yourself
you were glad to be alive."   "You read my mind like a
gypsy—like the gypsy you are!"   "I feel like a gypsy
this morning.   And you?"   "Not like a half-Hamlet."
"Ah!   That phrase sticks."   "It doesn't fit.   I'm for
action.   Let's walk over Rome."   "Merci!   I have a
breakfast engagement with Mr. Saint-Hilary."   I must
have looked so displeased that she smiled one of her
smiles of half-pity.   I winced.   I was a mild mark for
her wit.   What did she think of me?   And to betray
my jealousy like a raw boy fresh from school!   I stiffened
my spine.   The crisp sunshine painted her as a most
desirable picture.   "If we are to be friends," she soberly
suggested, "let us not mind the pebbles in our own
shoes.   Because you feel like a freed balloon to-day, you
fancy that the cityful should rejoice with your joy.
How like a poet.   What if I told you that I came out here

to be alone, so utterly miserable am I. What would you
say?" "That I don't believe it, my dear Mrs. Saint-
Hilary. I ask your pardon for my selfishness. I feel
well this morning, and, manlike, I wish you to feel the
same."

Then in tremulous anticipation I gazed at her. What
had operated on my spirits to liberate such emotions?
Compared with this minute, my life had been a-slumber-
ing. To my scrutiny she seemed more buoyant than the
other night at the Bernervilles. I endeavoured to grasp
the secret of her fleeting expression; but her eyes were
the guardians of mute treasures, they had no message for
me. I suppressed my eagerness. I determined not to
be cajoled into self-betrayal. We walked in the direction of the Villa Medici. We did not enter; instead,
turned into a road that follows the curves of the bridle-
path, and if we did not speak, our brains were busy building—what? I don't know. So little had happened to
me, so little of value, that I could not help pondering
the possibilities of my companion's career. There was she
walking, almost touching me, and I knew no more about
her soul than if she hailed from a neighbouring planet.
I had grown to distrust my early belief that women were
easy to read because of their being more instinctive than
men, and therefore wore their hearts exposed. But no
one is easy to read, men no more than women. Each
human is an isolated complex of organs. The greatest
readers of the human heart are those who more fully
than others interpret themselves. Humility itself in the
presence of my new friend, I asked myself whether I
could seal my lips so effectually that she might seek in
vain for my secret. I firmly believed it to be a secret.
Suddenly I spoke: "Let us talk of your Celtic poets. I

read them.   I love but I can't always understand them."
She turned moist eyes towards me.   She moved my heart
like the faint sound of nocturnal fountains.   "Ireland is
all my life.   When I'm there, I'm unhappy.   That's
because I'm Irish.   But when I'm away, I'm unhappy,
and that is Irish, too."   Everything about her seemed
to live; the flower in her hair was faded in comparison
with the sparkle in her flower-like eyes.   Her smile was
as tricksy as the new moon seen through flying cloud-scud.

I was delighted.   I had come out with an unusual
fund of good humour, and here I was expending it upon
my companion.   I hardly thought of myself.   Truly a
novel, refreshing experience for an egotist.   She was
conscious that she puzzled me, for she stopped and in
her cheerful every-day voice commanded: "About face!
march!"   My heart beat heavily; though it was midday and the sun blazing hot for October, the air seemed
cooler.   Obeying, I kept in rhythm with her impetuous
gait.   We soon passed out before the Piazzo Margherita.
She signalled a negative.   Then, at last, to the Piazza
Barberini?   No!   She would say good-by at the church.
I looked at her so earnestly that she coloured.   Nothing
was said about a future meeting.   I became doleful.
"Ah! half-Hamlet," she teasingly protested.   And she
quickly walked along the Via Sistina.   "Celt!" I cried,
as I watched her graceful, swaying figure.   I then went
indoors, drank tea, and smoked till dinner-time.   Oh! if
only I had the courage at the moment when most needed.
To be a thunderbolt in action—that was my unrealised
ambition.   But a half-Hamlet!

IV

That night at the Teatro Costanzi I saw a play by D'Annunzio, a violent tragedy related in the golden voice of the poet, but not akin to my mood. I wished myself far away from this huge theatre, sonorous with applause. I left before the culminating act and paced the streets. The moon had blotted out the stars and, like a silver-white pyx, swung in the firmament; there was a cloud-shine on the fleecy boulders that nimbly accompanied it through the blue. This sky incited me to vague heroisms, yet I was more curious about the look of Rome in the moon-rays—so ingrained my romantic imagination. It was not long before I turned off the Corso. The Piazza de Spagna was deserted; not even a carriage disturbed its august emptiness. The moon transposed the trees of the Pincio into ebon music and the Spanish Stairs were streaked with bars of light. As I neared the top I discerned the figure of a woman, closely hooded, who recklessly ran down the steps. If she had not recoiled as she passed me I should not have paused to look at her. "Mrs. Saint-Hilary!" She went on, taking two steps at a time. So swift was her flight that instinctively I gazed above for her pursuer. I saw none. I followed her, but not far; the encounter had unnerved her. She stopped at the bottom of the steps. I could not distinguish her features. I took her hand and found it icy. "Dear, dear lady, what troubles you so? Are you ill?" She did not reply. I could feel that she trembled. "Let me bring you home. You are frightened. I'll ask no questions. It is not well for you to be out alone at this hour." I sought to lead up the stairs. She snatched her hand from mine. "No, no, not that way!

Good God—not home!" I was appalled by the extravagant misery of her tone. Here was the last act of
the drama I had not sat out, and one infinitely more
poignant than the fiction of the Italian poet. Without
artifice was the soul of the woman bared to me. I was
dumb with the horror of my imagining. What else could
have driven this gentle creature out on the streets of a
strange city—what else but—! I ground my teeth in
rage. My phlegmatic ego dissolved in the fire of her
sorrow. Like a flash it came upon me. I loved her. I
had loved her from the first. And she had been driven
from her husband by reason of some nameless outrage
at his hands. Brute! I uttered a hoarse cry and gripped
her. "Come," I whispered. "Come. I'll not trouble
you with a single question. I understand everything.
Come with me—up the stairs. There is refuge for you
at the hotel. I'll not worry you with my company."
She regarded me with blank eyes—I caught their inter-
mittent glint. When she spoke, her voice was toneless.
"I'll go with you, but you must take me to my home.
In the Ludovisi Quarter. You've brought me to my
senses. Don't, dear friend, set me down as a mad-
woman. I was crazy. There was provocation. It's
past. I'll go back. Forget all about this when we
part." I felt moonstruck, my personality evaporating.
This was our farewell, the end of my brief romance.
She would go back to the man she loved despite his bru-
tality. The reason for this love! Whistle down the
wind for the answer. I brought her to the door of her
hotel and went away without a word. Twice she had
sent me from her—once playfully and now in sorrow.
Celtic she was. She had the cruel heart of the Celt.
. . . Was the music in her worth the hearing?

V

My ill-luck pursued me to Venice. When it rains in Rome there are the palaces, the picture-galleries, the marbles, the churches; but at Venice the meeting of the waters proves doubly monotonous. The wet of the canal enters the soul. The drippings of the sky are as the eternal tears of the banished gods. In the Ducal Palace sombre dampness dowers with humid eyes immemorial portraits. Along the waterways the wind howls as it transfixes the wanderer with lance-like thrusts. I execrated life when I stepped into the hotel gondola at the station, and sat shivering and propelled through the desolate darkness of narrow waterways where murder and mystery might lurk under mean, flickering gas-jets. The melancholy challenge of my gondolier failed to evoke poetic visions of nocturnal Venice. I was glad to gain the steps of my hotel. Everyone was congealed by the cold, everything saturated with the rain. I did not long remain in my apartment. Without, the storm-drums of the Adriatic were ruffling; the shape of the gale was lost in the wrack of spilt mist.

At Bauer-Grunwald's it was cheerful, the most cheerful café on the lagoons. Crowded with tourists, eating, drinking, smoking, talking, the picture appealed to me because of its human quality. Nevertheless, I was homesick for Rome, for the hospitable, if tiresome, Bernervilles—the Madame with her teasing chatter, her husband with his malicious wit. Sick, too, though in another way, for the sight of a woman's face. . . . "What an ass I am! Very well, garçon, I'll sit at this table. First give me the wine-card." I had not immediately quitted Rome after that night. But I avoided my friends.

I wished to hear no gossip. I could surmise without being boldly told that unhappiness camped in the household of the Saint-Hilarys. After a week the city became intolerable and I fled to Venice—where it rained, where it would rain forever. I ordered some cold meat, a salad, a bottle of Bordeaux. Then, relieved of the head waiter's presence, I looked about me. Yes, those visitors from the world over were practical; bad weather didn't daunt them. And then my roving eye took in a man who sat smiling opposite me. Affrightedly, I clutched my knees. Was I dreaming? No, the vision was too real, too burly, too much of the flesh. His big red fist extended, Saint-Hilary crossed the aisle. "You here! What luck! I thought I'd be forced to put in an interminable evening drinking and talking to the waiter." I tried not to see the offered hand, but I felt it as it squeezed with unaffected vigour my thin fingers. I loathed the monster. I had expended my nervous energy for a week damning him, and here he was—but why in Venice? And alone. More ill-luck.

"I've been drinking a lot for the last ten days," Saint-Hilary confessed in a husky voice. "You won't mind, will you? You're a good chap; hard to make out. I'm in a heap of trouble. Let me bother you. I'm alone. Here, waiter! Fetch my glass to this gentleman's table. Hurry up!" The order was given with characteristic energy as he dropped into a chair beside me, bidding me go ahead and eat my supper. "I'll be all right soon." Sick at heart, I swallowed the food, sawdust and ashes to my taste. After some wine, I plucked up wit enough to ask Saint-Hilary what he was doing away from Rome. "Doing? I'll just tell you, my boy. I'm up here looking for Mrs. Saint-Hilary, for my wife.

What are you doing here, may I ask?" The question, though put without ill-temper, made me pale. "Why, Mr. Saint-Hilary, I only arrived an hour ago on the morning train from Rome." I stammered, actually feeling guilty. "I know it, my boy, I know it. You are on the safe side, but a little soft on Dottie—all the young painters, poets, composers are. I'm not blaming you for her running away from me. She vamoosed the ranch after you brought her back from the Spanish Stairs." "She told you?" I struggled not to appear embarrassed. "Yes, and told what a trump you were. You behaved like a gentleman. I acted like a brute. Don't scold. I am a brute. When I accused her of taking too much interest in you—say, man, don't get up so suddenly, my nerves are all taut from brandy! I meant no offence—why, she turned on me like a tigress. Oh! She has a sweet temper. She is poetic. Such a talent! I honestly think she has used you for 'copy.' Sit down! You can't go away now and leave me alone. I'll go nutty. All right, I promise to say nothing more. I'm to blame—entirely. No, I'm not jealous—of you. There's always a lot of chaps hanging around her skirts. I wonder how she keeps from mixing up their schedules. I simply couldn't let the brandy alone— Do you see this book? Have you read it?" He handed me a little volume bound in gold and green. I recognised it. "Yes," I answered. "I read Meryona on the train. It's exquisite. Who wrote it? Who is this Rosa Mystica? She might belong to the new group of Irish writers of whom your wife—Mrs. Saint-Hilary—is so fond. I was puzzled by faint echoes of Keats, George Russell—" I was only too glad to lead the conversation into a different channel. But my heart was a lump in my bosom. I

longed to hear more news of her, to learn the cause of
her trouble. And her whereabouts.

"You'll never learn from me who Rosa Mystica is,"
replied Saint-Hilary. His expansive mood had vanished.
In a halting manner he read paragraphs from the book,
paragraphs of rich meanings, of richer prose. Nervous
as he was, he exposed in trained voice the densely woven
patterns of this new prose with its undertones of Celtic
sorrow, its veiled passion, rhythmic pathos, mystical
overtones, and its wild call from the heart of Erin. . . .
Meryona! The title was an evocation. And surely no
man could have written it. "Yes, my boy, that's great
art, great soul. Do you know," he whispered, "they
have saddled me with the authorship? Even Dottie
has asked me the question, asked me, this good old newspaper hack. Have a drink." He paused. I paid my
score and arose. "Not going! Listen to the rain on the
roof. Stay a bit. I return to Rome early in the morning.
I think I'll find Dottie at home. Lord, what a face you
pull— Well, good night to you. I'm glad I met you. If
you ever publish anything, send me a copy and I'll give
it a good review. Where are you stopping?" I hurried
away. I would have struck him in another minute—
that is what I said to myself as I went over the bridge
across Campo St. Moisé into the hotel. But I did not
sleep that night. I found a pencilled card in the morning. It told that he hoped to see me in Rome soon.
No more. I tore it up and went for coffee. It still
rained, ferociously. "I'll go up to Milan to-night," I
planned. "At least I can hear Duse. Here!" I asked
for a railway guide and marked down my train. It
would leave in the afternoon. I breasted the wind

shrieking through the Piazzetta and stumbled along the Riva degli Schiavoni. I could hardly see Santa Maria della Salute for the grey rain that came obliquely across the lagoon, titillating the shallow waters into foam. The Guidecca was a nebulous patch. And the sharp, salty odours that were abroad in the air set me dreaming of mid-ocean. Turning off the unprotected Riva I walked at hazard, arriving on the Rio della Picta. There I found the Church of San Giorgio degli Schiavoni, and entered more for protection than from piety.

In front of Carpaccio's "Saint George and the Dragon" I saw her. At once the poorly lighted church was flooded as if by a Turner sunburst. Forgotten the wet, forgotten Venice, forgotten Saint-Hilary with his odious confidences. She stood there, in devotional attitude, before the masterpiece. I almost expected her to kneel in prayer as she had knelt that first day in the cemetery. Then the lame cicerone, who sews when he is not explaining the pictures to Ruskin-bewildered tourists, spoke to me. Would the Signor Inglese care to look? My threatening expression silenced him. But it was too late to retreat; attracted by the voices, she turned. I could have called her Blesséd as in an unconcerned manner she crossed to me. She saved me a wilderness of explanations. "Suppose we go to the hotel," she remarked in her accustomed cool tones. The wind twisted our umbrellas and beat rain into our faces so that an exchange of words was not easy. An idea overtook me; as we passed the gondolas at the Piazzetta I shouted in her ears: "The Giardino Reale! Let's go." In a few minutes two barelegged men were fighting as inch by inch they slowly paddled their craft through toppling seas. It was a daring excursion; the little steamer would have carried us more safely; but then

we could not have sat so intimately as in the gondola.
Drenched, we entered the picture-gallery in the Royal
Gardens and stopped to breathe; we soon found a café,
where I ordered something. I did not attempt to ask
questions. Her grateful eyes rewarded me, but the events
of the past few hours were telling on my nerves, on my
imagination. I felt bolder than in Rome. The woman
I adored was with me, apparently contented in my company. And how lovely she looked. The damp air had
set burning her rich Irish complexion. Her grey eyes,
enlarged by sorrow, did not avoid my gaze. Subtle
curves were in her smile. She was more radiant than
I had ever seen her at Rome.

Emboldened by the old Chianti, I exclaimed:
"I'm so happy, Dorothea." She wider opened her
eyes. I placed my hand in hers. "I'm so happy. O
to be in Venice! And with you. I—" "Hadn't we
better return to the hotel?" she asked. I hesitated.
The man who hesitates is sometimes saved. "I hope
you will pardon my crazy tongue. I'm only telling you
the truth. How I supposed since that night—" She
interrupted: "But you are too nervous to talk. You
have not said anything, told any truth—and you must
not. I am alone. Be my friend. A woman alone is
always in the wrong. Here is the waiter. Pay him and
let me go. Please!" Despairingly, I settled. We went
into the gale and walked, crossing slippery marble
bridges, deserted quays, and to the howling tune of the
wind. When we at last reached the Hotel Danieli, she
bowed her head and entered. This was too much. I
followed, and in the salon called to her. I felt myself
wilting under her piercing gaze, but I would not be

silenced. "Listen to me—Mrs. Saint-Hilary. I may
be the victim of an artistic vivisection, yet in Rome
when you were with your husband, I held my tongue.
But this is Venice. I refuse to be tortured any longer.
Last night I saw him, saw Saint-Hilary—" She started,
then blushed hotly. "Last night—here?" "Here," I
persisted. "He told me all," I defiantly continued,
though I knew I was becoming melodramatic in my
manner. "He told me all. I know who wrote Meryona,
that beautiful book. Oh! Dorothea, you wonderful poet,
how can you endure your life?" "He said I wrote Meryona?" "No, not exactly. He said that he had been
credited with the book." "He is the author, do you hear
me? My husband is the author of the books signed Rosa
Mystica." She was a blazing sunset. She fairly glit-
tered in her wrath. "I don't believe it—I don't believe
it." "You must believe it," and then her humour
changed. "Now, sit down and be quiet. Let us think
the matter out." Bewildered, I followed her movements.
For five minutes she paced the room. I could hear the
thumping of my heart. "I'll go back to Rome with
you," she gravely announced, her eyes narrowed to slits,
her voice filed to a provocative murmur. Joyfully I
sprang towards her—at last the violin had vibrated to
my key-note. "No, no—not yet!" The silky smile of
her set me crazy. "Do you return to your hotel. Come
for me in an hour. I'll be ready." Happily dismissed,
I rushed back to my room, packed, paid my bill, and
before the sixty minutes had passed I was again at the
Danieli. The portier solemnly looked at me. The lady
had gone away half an hour ago. "Gone! Why, I
had an engagement with her." "A big gentleman called
a few minutes after you left," soothingly replied the

fellow as he held out his hand. "Her husband!" I mechanically cried but in a chilly rage, determined to wear a brave face. "Oh, yes, her husband—thank you, Signor." With women the unexpected rules, I ruminated. When they pipe, men must dance, and once I had believed the contrary. Life is very different from books. As the train traversed the interminable bridge, I looked at Venice storm-begirt, sea and sky in watery embrace, and, my throat choking, I tried to hum: "Oh, to be a woman and a nomad's heart in me!" But I was only a sentimental comedian, and soon my eyes were wet, like Venice.

VI

What had I done, what had I said? I often asked myself. I had loved a woman with a lyric bird nesting in her bosom, neglected by a coarse husband, one who smirkingly had taken upon himself the honours due his wife. (I have since noted that the husband of the woman you desire is always "coarse," though on closer acquaintance he is very nice; nicer, perhaps, than his "misunderstood" spouse; and I have known more than one case where a man has regretted the lost friendship of a man in exchange for the doubtful favours of the woman who betrayed him.) Who breaks, pays. And I had not been allowed to tell her of my sincere affection; under the sting of her husband's indirect revelations, and the wine and the weather (curse that Chianti!), I had whimpered and she had left me. Had she not throughout our brief acquaintance always sent me away from her? Oh! what an ass was I! The woman had never ceased loving her husband—not even when ill-treated. And I fancied I understood the uneasy sex. Oh! what a dolt! And to seek her love in such a hurried style—like a train that must be overtaken. . . .

One day in Paris I read of the sudden death from apoplexy of the noted writer Lewis Saint-Hilary; and the chronicles were full of the past doings of this robust worthy, who, in addition to having been a journalist of experience, unexpectedly proved to be the author of Meryona, that prose epic of Erin, the first impulse to the Neo-Celtic renascence. I rubbed my eyes and returned to Rome. There I did not find the Bernervilles. They had gone to Egypt, taking with them Prince Abbazia, whose health was far from reassuring—the sympathetic Cameriere added that Burgundy and brandy were poor props to a long life. And Madame Saint-Hilary! Ah! He threw out his skinny hands, palms upwards; she never came now to the Palazzo Barbarini. She is the widow of a distinguished poet—addio, Signor, addio! . . .

Another October sun slanted its yellow glory from the western sky as I entered the narrow gate of the Protestant cemetery, which still wore its air of delicate desolation. One year earlier I had here encountered my fate, the first woman, I am certain, who understood me. My step was heavy as up the slope I went to the remains of my poets. Was it a trick of memory or hallucination that pictured for me a kneeling figure; but at a newly made grave, not Shelley's this time! Increasing my speed, I sprang up the incline. She did not turn as I came to the tomb. It was, indeed, the widow of Lewis Saint-Hilary, garbed in green, and so immersed in her meditations that I feared to disturb her. For minutes I kept silence, then my temperament mastered my tongue—

besides, the colour of her hair worried me; it had been black, now it was blonde, a true Botticellian blonde. The change made me doubly curious. "Dorothea," I softly called. "Dorothea." She did not move. "Do you know who is speaking, Mrs. Saint-Hilary?" I continued, my courage oozing through the very cadences of my voice. "I know—yes." "Won't you see me again?" This imploringly. She sternly replied: "No." "Is this—is this all?" "All," and compressed in the answer was the Venice of our last day—cold, rainy, charmless. Stung to the centre of my dearest vanity, I left her. For me she was a cracked fiddle. She was married to the memory of her dead: a spiritual Suttee. With a final gesture I bade my hopes take flight. It was the first brave act in my irresolute life. As I passed through the portal of the cemetery, I felt like a man who had at last escaped the burdens of a corroding conscience. If marriage depended alone on woman, how long would the institution endure?

For years the literary world was startled by posthumous works of the late fecund and brilliant Lewis Saint-Hilary. His widow proved an admirable editor of the deceased man's manuscripts. Epical and dramatic, lyric, pathetic, saturated with patriotism and wistful poesy, the note of the Gaelic race, these books in verse and prose set us all wondering why we had so underestimated the powers of Saint-Hilary. Even his wife had called him lazy. Parallel cases may be remembered with the widows of a celebrated French historian, and of an Englishman who wrote so significantly about Gaelic lore; both the widows edited posthumous works, and the Frenchwoman's devotion was so great, so it has been rumoured, that she outran her prudence and wrote some books herself—but

MY MAIDEN FLIGHT
Atlantic City, September, 1915

that's stale literary gossip.   Certainly Mrs. Saint-Hilary did not write Meryona.   She told me so.   And yet—I often think that if Dorothea had but realised the golden opportunity she lost when she refused to transform a half-Hamlet into a singing poet and do for the living what she accomplished for the dead, perhaps I might have mastered my emotional reticence; perhaps. . . .   But why, psychologically speaking, did she become a Botticellian blonde?   Did she have the feminine thirst for a second submission?   That is a more provocative and fascinating enigma than the disputed authorship of Meryona.

CODA

And now it is time to ring down the final curtain on the show. I might go on tapping new levels of energy, to use the striking phrase of William James, but to what purpose! Life is like an onion. You may peel off layer after layer until you reach the core—and then there is nothing. So could I skin my little symphony, in which there has been more dissonance than harmony, and enumerate my leading-motives; my mediocrity; my resigned attitude as a contemporary; my steeplejackism—I am still an impenitent steeplejack and hope to die with my boots on; my disgust with Barmecide banquets; my vanity, selfishness, and egotism; my mannerisms, limitations; my many sins of omission and commission, including my regrets for girls unkissed; my garrulity, discursiveness, and vice of allusiveness; the list might be made much longer, only you must be weary of the personal pronoun stitched in the palimpsest of my adventure. The truth is seldom amusing, and my velleities too often graze the fantastic. But you may put your hand in this rag-bag of mine and pull out a quotation worth remembering; indeed, this may be critically judged from the protasis to the catastrophe as a book of beautiful quotations. Fancy, if I had followed the pattern of Dostoievsky and devoted several hundred thousand words to one day's happenings in life! It is at least a negative virtue that I did not do this. Other ears, other songs. I forgot my belief in a personal devil as a leading-motive, that devil who could say in jocular accents, for he is a sound Latinist, even if he likes to twist a text to suit his diabolic purpose: "Sathanas sum, et nihil humanum a me alienum puto." After that Terence may go hang. And don't forget the devil is a believer.

The genesis of these avowals was simple enough. My editor wagered me that I could write them and I wagered him I could not. I lost, but as nothing was staked, he, too, lost. It was galley-slave work, as not a line was written till May 15, 1918. Yet not altogether an unpleasant task. And finished in exactly fifteen weeks, written with a pen. As I once said to Theodore Presser: How happy we were in the days when we were starving! And the mighty maw of the printing-press engulfing "copy" by the mile! I often felt like that Russian peasant, who, chased by a bear, finally reached his house, swimming the last mile; happy, exhausted, but perspiring rivers. I have covered a period of at least fifty years. Need I tell you that my cosmopolitanism peeled off like dry paint from a cracked wall when President Wilson proclaimed our nation at war? I shall never forget the amazed expression of Colonel Roosevelt as I admitted that I was in Paris when I attained my majority, and did not cast a vote in our presidential election. And he was justified in his gesture of disapproval; cosmopolitanism is all very well for the dilettante, but for a young man on the threshold of life it is sometimes deadly poison. Our country first. This is a fighting planet. Pacificism is a pipe-dream. The Lord is a man of war. Tolle, lege!

After sixty a man's future lies behind him. The thing that hath been, it is that which shall be. He dwells in memory-images. Years ago I lived in the Impasse du Maine, on the left bank, Paris. Every morning I was annoyed because awakened by piano-playing, evidently that of a mediocre amateur (some amateurs are not mediocre). I asked that handy busybody of all work, the concierge, if he knew the name of the relentless pianist. "Ah, that is M. le Comte. He is very old and is spending his time pleasantly before he dies." Later I saw M. le Comte. White of beard, spry for an octogenarian, his muscles still capable of pounding, he seemed far from the end of every man's desire. The words of the concierge now made their appeal to me: "He is spending his time pleasantly before he dies." Can you think of anything more reasonable? He played cards, no doubt, did M. le Comte, and went to his pet café to sip coffee, smoke, and read the newspaper, stuffed with his favourite prejudices. But the main business of the day was his hour at the keyboard. The music must have made his rusty old bones sweeter. I recall that he always finished with the Souvenir de Kiev, by a Bohemian composer, a friend of Chopin, Jules Schulhoff. There was a prodigious amount of bang and clatter, and then the old nobleman, who probably remembered Louis Philippe, would saunter forth, in his buttonhole a rose, a malacca cane jauntily switching the earth. I envied this serene sunset of a long, useless, and no doubt troubled existence. Who wrote "It is wonderful what one ray of sunshine can do for the soul of man"? Music was this old chap's sunshine.

I can't play cards or billiards. I can't read day and night. I take no interest in the chess-board of politics, and I am not too pious. What shall I do? Music, always music! There are certain compositions by my beloved Chopin to master which eternity itself would not be too long. That last page of the Second Ballade as

Anton Rubinstein played it, in apocalyptic thunder-
tones! Or the study in double-thirds rippled off by the
velvety fingers of de Pachmann! I once more place
the notes on the piano-desk. Courage! Time is fuga-
cious. How many years have I not played that magic
music? Music the flying vision . . . music that merges
with the tender air . . . its image melts in shy misty
shadows . . . the cloud, the cloud, the singing, shining
cloud . . . over the skies and far away . . . the beckon-
ing cloud. . . .

FINIS

INDEX

What some distinguished writers have said of them:

Maurice Maeterlinck wrote, May 15, 1905: "Do you know that 'Iconoclasts' is the only book of high and universal critical worth that we have had for years—to be precise, since Georg Brandes. It is at once strong and fine, supple and firm, indulgent and sure."

And of "Ivory Apes and Peacocks" he said, among other things: "I have marvelled at the vigilance and clarity with which you follow and judge the new literary and artistic movements in all countries. I do not know of criticism more pure and sure than yours." (October, 1915.)

———

"The Mercure de France translated the other day from Scribner's one of the best studies which have been written on Stendhal for a long time, in which there was no evasion of the question of Stendhal's immorality. The author of that article, James Huneker, is, among foreign critics, the one best acquainted with French literature and the one who judges us with the greatest sympathy and with the most freedom. He has protested with force in numerous American journals against the campaign of defamation against France, and he has easily proved that those who participate in it are ignorant and fanatical." —*"Promenades Littéraires"* (*Troisième Série*), *Remy de Gourmont.* (Translated by Burton Rascoe for the Chicago *Tribune.*)

———

Paul Bourget wrote, Lundi de Paques, 1909, of "Egoists": "I have browsed through the pages of your book and found that you touch in a sympathetic style on diverse problems, artistic and literary. In the case of Stendhal your catholicity of treatment is extremely rare and courageous."

———

Dr. Georg Brandes, the versatile and profound Danish critic, wrote: "I find your breadth of view and its expression more European than American; but the essential thing is that you are an artist to your very marrow."

BEDOUINS

Mary Garden; Debussy; Chopin or the Circus; Botticelli; Poe; Brahmsody; Anatole France; Mirbeau; Caruso on Wheels; Calico Cats; the Artistic Temperament; Idols and Ambergris; With the Supreme Sin; Grindstones; A Masque of Music, and The Vision Malefic.

"Indeed, Mr. Huneker knows the magic of turning the commonest fact of literature or art into a gorgeous fiction. . . . 'Bedouins,' like all of the author's books, is a thing apart in our literature."—BENJAMIN DE CASSERES, *New York Times.*

"If there is ever a real culture in this country its roots will run in many directions; but historians will not dig very far before they run across the Huneker-root, not only because of its tremendous vitality and world-tentacles, but because of its stark individualism and militant sap. He is the greatest of patriots who raises the intellectual levels of his country; and James Huneker is therefore, to me, the greatest of living Americans."—*Musical America.*

IVORY APES AND PEACOCKS

"His critical tact is well-nigh infallible. . . . His position among writers on æsthetics is anomalous and incredible: no merchant traffics in his heart, yet he commands a large, an eager, an affectionate public. Is it because he is both vivid and acute, robust yet fine-fingered, tolerant yet unyielding, astringent yet tender—a mellow pessimist, a kindly cynic? Or is it rather because he is, primarily, a temperament—dynamic, contagious, lovable, inveterately alive—expressing itself through the most transparent of the arts?"
—LAWRENCE GILMAN, in *North American Review* (October, 1915).

NEW COSMOPOLIS

"Mr. James Huneker, critic of music in the first place, is a craftsman of diverse accomplishment who occupies a distinctive and distinguished place among present-day American essayists. He is intensely 'modern,' well read in recent European writers, and not lacking sympathy with the more rebellious spirits. He flings off his impressions at fervent heat; he is not ashamed to be enthusiastic; and he cannot escape that large sentimentality which, to less disciplined transatlantic writers, is known nakedly as 'heart interest.' Out of his chaos of reading and observation he has, however, evolved a criticism of life that makes for intellectual cultivation, although it is of a Bohemian rather than an academic kind."—*London Athenæum* (November 6, 1915).

UNICORNS

"The essays are short, full of a satisfying—and fascinating—crispness, both memorable and delightful. And they are full of fancy, too, of the gayest humor, the quickest appreciation, the gentlest sympathy, sometimes of an enchanting extravagance."

—*New York Times.*

MELOMANIACS

"It wou'd be difficult to sum up 'Melomaniacs' in a phrase. Never did a book, in my opinion at any rate, exhibit greater contrasts, not, perhaps, of strength and weakness, but of clearness and obscurity."

—HAROLD E. GORST, in *London Saturday Review* (Dec. 8, 1906).

VISIONARIES

"In 'The Spiral Road' and in some of the other stories both fantasy and narrative may be compared with Hawthorne in his most unearthly moods. The younger man has read his Nietzsche and has cast off his heritage of simple morals. Hawthorne's Puritanism finds no echo in these modern souls, all sceptical, wavering, and unblessed. But Hawthorne's splendor of vision and his power of sympathy with a tormented mind do live again in the best of Mr. Huneker's stories."

—*London Academy* (Feb. 3, 1906).

ICONOCLASTS: A Book of Dramatists

"His style is a little jerky, but is one of those rare styles in which we are led to expect some significance, if not wit, in every sentence."—G. K. CHESTERTON, in *London Daily News.*

MEZZOTINTS IN MODERN MUSIC

"Mr. Huneker is, in the best sense, a critic; he listens to the music and gives you his impressions as rapidly and in as few words as possible; or he sketches the composers in fine, broad, sweeping strokes with a magnificent disregard for unimportant details. And as Mr. Huneker is, as I have said, a powerful personality, a man of quick brain and an energetic imagination, a man of moods and temperament—a string that vibrates and sings in response to music—we get in these essays of his a distinctly original and very valuable contribution to the world's tiny musical literature."

—J. F. RUNCIMAN, in *London Saturday Review.*